EDI Teaching Materials Series
Number 1

COMPOUNDING AND DISCOUNTING TABLES
for Project Evaluation

Edited by
J. Price Gittinger

Economic Development Institute
INTERNATIONAL BANK
FOR RECONSTRUCTION AND DEVELOPMENT
Washington, D.C.

1973

Second Printing, June 1973

CONTENTS

FOREWORD

This book grew in response to the need of the Economic Development Institute for easily comprehensible tables to be used for teaching project analysis. It also became evident that the book would meet a need of the Bank Group staff for readily available, convenient tables to use in project preparation. We have decided to make it available in this form for wider circulation in the hope that it will be useful to those in other organizations who teach project analysis and to economists and noneconomists in our member countries who may find it convenient in preparing development projects.

The book was prepared in close consultation with the Bank's Projects Departments and the Computing Activities Department; it was largely completed during K. S. Krishnaswamy's tour as Director of the Institute.

The work is the first in a new series of EDI Teaching Materials that we are planning to publish. The series, well exemplified by the present publication, is to be based on material prepared for and tested in teaching in the Economic Development Institute that we have reason to believe would be useful for similar purposes elsewhere. We also hope that it will be of help to the Fellows of the EDI, many of whom made a sizable contribution to the material to be published in the series, through their participation in courses.

Andrew M. Kamarck
Director
Economic Development Institute

RATE
1%

Year	COMPOUNDING FACTOR FOR 1 What an initial amount becomes when growing at compound interest	COMPOUNDING FACTOR FOR 1 PER ANNUM Growth of equal year-end deposits all growing at compound interest	SINKING FUND FACTOR Level deposit required each year to reach 1 by a given year
1	1.010 000	1.000 000	1.000 000
2	1.020 100	2.010 000	.497 512
3	1.030 301	3.030 100	.330 022
4	1.040 604	4.060 401	.246 281
5	1.051 010	5.101 005	.196 040
6	1.061 520	6.152 015	.162 548
7	1.072 135	7.213 535	.138 628
8	1.082 857	8.285 671	.120 690
9	1.093 685	9.368 527	.106 740
10	1.104 622	10.462 213	.095 582
11	1.115 668	11.566 835	.086 454
12	1.126 825	12.682 503	.078 849
13	1.138 093	13.809 328	.072 415
14	1.149 474	14.947 421	.066 901
15	1.160 969	16.096 896	.062 124
16	1.172 579	17.257 864	.057 945
17	1.184 304	18.430 443	.054 258
18	1.196 147	19.614 748	.050 982
19	1.208 109	20.810 895	.048 052
20	1.220 190	22.019 004	.045 415
21	1.232 392	23.239 194	.043 031
22	1.244 716	24.471 586	.040 864
23	1.257 163	25.716 302	.038 886
24	1.269 735	26.973 465	.037 073
25	1.282 432	28.243 200	.035 407
26	1.295 256	29.525 631	.033 869
27	1.308 209	30.820 888	.032 446
28	1.321 291	32.129 097	.031 124
29	1.334 504	33.450 388	.029 895
30	1.347 849	34.784 892	.028 748
31	1.361 327	36.132 740	.027 676
32	1.374 941	37.494 068	.026 671
33	1.388 690	38.869 009	.025 727
34	1.402 577	40.257 699	.024 840
35	1.416 603	41.660 276	.024 004
36	1.430 769	43.076 878	.023 214
37	1.445 076	44.507 647	.022 468
38	1.459 527	45.952 724	.021 761
39	1.474 123	47.412 251	.021 092
40	1.488 864	48.886 373	.020 456
41	1.503 752	50.375 237	.019 851
42	1.518 790	51.878 989	.019 276
43	1.533 978	53.397 779	.018 727
44	1.549 318	54.931 757	.018 204
45	1.564 811	56.481 075	.017 705
46	1.580 459	58.045 885	.017 228
47	1.596 263	59.626 344	.016 771
48	1.612 226	61.222 608	.016 334
49	1.628 348	62.834 834	.015 915
50	1.644 632	64.463 182	.015 513

RATE 1%

DISCOUNT FACTOR How much 1 at a future date is worth today	PRESENT WORTH OF AN ANNUITY FACTOR How much 1 received or paid annually for X years is worth today	CAPITAL RECOVERY FACTOR Annual payment that will repay a $1 loan in X years with compound interest on the unpaid balance	Year
.990 099	.990 099	1.010 000	1
.980 296	1.970 395	.507 512	2
.970 590	2.940 985	.340 022	3
.960 980	3.901 966	.256 281	4
.951 466	4.853 431	.206 040	5
.942 045	5.795 476	.172 548	6
.932 718	6.728 195	.148 628	7
.923 483	7.651 678	.130 690	8
.914 340	8.566 018	.116 740	9
.905 287	9.471 305	.105 582	10
.896 324	10.367 628	.096 454	11
.887 449	11.255 077	.088 849	12
.878 663	12.133 740	.082 415	13
.869 963	13.003 703	.076 901	14
.861 349	13.865 053	.072 124	15
.852 821	14.717 874	.067 945	16
.844 377	15.562 251	.064 258	17
.836 017	16.398 269	.060 982	18
.827 740	17.226 008	.058 052	19
.819 544	18.045 553	.055 415	20
.811 430	18.856 983	.053 031	21
.803 396	19.660 379	.050 864	22
.795 442	20.455 821	.048 886	23
.787 566	21.243 387	.047 073	24
.779 768	22.023 156	.045 407	25
.772 048	22.795 204	.043 869	26
.764 404	23.559 608	.042 446	27
.756 836	24.316 443	.041 124	28
.749 342	25.065 785	.039 895	29
.741 923	25.807 708	.038 748	30
.734 577	26.542 285	.037 676	31
.727 304	27.269 589	.036 671	32
.720 103	27.989 693	.035 727	33
.712 973	28.702 666	.034 840	34
.705 914	29.408 580	.034 004	35
.698 925	30.107 505	.033 214	36
.692 005	30.799 510	.032 468	37
.685 153	31.484 663	.031 761	38
.678 370	32.163 033	.031 092	39
.671 653	32.834 686	.030 456	40
.665 003	33.499 689	.029 851	41
.658 419	34.158 108	.029 276	42
.651 900	34.810 008	.028 727	43
.645 445	35.455 454	.028 204	44
.639 055	36.094 508	.027 705	45
.632 728	36.727 236	.027 228	46
.626 463	37.353 699	.026 771	47
.620 260	37.973 959	.026 334	48
.614 119	38.588 079	.025 915	49
.608 039	39.196 118	.025 513	50

RATE
2%

Year	COMPOUNDING FACTOR FOR 1 What an initial amount becomes when growing at compound interest	COMPOUNDING FACTOR FOR 1 PER ANNUM Growth of equal year-end deposits all growing at compound interest	SINKING FUND FACTOR Level deposit required each year to reach 1 by a given year
1	1.020 000	1.000 000	1.000 000
2	1.040 400	2.020 000	.495 050
3	1.061 208	3.060 400	.326 755
4	1.082 432	4.121 608	.242 624
5	1.104 081	5.204 040	.192 158
6	1.126 162	6.308 121	.158 526
7	1.148 686	7.434 283	.134 512
8	1.171 659	8.582 969	.116 510
9	1.195 093	9.754 628	.102 515
10	1.218 994	10.949 721	.091 327
11	1.243 374	12.168 715	.082 178
12	1.268 242	13.412 090	.074 560
13	1.293 607	14.680 332	.068 118
14	1.319 479	15.973 938	.062 602
15	1.345 868	17.293 417	.057 825
16	1.372 786	18.639 285	.053 650
17	1.400 241	20.012 071	.049 970
18	1.428 246	21.412 312	.046 702
19	1.456 811	22.840 559	.043 782
20	1.485 947	24.297 370	.041 157
21	1.515 666	25.783 317	.038 785
22	1.545 980	27.298 984	.036 631
23	1.576 899	28.844 963	.034 668
24	1.608 437	30.421 862	.032 871
25	1.640 606	32.030 300	.031 220
26	1.673 418	33.670 906	.029 699
27	1.706 886	35.344 324	.028 293
28	1.741 024	37.051 210	.026 990
29	1.775 845	38.792 235	.025 778
30	1.811 362	40.568 079	.024 650
31	1.847 589	42.379 441	.023 596
32	1.884 541	44.227 030	.022 611
33	1.922 231	46.111 570	.021 687
34	1.960 676	48.033 802	.020 819
35	1.999 890	49.994 478	.020 002
36	2.039 887	51.994 367	.019 233
37	2.080 685	54.034 255	.018 507
38	2.122 299	56.114 940	.017 821
39	2.164 745	58.237 238	.017 171
40	2.208 040	60.401 983	.016 556
41	2.252 200	62.610 023	.015 972
42	2.297 244	64.862 223	.015 417
43	2.343 189	67.159 468	.014 890
44	2.390 053	69.502 657	.014 388
45	2.437 854	71.892 710	.013 910
46	2.486 611	74.330 564	.013 453
47	2.536 344	76.817 176	.013 018
48	2.587 070	79.353 519	.012 602
49	2.638 812	81.940 590	.012 204
50	2.691 588	84.579 401	.011 823

RATE
2%

DISCOUNT FACTOR How much 1 at a future date is worth today	PRESENT WORTH OF AN ANNUITY FACTOR How much 1 received or paid annually for X years is worth today	CAPITAL RECOVERY FACTOR Annual payment that will repay a $1 loan in X years with compound interest on the unpaid balance	Year
.980 392	.980 392	1.020 000	1
.961 169	1.941 561	.515 050	2
.942 322	2.883 883	.346 755	3
.923 845	3.807 729	.262 624	4
.905 731	4.713 460	.212 158	5
.887 971	5.601 431	.178 526	6
.870 560	6.471 991	.154 512	7
.853 490	7.325 481	.136 510	8
.836 755	8.162 237	.122 515	9
.820 348	8.982 585	.111 327	10
.804 263	9.786 848	.102 178	11
.788 493	10.575 341	.094 560	12
.773 033	11.348 374	.088 118	13
.757 875	12.106 249	.082 602	14
.743 015	12.849 264	.077 825	15
.728 446	13.577 709	.073 650	16
.714 163	14.291 872	.069 970	17
.700 159	14.992 031	.066 702	18
.686 431	15.678 462	.063 782	19
.672 971	16.351 433	.061 157	20
.659 776	17.011 209	.058 785	21
.646 839	17.658 048	.056 631	22
.634 156	18.292 204	.054 668	23
.621 721	18.913 926	.052 871	24
.609 531	19.523 456	.051 220	25
.597 579	20.121 036	.049 699	26
.585 862	20.706 898	.048 293	27
.574 375	21.281 272	.046 990	28
.563 112	21.844 385	.045 778	29
.552 071	22.396 456	.044 650	30
.541 246	22.937 702	.043 596	31
.530 633	23.468 335	.042 611	32
.520 229	23.988 564	.041 687	33
.510 028	24.498 592	.040 819	34
.500 028	24.998 619	.040 002	35
.490 223	25.488 842	.039 233	36
.480 611	25.969 453	.038 507	37
.471 187	26.440 641	.037 821	38
.461 948	26.902 589	.037 171	39
.452 890	27.355 479	.036 556	40
.444 010	27.799 489	.035 972	41
.435 304	28.234 794	.035 417	42
.426 769	28.661 562	.034 890	43
.418 401	29.079 963	.034 388	44
.410 197	29.490 160	.033 910	45
.402 154	29.892 314	.033 453	46
.394 268	30.286 582	.033 018	47
.386 538	30.673 120	.032 602	48
.378 958	31.052 078	.032 204	49
.371 528	31.423 606	.031 823	50

RATE
3%

Year	COMPOUNDING FACTOR FOR 1 What an initial amount becomes when growing at compound interest	COMPOUNDING FACTOR FOR 1 PER ANNUM Growth of equal year-end deposits all growing at compound interest	SINKING FUND FACTOR Level deposit required each year to reach 1 by a given year
1	1.030 000	1.000 000	1.000 000
2	1.060 900	2.030 000	.492 611
3	1.092 727	3.090 900	.323 530
4	1.125 509	4.183 627	.239 027
5	1.159 274	5.309 136	.188 355
6	1.194 052	6.468 410	.154 598
7	1.229 874	7.662 462	.130 506
8	1.266 770	8.892 336	.112 456
9	1.304 773	10.159 106	.098 434
10	1.343 916	11.463 879	.087 231
11	1.384 234	12.807 796	.078 077
12	1.425 761	14.192 030	.070 462
13	1.468 534	15.617 790	.064 030
14	1.512 590	17.086 324	.058 526
15	1.557 967	18.598 914	.053 767
16	1.604 706	20.156 881	.049 611
17	1.652 848	21.761 588	.045 953
18	1.702 433	23.414 435	.042 709
19	1.753 506	25.116 868	.039 814
20	1.806 111	26.870 374	.037 216
21	1.860 295	28.676 486	.034 872
22	1.916 103	30.536 780	.032 747
23	1.973 587	32.452 884	.030 814
24	2.032 794	34.426 470	.029 047
25	2.093 778	36.459 264	.027 428
26	2.156 591	38.553 042	.025 938
27	2.221 289	40.709 634	.024 564
28	2.287 928	42.930 923	.023 293
29	2.356 566	45.218 850	.022 115
30	2.427 262	47.575 416	.021 019
31	2.500 080	50.002 678	.019 999
32	2.575 083	52.502 759	.019 047
33	2.652 335	55.077 841	.018 156
34	2.731 905	57.730 177	.017 322
35	2.813 862	60.462 082	.016 539
36	2.898 278	63.275 944	.015 804
37	2.985 227	66.174 223	.015 112
38	3.074 783	69.159 449	.014 459
39	3.167 027	72.234 233	.013 844
40	3.262 038	75.401 260	.013 262
41	3.359 899	78.663 298	.012 712
42	3.460 696	82.023 196	.012 192
43	3.564 517	85.483 892	.011 698
44	3.671 452	89.048 409	.011 230
45	3.781 596	92.719 861	.010 785
46	3.895 044	96.501 457	.010 363
47	4.011 895	100.396 501	.009 961
48	4.132 252	104.408 396	.009 578
49	4.256 219	108.540 648	.009 213
50	4.383 906	112.796 867	.008 865

RATE
3%

DISCOUNT FACTOR How much 1 at a future date is worth today	PRESENT WORTH OF AN ANNUITY FACTOR How much 1 received or paid annually for X years is worth today	CAPITAL RECOVERY FACTOR Annual payment that will repay a $1 loan in X years with compound interest on the unpaid balance	Year
.970 874	.970 874	1.030 000	1
.942 596	1.913 470	.522 611	2
.915 142	2.828 611	.353 530	3
.888 487	3.717 098	.269 027	4
.862 609	4.579 707	.218 355	5
.837 484	5.417 191	.184 598	6
.813 092	6.230 283	.160 506	7
.789 409	7.019 692	.142 456	8
.766 417	7.786 109	.128 434	9
.744 094	8.530 203	.117 231	10
.722 421	9.252 624	.108 077	11
.701 380	9.954 004	.100 462	12
.680 951	10.634 955	.094 030	13
.661 118	11.296 073	.088 526	14
.641 862	11.937 935	.083 767	15
.623 167	12.561 102	.079 611	16
.605 016	13.166 118	.075 953	17
.587 395	13.753 513	.072 709	18
.570 286	14.323 799	.069 814	19
.553 676	14.877 475	.067 216	20
.537 549	15.415 024	.064 872	21
.521 893	15.936 917	.062 747	22
.506 692	16.443 608	.060 814	23
.491 934	16.935 542	.059 047	24
.477 606	17.413 148	.057 428	25
.463 695	17.876 842	.055 938	26
.450 189	18.327 031	.054 564	27
.437 077	18.764 108	.053 293	28
.424 346	19.188 455	.052 115	29
.411 987	19.600 441	.051 019	30
.399 987	20.000 428	.049 999	31
.388 337	20.388 766	.049 047	32
.377 026	20.765 792	.048 156	33
.366 045	21.131 837	.047 322	34
.355 383	21.487 220	.046 539	35
.345 032	21.832 252	.045 804	36
.334 983	22.167 235	.045 112	37
.325 226	22.492 462	.044 459	38
.315 754	22.808 215	.043 844	39
.306 557	23.114 772	.043 262	40
.297 628	23.412 400	.042 712	41
.288 959	23.701 359	.042 192	42
.280 543	23.981 902	.041 698	43
.272 372	24.254 274	.041 230	44
.264 439	24.518 713	.040 785	45
.256 737	24.775 449	.040 363	46
.249 259	25.024 708	.039 961	47
.241 999	25.266 707	.039 578	48
.234 950	25.501 657	.039 213	49
.228 107	25.729 764	.038 865	50

RATE
4%

Year	COMPOUNDING FACTOR FOR 1 What an initial amount becomes when growing at compound interest	COMPOUNDING FACTOR FOR 1 PER ANNUM Growth of equal year-end deposits all growing at compound interest	SINKING FUND FACTOR Level deposit required each year to reach 1 by a given year
1	1.040 000	1.000 000	1.000 000
2	1.081 600	2.040 000	.490 196
3	1.124 864	3.121 600	.320 349
4	1.169 859	4.246 464	.235 490
5	1.216 653	5.416 323	.184 627
6	1.265 319	6.632 975	.150 762
7	1.315 932	7.898 294	.126 610
8	1.368 569	9.214 226	.108 528
9	1.423 312	10.582 795	.094 493
10	1.480 244	12.006 107	.083 291
11	1.539 454	13.486 351	.074 149
12	1.601 032	15.025 805	.066 552
13	1.665 074	16.626 838	.060 144
14	1.731 676	18.291 911	.054 669
15	1.800 944	20.023 588	.049 941
16	1.872 981	21.824 531	.045 820
17	1.947 900	23.697 512	.042 199
18	2.025 817	25.645 413	.038 993
19	2.106 849	27.671 229	.036 139
20	2.191 123	29.778 079	.033 582
21	2.278 768	31.969 202	.031 280
22	2.369 919	34.247 970	.029 199
23	2.464 716	36.617 889	.027 309
24	2.563 304	39.082 604	.025 587
25	2.665 836	41.645 908	.024 012
26	2.772 470	44.311 745	.022 567
27	2.883 369	47.084 214	.021 239
28	2.998 703	49.967 583	.020 013
29	3.118 651	52.966 286	.018 880
30	3.243 398	56.084 938	.017 830
31	3.373 133	59.328 335	.016 855
32	3.508 059	62.701 469	.015 949
33	3.648 381	66.209 527	.015 104
34	3.794 316	69.857 909	.014 315
35	3.946 089	73.652 225	.013 577
36	4.103 933	77.598 314	.012 887
37	4.268 090	81.702 246	.012 240
38	4.438 813	85.970 336	.011 632
39	4.616 366	90.409 150	.011 061
40	4.801 021	95.025 516	.010 523
41	4.993 061	99.826 536	.010 017
42	5.192 784	104.819 598	.009 540
43	5.400 495	110.012 382	.009 090
44	5.616 515	115.412 877	.008 665
45	5.841 176	121.029 392	.008 262
46	6.074 823	126.870 568	.007 882
47	6.317 816	132.945 390	.007 522
48	6.570 528	139.263 206	.007 181
49	6.833 349	145.833 734	.006 857
50	7.106 683	152.667 084	.006 550

RATE 4%

DISCOUNT FACTOR How much 1 at a future date is worth today	PRESENT WORTH OF AN ANNUITY FACTOR How much 1 received or paid annually for X years is worth today	CAPITAL RECOVERY FACTOR Annual payment that will repay a $1 loan in X years with compound interest on the unpaid balance	Year
.961 538	.961 538	1.040 000	1
.924 556	1.886 095	.530 196	2
.888 996	2.775 091	.360 349	3
.854 804	3.629 895	.275 490	4
.821 927	4.451 822	.224 627	5
.790 315	5.242 137	.190 762	6
.759 918	6.002 055	.166 610	7
.730 690	6.732 745	.148 528	8
.702 587	7.435 332	.134 493	9
.675 564	8.110 896	.123 291	10
.649 581	8.760 477	.114 149	11
.624 597	9.385 074	.106 552	12
.600 574	9.985 648	.100 144	13
.577 475	10.563 123	.094 669	14
.555 265	11.118 387	.089 941	15
.533 908	11.652 296	.085 820	16
.513 373	12.165 669	.082 199	17
.493 628	12.659 297	.078 993	18
.474 642	13.133 939	.076 139	19
.456 387	13.590 326	.073 582	20
.438 834	14.029 160	.071 280	21
.421 955	14.451 115	.069 199	22
.405 720	14.856 842	.067 309	23
.390 121	15.246 963	.065 587	24
.375 117	15.622 080	.064 012	25
.360 689	15.982 769	.062 567	26
.346 817	16.329 586	.061 239	27
.333 477	16.663 063	.060 013	28
.320 651	16.983 715	.058 880	29
.308 319	17.292 033	.057 830	30
.296 460	17.588 494	.056 855	31
.285 058	17.873 551	.055 949	32
.274 094	18.147 646	.055 104	33
.263 552	18.411 198	.054 315	34
.253 415	18.664 613	.053 577	35
.243 669	18.908 282	.052 887	36
.234 297	19.142 579	.052 240	37
.225 285	19.367 864	.051 632	38
.216 621	19.584 485	.051 061	39
.208 289	19.792 774	.050 523	40
.200 278	19.993 052	.050 017	41
.192 575	20.185 627	.049 540	42
.185 168	20.370 795	.049 090	43
.178 046	20.548 841	.048 665	44
.171 198	20.720 040	.048 262	45
.164 614	20.884 654	.047 882	46
.158 283	21.042 936	.047 522	47
.152 195	21.195 131	.047 181	48
.146 341	21.341 472	.046 857	49
.140 713	21.482 185	.046 550	50

RATE
5%

Year	COMPOUNDING FACTOR FOR 1 What an initial amount becomes when growing at compound interest	COMPOUNDING FACTOR FOR 1 PER ANNUM Growth of equal year-end deposits all growing at compound interest	SINKING FUND FACTOR Level deposit required each year to reach 1 by a given year
1	1.050 000	1.000 000	1.000 000
2	1.102 500	2.050 000	.487 805
3	1.157 625	3.152 500	.317 209
4	1.215 506	4.310 125	.232 012
5	1.276 282	5.525 631	.180 975
6	1.340 096	6.801 913	.147 017
7	1.407 100	8.142 008	.122 820
8	1.477 455	9.549 109	.104 722
9	1.551 328	11.026 564	.090 690
10	1.628 895	12.577 893	.079 505
11	1.710 339	14.206 787	.070 389
12	1.795 856	15.917 127	.062 825
13	1.885 649	17.712 983	.056 456
14	1.979 932	19.598 632	.051 024
15	2.078 928	21.578 564	.046 342
16	2.182 875	23.675 492	.042 270
17	2.292 018	25.840 366	.038 699
18	2.406 619	28.132 385	.035 546
19	2.526 950	30.539 004	.032 745
20	2.653 298	33.065 954	.030 243
21	2.785 963	35.719 252	.027 996
22	2.925 261	38.505 214	.025 971
23	3.071 524	41.430 475	.024 137
24	3.225 100	44.501 999	.022 471
25	3.386 355	47.727 099	.020 952
26	3.555 673	51.113 454	.019 564
27	3.733 456	54.669 126	.018 292
28	3.920 129	58.402 583	.017 123
29	4.116 136	62.322 712	.016 046
30	4.321 942	66.438 848	.015 051
31	4.538 039	70.760 790	.014 132
32	4.764 941	75.298 829	.013 280
33	5.003 189	80.063 771	.012 490
34	5.253 348	85.066 959	.011 755
35	5.516 015	90.320 307	.011 072
36	5.791 816	95.836 323	.010 434
37	6.081 407	101.628 139	.009 840
38	6.385 477	107.709 546	.009 284
39	6.704 751	114.095 023	.008 765
40	7.039 989	120.799 774	.008 278
41	7.391 988	127.839 763	.007 822
42	7.761 588	135.231 751	.007 395
43	8.149 667	142.993 339	.006 993
44	8.557 150	151.143 006	.006 616
45	8.985 008	159.700 156	.006 262
46	9.434 258	168.685 164	.005 928
47	9.905 971	178.119 422	.005 614
48	10.401 270	188.025 393	.005 318
49	10.921 333	198.426 663	.005 040
50	11.467 400	209.347 996	.004 777

RATE 5%

DISCOUNT FACTOR How much 1 at a future date is worth today	PRESENT WORTH OF AN ANNUITY FACTOR How much 1 received or paid annually for X years is worth today	CAPITAL RECOVERY FACTOR Annual payment that will repay a $1 loan in X years with compound interest on the unpaid balance	Year
.952 381	.952 381	1.050 000	1
.907 029	1.859 410	.537 805	2
.863 838	2.723 248	.367 209	3
.822 702	3.545 951	.282 012	4
.783 526	4.329 477	.230 975	5
.746 215	5.075 692	.197 017	6
.710 681	5.786 373	.172 820	7
.676 839	6.463 213	.154 722	8
.644 609	7.107 822	.140 690	9
.613 913	7.721 735	.129 505	10
.584 679	8.306 414	.120 389	11
.556 837	8.863 252	.112 825	12
.530 321	9.393 573	.106 456	13
.505 068	9.898 641	.101 024	14
.481 017	10.379 658	.096 342	15
.458 112	10.837 770	.092 270	16
.436 297	11.274 066	.088 699	17
.415 521	11.689 587	.085 546	18
.395 734	12.085 321	.082 745	19
.376 889	12.462 210	.080 243	20
.358 942	12.821 153	.077 996	21
.341 850	13.163 003	.075 971	22
.325 571	13.488 574	.074 137	23
.310 068	13.798 642	.072 471	24
.295 303	14.093 945	.070 952	25
.281 241	14.375 185	.069 564	26
.267 848	14.643 034	.068 292	27
.255 094	14.898 127	.067 123	28
.242 946	15.141 074	.066 046	29
.231 377	15.372 451	.065 051	30
.220 359	15.592 811	.064 132	31
.209 866	15.802 677	.063 280	32
.199 873	16.002 549	.062 490	33
.190 355	16.192 904	.061 755	34
.181 290	16.374 194	.061 072	35
.172 657	16.546 852	.060 434	36
.164 436	16.711 287	.059 840	37
.156 605	16.867 893	.059 284	38
.149 148	17.017 041	.058 765	39
.142 046	17.159 086	.058 278	40
.135 282	17.294 368	.057 822	41
.128 840	17.423 208	.057 395	42
.122 704	17.545 912	.056 993	43
.116 861	17.662 773	.056 616	44
.111 297	17.774 070	.056 262	45
.105 997	17.880 066	.055 928	46
.100 949	17.981 016	.055 614	47
.096 142	18.077 158	.055 318	48
.091 564	18.168 722	.055 040	49
.087 204	18.255 925	.054 777	50

RATE
6%

Year	COMPOUNDING FACTOR FOR 1 What an initial amount becomes when growing at compound interest	COMPOUNDING FACTOR FOR 1 PER ANNUM Growth of equal year-end deposits all growing at compound interest	SINKING FUND FACTOR Level deposit required each year to reach 1 by a given year
1	1.060 000	1.000 000	1.000 000
2	1.123 600	2.060 000	.485 437
3	1.191 016	3.183 600	.314 110
4	1.262 477	4.374 616	.228 591
5	1.338 226	5.637 093	.177 396
6	1.418 519	6.975 319	.143 363
7	1.503 630	8.393 838	.119 135
8	1.593 848	9.897 468	.101 036
9	1.689 479	11.491 316	.087 022
10	1.790 848	13.180 795	.075 868
11	1.898 299	14.971 643	.066 793
12	2.012 196	16.869 941	.059 277
13	2.132 928	18.882 138	.052 960
14	2.260 904	21.015 066	.047 585
15	2.396 558	23.275 970	.042 963
16	2.540 352	25.672 528	.038 952
17	2.692 773	28.212 880	.035 445
18	2.854 339	30.905 653	.032 357
19	3.025 600	33.759 992	.029 621
20	3.207 135	36.785 591	.027 185
21	3.399 564	39.992 727	.025 005
22	3.603 537	43.392 290	.023 046
23	3.819 750	46.995 828	.021 278
24	4.048 935	50.815 577	.019 679
25	4.291 871	54.864 512	.018 227
26	4.549 383	59.156 383	.016 904
27	4.822 346	63.705 766	.015 697
28	5.111 687	68.528 112	.014 593
29	5.418 388	73.639 798	.013 580
30	5.743 491	79.058 186	.012 649
31	6.088 101	84.801 677	.011 792
32	6.453 387	90.889 778	.011 002
33	6.840 590	97.343 165	.010 273
34	7.251 025	104.183 755	.009 598
35	7.686 087	111.434 780	.008 974
36	8.147 252	119.120 867	.008 395
37	8.636 087	127.268 119	.007 857
38	9.154 252	135.904 206	.007 358
39	9.703 507	145.058 458	.006 894
40	10.285 718	154.761 966	.006 462
41	10.902 861	165.047 684	.006 059
42	11.557 033	175.950 545	.005 683
43	12.250 455	187.507 577	.005 333
44	12.985 482	199.758 032	.005 006
45	13.764 611	212.743 514	.004 700
46	14.590 487	226.508 125	.004 415
47	15.465 917	241.098 612	.004 148
48	16.393 872	256.564 529	.003 898
49	17.377 504	272.958 401	.003 664
50	18.420 154	290.335 905	.003 444

RATE 6%

DISCOUNT FACTOR How much 1 at a future date is worth today	PRESENT WORTH OF AN ANNUITY FACTOR How much 1 received or paid annually for X years is worth today	CAPITAL RECOVERY FACTOR Annual payment that will repay a $1 loan in X years with compound interest on the unpaid balance	Year
.943 396	.943 396	1.060 000	1
.889 996	1.833 393	.545 437	2
.839 619	2.673 012	.374 110	3
.792 094	3.465 106	.288 591	4
.747 258	4.212 364	.237 396	5
.704 961	4.917 324	.203 363	6
.665 057	5.582 381	.179 135	7
.627 412	6.209 794	.161 036	8
.591 898	6.801 692	.147 022	9
.558 395	7.360 087	.135 868	10
.526 788	7.886 875	.126 793	11
.496 969	8.383 844	.119 277	12
.468 839	8.852 683	.112 960	13
.442 301	9.294 984	.107 585	14
.417 265	9.712 249	.102 963	15
.393 646	10.105 895	.098 952	16
.371 364	10.477 260	.095 445	17
.350 344	10.827 603	.092 357	18
.330 513	11.158 116	.089 621	19
.311 805	11.469 921	.087 185	20
.294 155	11.764 077	.085 005	21
.277 505	12.041 582	.083 046	22
.261 797	12.303 379	.081 278	23
.246 979	12.550 358	.079 679	24
.232 999	12.783 356	.078 227	25
.219 810	13.003 166	.076 904	26
.207 368	13.210 534	.075 697	27
.195 630	13.406 164	.074 593	28
.184 557	13.590 721	.073 580	29
.174 110	13.764 831	.072 649	30
.164 255	13.929 086	.071 792	31
.154 957	14.084 043	.071 002	32
.146 186	14.230 230	.070 273	33
.137 912	14.368 141	.069 598	34
.130 105	14.498 246	.068 974	35
.122 741	14.620 987	.068 395	36
.115 793	14.736 780	.067 857	37
.109 239	14.846 019	.067 358	38
.103 056	14.949 075	.066 894	39
.097 222	15.046 297	.066 462	40
.091 719	15.138 016	.066 059	41
.086 527	15.224 543	.065 683	42
.081 630	15.306 173	.065 333	43
.077 009	15.383 182	.065 006	44
.072 650	15.455 832	.064 700	45
.068 538	15.524 370	.064 415	46
.064 658	15.589 028	.064 148	47
.060 998	15.650 027	.063 898	48
.057 546	15 707 572	.063 664	49
.054 288	15.761 861	.063 444	50

RATE 7%

Year	COMPOUNDING FACTOR FOR 1 What an initial amount becomes when growing at compound interest	COMPOUNDING FACTOR FOR 1 PER ANNUM Growth of equal year-end deposits all growing at compound interest	SINKING FUND FACTOR Level deposit required each year to reach 1 by a given year
1	1.070 000	1.000 000	1.000 000
2	1.144 900	2.070 000	.483 092
3	1.225 043	3.214 900	.311 052
4	1.310 796	4.439 943	.225 228
5	1.402 552	5.750 739	.173 891
6	1.500 730	7.153 291	.139 796
7	1.605 781	8.654 021	.115 553
8	1.718 186	10.259 803	.097 468
9	1.838 459	11.977 989	.083 486
10	1.967 151	13.816 448	.072 378
11	2.104 852	15.783 599	.063 357
12	2.252 192	17.888 451	.055 902
13	2.409 845	20.140 643	.049 651
14	2.578 534	22.550 488	.044 345
15	2.759 032	25.129 022	.039 795
16	2.952 164	27.888 054	.035 858
17	3.158 815	30.840 217	.032 425
18	3.379 932	33.999 033	.029 413
19	3.616 528	37.378 965	.026 753
20	3.869 684	40.995 492	.024 393
21	4.140 562	44.865 177	.022 289
22	4.430 402	49.005 739	.020 406
23	4.740 530	53.436 141	.018 714
24	5.072 367	58.176 671	.017 189
25	5.427 433	63.249 038	.015 811
26	5.807 353	68.676 470	.014 561
27	6.213 868	74.483 823	.013 426
28	6.648 838	80.697 691	.012 392
29	7.114 257	87.346 529	.011 449
30	7.612 255	94.460 786	.010 586
31	8.145 113	102.073 041	.009 797
32	8.715 271	110.218 154	.009 073
33	9.325 340	118.933 425	.008 408
34	9.978 114	128.258 765	.007 797
35	10.676 581	138.236 878	.007 234
36	11.423 942	148.913 460	.006 715
37	12.223 618	160.337 402	.006 237
38	13.079 271	172.561 020	.005 795
39	13.994 820	185.640 292	.005 387
40	14.974 458	199.635 112	.005 009
41	16.022 670	214.609 570	.004 660
42	17.144 257	230.632 240	.004 336
43	18.344 355	247.776 496	.004 036
44	19.628 460	266.120 851	.003 758
45	21.002 452	285.749 311	.003 500
46	22.472 623	306.751 763	.003 260
47	24.045 707	329.224 386	.003 037
48	25.728 907	353.270 093	.002 831
49	27.529 930	378.999 000	.002 639
50	29.457 025	406.528 929	.002 460

RATE
7%

DISCOUNT FACTOR How much 1 at a future date is worth today	PRESENT WORTH OF AN ANNUITY FACTOR How much 1 received or paid annually for X years is worth today	CAPITAL RECOVERY FACTOR Annual payment that will repay a $1 loan in X years with compound interest on the unpaid balance	Year
.934 579	.934 579	1.070 000	1
.873 439	1.808 018	.553 092	2
.816 298	2.624 316	.381 052	3
.762 895	3.387 211	.295 228	4
.712 986	4.100 197	.243 891	5
.666 342	4.766 540	.209 796	6
.622 750	5.389 289	.185 553	7
.582 009	5.971 299	.167 468	8
.543 934	6.515 232	.153 486	9
.508 349	7.023 582	.142 378	10
.475 093	7.498 674	.133 357	11
.444 012	7.942 686	.125 902	12
.414 964	8.357 651	.119 651	13
.387 817	8.745 468	.114 345	14
.362 446	9.107 914	.109 795	15
.338 735	9.446 649	.105 858	16
.316 574	9.763 223	.102 425	17
.295 864	10.059 087	.099 413	18
.276 508	10.335 595	.096 753	19
.258 419	10.594 014	.094 393	20
.241 513	10.835 527	.092 289	21
.225 713	11.061 240	.090 406	22
.210 947	11.272 187	.088 714	23
.197 147	11.469 334	.087 189	24
.184 249	11.653 583	.085 811	25
.172 195	11.825 779	.084 561	26
.160 930	11.986 709	.083 426	27
.150 402	12.137 111	.082 392	28
.140 563	12.277 674	.081 449	29
.131 367	12.409 041	.080 586	30
.122 773	12.531 814	.079 797	31
.114 741	12.646 555	.079 073	32
.107 235	12.753 790	.078 408	33
.100 219	12.854 009	.077 797	34
.093 663	12.947 672	.077 234	35
.087 535	13.035 208	.076 715	36
.081 809	13.117 017	.076 237	37
.076 457	13.193 473	.075 795	38
.071 455	13.264 928	.075 387	39
.066 780	13.331 709	.075 009	40
.062 412	13.394 120	.074 660	41
.058 329	13.452 449	.074 336	42
.054 513	13.506 962	.074 036	43
.050 946	13.557 908	.073 758	44
.047 613	13.605 522	.073 500	45
.044 499	13.650 020	.073 260	46
.041 587	13.691 608	.073 037	47
.038 867	13.730 474	.072 831	48
.036 324	13.766 799	.072 639	49
.033 948	13.800 746	.072 460	50

RATE 8%

Year	COMPOUNDING FACTOR FOR 1 What an initial amount becomes when growing at compound interest	COMPOUNDING FACTOR FOR 1 PER ANNUM Growth of equal year-end deposits all growing at compound interest	SINKING FUND FACTOR Level deposit required each year to reach 1 by a given year
1	1.080 000	1.000 000	1.000 000
2	1.166 400	2.080 000	.480 769
3	1.259 712	3.246 400	.308 034
4	1.360 489	4.506 112	.221 921
5	1.469 328	5.866 601	.170 456
6	1.586 874	7.335 929	.136 315
7	1.713 824	8.922 803	.112 072
8	1.850 930	10.636 628	.094 015
9	1.999 005	12.487 558	.080 080
10	2.158 925	14.486 562	.069 029
11	2.331 639	16.645 487	.060 076
12	2.518 170	18.977 126	.052 695
13	2.719 624	21.495 297	.046 522
14	2.937 194	24.214 920	.041 297
15	3.172 169	27.152 114	.036 830
16	3.425 943	30.324 283	.032 977
17	3.700 018	33.750 226	.029 629
18	3.996 019	37.450 244	.026 702
19	4.315 701	41.446 263	.024 128
20	4.660 957	45.761 964	.021 852
21	5.033 834	50.422 921	.019 832
22	5.436 540	55.456 755	.018 032
23	5.871 464	60.893 296	.016 422
24	6.341 181	66.764 759	.014 978
25	6.848 475	73.105 940	.013 679
26	7.396 353	79.954 415	.012 507
27	7.988 061	87.350 768	.011 448
28	8.627 106	95.338 830	.010 489
29	9.317 275	103.965 936	.009 619
30	10.062 657	113.283 211	.008 827
31	10.867 669	123.345 868	.008 107
32	11.737 083	134.213 537	.007 451
33	12.676 050	145.950 620	.006 852
34	13.690 134	158.626 670	.006 304
35	14.785 344	172.316 804	.005 803
36	15.968 172	187.102 148	.005 345
37	17.245 626	203.070 320	.004 924
38	18.625 276	220.315 945	.004 539
39	20.115 298	238.941 221	.004 185
40	21.724 521	259.056 519	.003 860
41	23.462 483	280.781 040	.003 561
42	25.339 482	304.243 523	.003 287
43	27.366 640	329.583 005	.003 034
44	29.555 972	356.949 646	.002 802
45	31.920 449	386.505 617	.002 587
46	34.474 085	418.426 067	.002 390
47	37.232 012	452.900 152	.002 208
48	40.210 573	490.132 164	.002 040
49	43.427 419	530.342 737	.001 886
50	46.901 613	573.770 156	.001 743

DISCOUNT FACTOR How much 1 at a future date is worth today	PRESENT WORTH OF AN ANNUITY FACTOR How much 1 received or paid annually for X years is worth today	CAPITAL RECOVERY FACTOR Annual payment that will repay a $1 loan in X years with compound interest on the unpaid balance	Year
.925 926	.925 926	1.080 000	1
.857 339	1.783 265	.560 769	2
.793 832	2.577 097	.388 034	3
.735 030	3.312 127	.301 921	4
.680 583	3.992 710	.250 456	5
.630 170	4.622 880	.216 315	6
.583 490	5.206 370	.192 072	7
.540 269	5.746 639	.174 015	8
.500 249	6.246 888	.160 080	9
.463 193	6.710 081	.149 029	10
.428 883	7.138 964	.140 076	11
.397 114	7.536 078	.132 695	12
.367 698	7.903 776	.126 522	13
.340 461	8.244 237	.121 297	14
.315 242	8.559 479	.116 830	15
.291 890	8.851 369	.112 977	16
.270 269	9.121 638	.109 629	17
.250 249	9.371 887	.106 702	18
.231 712	9.603 599	.104 128	19
.214 548	9.818 147	.101 852	20
.198 656	10.016 803	.099 832	21
.183 941	10.200 744	.098 032	22
.170 315	10.371 059	.096 422	23
.157 699	10.528 758	.094 978	24
.146 018	10.674 776	.093 679	25
.135 202	10.809 978	.092 507	26
.125 187	10.935 165	.091 448	27
.115 914	11.051 078	.090 489	28
.107 328	11.158 406	.089 619	29
.099 377	11.257 783	.088 827	30
.092 016	11.349 799	.088 107	31
.085 200	11.434 999	.087 451	32
.078 889	11.513 888	.086 852	33
.073 045	11.586 934	.086 304	34
.067 635	11.654 568	.085 803	35
.062 625	11.717 193	.085 345	36
.057 986	11.775 179	.084 924	37
.053 690	11.828 869	.084 539	38
.049 713	11.878 582	.084 185	39
.046 031	11.924 613	.083 860	40
.042 621	11.967 235	.083 561	41
.039 464	12.006 699	.083 287	42
.036 541	12.043 240	.083 034	43
.033 834	12.077 074	.082 802	44
.031 328	12.108 402	.082 587	45
.029 007	12.137 409	.082 390	46
.026 859	12.164 267	.082 208	47
.024 869	12.189 136	.082 040	48
.023 027	12.212 163	.081 886	49
.021 321	12.233 485	.081 743	50

RATE
9%

Year	COMPOUNDING FACTOR FOR 1 What an initial amount becomes when growing at compound interest	COMPOUNDING FACTOR FOR 1 PER ANNUM Growth of equal year-end deposits all growing at compound interest	SINKING FUND FACTOR Level deposit required each year to reach 1 by a given year
1	1.090 000	1.000 000	1.000 000
2	1.188 100	2.090 000	.478 469
3	1.295 029	3.278 100	.305 055
4	1.411 582	4.573 129	.218 669
5	1.538 624	5.984 711	.167 092
6	1.677 100	7.523 335	.132 920
7	1.828 039	9.200 435	.108 691
8	1.992 563	11.028 474	.090 674
9	2.171 893	13.021 036	.076 799
10	2.367 364	15.192 930	.065 820
11	2.580 426	17.560 293	.056 947
12	2.812 665	20.140 720	.049 651
13	3.065 805	22.953 385	.043 567
14	3.341 727	26.019 189	.038 433
15	3.642 482	29.360 916	.034 059
16	3.970 306	33.003 399	.030 300
17	4.327 633	36.973 705	.027 046
18	4.717 120	41.301 338	.024 212
19	5.141 661	46.018 458	.021 730
20	5.604 411	51.160 120	.019 546
21	6.108 808	56.764 530	.017 617
22	6.658 600	62.873 338	.015 905
23	7.257 874	69.531 939	.014 382
24	7.911 083	76.789 813	.013 023
25	8.623 081	84.700 896	.011 806
26	9.399 158	93.323 977	.010 715
27	10.245 082	102.723 135	.009 735
28	11.167 140	112.968 217	.008 852
29	12.172 182	124.135 356	.008 056
30	13.267 678	136.307 539	.007 336
31	14.461 770	149.575 217	.006 686
32	15.763 329	164.036 987	.006 096
33	17.182 028	179.800 315	.005 562
34	18.728 411	196.982 344	.005 077
35	20.413 968	215.710 755	.004 636
36	22.251 225	236.124 723	.004 235
37	24.253 835	258.375 948	.003 870
38	26.436 680	282.629 783	.003 538
39	28.815 982	309.066 463	.003 236
40	31.409 420	337.882 445	.002 960
41	34.236 268	369.291 865	.002 708
42	37.317 532	403.528 133	.002 478
43	40.676 110	440.845 665	.002 268
44	44.336 960	481.521 775	.002 077
45	48.327 286	525.858 734	.001 902
46	52.676 742	574.186 021	.001 742
47	57.417 649	626.862 762	.001 595
48	62.585 237	684.280 411	.001 461
49	68.217 908	746.865 648	.001 339
50	74.357 520	815.083 556	.001 227

RATE 9%

DISCOUNT FACTOR How much 1 at a future date is worth today	PRESENT WORTH OF AN ANNUITY FACTOR How much 1 received or paid annually for X years is worth today	CAPITAL RECOVERY FACTOR Annual payment that will repay a $1 loan in X years with compound interest on the unpaid balance	Year
.917 431	.917 431	1.090 000	1
.841 680	1.759 111	.568 469	2
.772 183	2.531 295	.395 055	3
.708 425	3.239 720	.308 669	4
.649 931	3.889 651	.257 092	5
.596 267	4.485 919	.222 920	6
.547 034	5.032 953	.198 691	7
.501 866	5.534 819	.180 674	8
.460 428	5.995 247	.166 799	9
.422 411	6.417 658	.155 820	10
.387 533	6.805 191	.146 947	11
.355 535	7.160 725	.139 651	12
.326 179	7.486 904	.133 567	13
.299 246	7.786 150	.128 433	14
.274 538	8.060 688	.124 059	15
.251 870	8.312 558	.120 300	16
.231 073	8.543 631	.117 046	17
.211 994	8.755 625	.114 212	18
.194 490	8.950 115	.111 730	19
.178 431	9.128 546	.109 546	20
.163 698	9.292 244	.107 617	21
.150 182	9.442 425	.105 905	22
.137 781	9.580 207	.104 382	23
.126 405	9.706 612	.103 023	24
.115 968	9.822 580	.101 806	25
.106 393	9.928 972	.100 715	26
.097 608	10.026 580	.099 735	27
.089 548	10.116 128	.098 852	28
.082 155	10.198 283	.098 056	29
.075 371	10.273 654	.097 336	30
.069 148	10.342 802	.096 686	31
.063 438	10.406 240	.096 096	32
.058 200	10.464 441	.095 562	33
.053 395	10.517 835	.095 077	34
.048 986	10.566 821	.094 636	35
.044 941	10.611 763	.094 235	36
.041 231	10.652 993	.093 870	37
.037 826	10.690 820	.093 538	38
.034 703	10.725 523	.093 236	39
.031 838	10.757 360	.092 960	40
.029 209	10.786 569	.092 708	41
.026 797	10.813 366	.092 478	42
.024 584	10.837 950	.092 268	43
.022 555	10.860 505	.092 077	44
.020 692	10.881 197	.091 902	45
.018 984	10.900 181	.091 742	46
.017 416	10.917 597	.091 595	47
.015 978	10.933 575	.091 461	48
.014 659	10.948 234	.091 339	49
.013 449	10.961 683	.091 227	50

RATE
10%

Year	COMPOUNDING FACTOR FOR 1 What an initial amount becomes when growing at compound interest	COMPOUNDING FACTOR FOR 1 PER ANNUM Growth of equal year-end deposits all growing at compound interest	SINKING FUND FACTOR Level deposit required each year to reach 1 by a given year
1	1.100 000	1.000 000	1.000 000
2	1.210 000	2.100 000	.476 190
3	1.331 000	3.310 000	.302 115
4	1.464 100	4.641 000	.215 471
5	1.610 510	6.105 100	.163 797
6	1.771 561	7.715 610	.129 607
7	1.948 717	9.487 171	.105 405
8	2.143 589	11.435 888	.087 444
9	2.357 948	13.579 477	.073 641
10	2.593 742	15.937 425	.062 745
11	2.853 117	18.531 167	.053 963
12	3.138 428	21.384 284	.046 763
13	3.452 271	24.522 712	.040 779
14	3.797 498	27.974 983	.035 746
15	4.177 248	31.772 482	.031 474
16	4.594 973	35.949 730	.027 817
17	5.054 470	40.544 703	.024 664
18	5.559 917	45.599 173	.021 930
19	6.115 909	51.159 090	.019 547
20	6.727 500	57.274 999	.017 460
21	7.400 250	64.002 499	.015 624
22	8.140 275	71.402 749	.014 005
23	8.954 302	79.543 024	.012 572
24	9.849 733	88.497 327	.011 300
25	10.834 706	98.347 059	.010 168
26	11.918 177	109.181 765	.009 159
27	13.109 994	121.099 942	.008 258
28	14.420 994	134.209 936	.007 451
29	15.863 093	148.630 930	.006 728
30	17.449 402	164.494 023	.006 079
31	19.194 342	181.943 425	.005 496
32	21.113 777	201.137 767	.004 972
33	23.225 154	222.251 544	.004 499
34	25.547 670	245.476 699	.004 074
35	28.102 437	271.024 368	.003 690
36	30.912 681	299.126 805	.003 343
37	34.003 949	330.039 486	.003 030
38	37.404 343	364.043 434	.002 747
39	41.144 778	401.447 778	.002 491
40	45.259 256	442.592 556	.002 259
41	49.785 181	487.851 811	.002 050
42	54.763 699	537.636 992	.001 860
43	60.240 069	592.400 692	.001 688
44	66.264 076	652.640 761	.001 532
45	72.890 484	718.904 837	.001 391
46	80.179 532	791.795 321	.001 263
47	88.197 485	871.974 853	.001 147
48	97.017 234	960.172 338	.001 041
49	106.718 957	1,057.189 572	.000 946
50	117.390 853	1,163.908 529	.000 859

RATE
10%

DISCOUNT FACTOR How much 1 at a future date is worth today	PRESENT WORTH OF AN ANNUITY FACTOR How much 1 received or paid annually for X years is worth today	CAPITAL RECOVERY FACTOR Annual payment that will repay a $1 loan in X years with compound interest on the unpaid balance	Year
.909 091	.909 091	1.100 000	1
.826 446	1.735 537	.576 190	2
.751 315	2.486 852	.402 115	3
.683 013	3.169 865	.315 471	4
.620 921	3.790 787	.263 797	5
.564 474	4.355 261	.229 607	6
.513 158	4.868 419	.205 405	7
.466 507	5.334 926	.187 444	8
.424 098	5.759 024	.173 641	9
.385 543	6.144 567	.162 745	10
.350 494	6.495 061	.153 963	11
.318 631	6.813 692	.146 763	12
.289 664	7.103 356	.140 779	13
.263 331	7.366 687	.135 746	14
.239 392	7.606 080	.131 474	15
.217 629	7.823 709	.127 817	16
.197 845	8.021 553	.124 664	17
.179 859	8.201 412	.121 930	18
.163 508	8.364 920	.119 547	19
.148 644	8.513 564	.117 460	20
.135 131	8.648 694	.115 624	21
.122 846	8.771 540	.114 005	22
.111 678	8.883 218	.112 572	23
.101 526	8.984 744	.111 300	24
.092 296	9.077 040	.110 168	25
.083 905	9.160 945	.109 159	26
.076 278	9.237 223	.108 258	27
.069 343	9.306 567	.107 451	28
.063 039	9.369 606	.106 728	29
.057 309	9.426 914	.106 079	30
.052 099	9.479 013	.105 496	31
.047 362	9.526 376	.104 972	32
.043 057	9.569 432	.104 499	33
.039 143	9.608 575	.104 074	34
.035 584	9.644 159	.103 690	35
.032 349	9.676 508	.103 343	36
.029 408	9.705 917	.103 030	37
.026 735	9.732 651	.102 747	38
.024 304	9.756 956	.102 491	39
.022 095	9.779 051	.102 259	40
.020 086	9.799 137	.102 050	41
.018 260	9.817 397	.101 860	42
.016 600	9.833 998	.101 688	43
.015 091	9.849 089	.101 532	44
.013 719	9.862 808	.101 391	45
.012 472	9.875 280	.101 263	46
.011 338	9.886 618	.101 147	47
.010 307	9.896 926	.101 041	48
.009 370	9.906 296	.100 946	49
.008 519	9.914 814	.100 859	50

RATE
11%

Year	COMPOUNDING FACTOR FOR 1 What an initial amount becomes when growing at compound interest	COMPOUNDING FACTOR FOR 1 PER ANNUM Growth of equal year-end deposits all growing at compound interest	SINKING FUND FACTOR Level deposit required each year to reach 1 by a given year
1	1.110 000	1.000 000	1.000 000
2	1.232 100	2.110 000	.473 934
3	1.367 631	3.342 100	.299 213
4	1.518 070	4.709 731	.212 326
5	1.685 058	6.227 801	.160 570
6	1.870 415	7.912 860	.126 377
7	2.076 160	9.783 274	.102 215
8	2.304 538	11.859 434	.084 321
9	2.558 037	14.163 972	.070 602
10	2.839 421	16.722 009	.059 801
11	3.151 757	19.561 430	.051 121
12	3.498 451	22.713 187	.044 027
13	3.883 280	26.211 638	.038 151
14	4.310 441	30.094 918	.033 228
15	4.784 589	34.405 359	.029 065
16	5.310 894	39.189 948	.025 517
17	5.895 093	44.500 843	.022 471
18	6.543 553	50.395 936	.019 843
19	7.263 344	56.939 488	.017 563
20	8.062 312	64.202 832	.015 576
21	8.949 166	72.265 144	.013 838
22	9.933 574	81.214 309	.012 313
23	11.026 267	91.147 884	.010 971
24	12.239 157	102.174 151	.009 787
25	13.585 464	114.413 307	.008 740
26	15.079 865	127.998 771	.007 813
27	16.738 650	143.078 636	.006 989
28	18.579 901	159.817 286	.006 257
29	20.623 691	178.397 187	.005 605
30	22.892 297	199.020 878	.005 025
31	25.410 449	221.913 174	.004 506
32	28.205 599	247.323 624	.004 043
33	31.308 214	275.529 222	.003 629
34	34.752 118	306.837 437	.003 259
35	38.574 851	341.589 555	.002 927
36	42.818 085	380.164 406	.002 630
37	47.528 074	422.982 490	.002 364
38	52.756 162	470.510 564	.002 125
39	58.559 340	523.266 726	.001 911
40	65.000 867	581.826 066	.001 719
41	72.150 963	646.826 934	.001 546
42	80.087 569	718.977 896	.001 391
43	88.897 201	799.065 465	.001 251
44	98.675 893	887.962 666	.001 126
45	109.530 242	986.638 559	.001 014
46	121.578 568	1,096.168 801	.000 912
47	134.952 211	1,217.747 369	.000 821
48	149.796 954	1,352.699 580	.000 739
49	166.274 619	1,502.496 534	.000 666
50	184.564 827	1,668.771 152	.000 599

RATE
11%

DISCOUNT FACTOR How much 1 at a future date is worth today	PRESENT WORTH OF AN ANNUITY FACTOR How much 1 received or paid annually for X years is worth today	CAPITAL RECOVERY FACTOR Annual payment that will repay a $1 loan in X years with compound interest on the unpaid balance	Year
.900 901	.900 901	1.110 000	1
.811 622	1.712 523	.583 934	2
.731 191	2.443 715	.409 213	3
.658 731	3.102 446	.322 326	4
.593 451	3.695 897	.270 570	5
.534 641	4.230 538	.236 377	6
.481 658	4.712 196	.212 215	7
.433 926	5.146 123	.194 321	8
.390 925	5.537 048	.180 602	9
.352 184	5.889 232	.169 801	10
.317 283	6.206 515	.161 121	11
.285 841	6.492 356	.154 027	12
.257 514	6.749 870	.148 151	13
.231 995	6.981 865	.143 228	14
.209 004	7.190 870	.139 065	15
.188 292	7.379 162	.135 517	16
.169 633	7.548 794	.132 471	17
.152 822	7.701 617	.129 843	18
.137 678	7.839 294	.127 563	19
.124 034	7.963 328	.125 576	20
.111 742	8.075 070	.123 838	21
.100 669	8.175 739	.122 313	22
.090 693	8.266 432	.120 971	23
.081 705	8.348 137	.119 787	24
.073 608	8.421 745	.118 740	25
.066 314	8.488 058	.117 813	26
.059 742	8.547 800	.116 989	27
.053 822	8.601 622	.116 257	28
.048 488	8.650 110	.115 605	29
.043 683	8.693 793	.115 025	30
.039 354	8.733 146	.114 506	31
.035 454	8.768 600	.114 043	32
.031 940	8.800 541	.113 629	33
.028 775	8.829 316	.113 259	34
.025 924	8.855 240	.112 927	35
.023 355	8.878 594	.112 630	36
.021 040	8.899 635	.112 364	37
.018 955	8.918 590	.112 125	38
.017 077	8.935 666	.111 911	39
.015 384	8.951 051	.111 719	40
.013 860	8.964 911	.111 546	41
.012 486	8.977 397	.111 391	42
.011 249	8.988 646	.111 251	43
.010 134	8.998 780	.111 126	44
.009 130	9.007 910	.111 014	45
.008 225	9.016 135	.110 912	46
.007 410	9.023 545	.110 821	47
.006 676	9.030 221	.110 739	48
.006 014	9.036 235	.110 666	49
.005 418	9.041 653	.110 599	50

RATE
12%

Year	COMPOUNDING FACTOR FOR 1 What an initial amount becomes when growing at compound interest	COMPOUNDING FACTOR FOR 1 PER ANNUM Growth of equal year-end deposits all growing at compound interest	SINKING FUND FACTOR Level deposit required each year to reach 1 by a given year
1	1.120 000	1.000 000	1.000 000
2	1.254 400	2.120 000	.471 698
3	1.404 928	3.374 400	.296 349
4	1.573 519	4.779 328	.209 234
5	1.762 342	6.352 847	.157 410
6	1.973 823	8.115 189	.123 226
7	2.210 681	10.089 012	.099 118
8	2.475 963	12.299 693	.081 303
9	2.773 079	14.775 656	.067 679
10	3.105 848	17.548 735	.056 984
11	3.478 550	20.654 583	.048 415
12	3.895 976	24.133 133	.041 437
13	4.363 493	28.029 109	.035 677
14	4.887 112	32.392 602	.030 871
15	5.473 566	37.279 715	.026 824
16	6.130 394	42.753 280	.023 390
17	6.866 041	48.883 674	.020 457
18	7.689 966	55.749 715	.017 937
19	8.612 762	63.439 681	.015 763
20	9.646 293	72.052 442	.013 879
21	10.803 848	81.698 736	.012 240
22	12.100 310	92.502 584	.010 811
23	13.552 347	104.602 894	.009 560
24	15.178 629	118.155 241	.008 463
25	17.000 064	133.333 870	.007 500
26	19.040 072	150.333 934	.006 652
27	21.324 881	169.374 007	.005 904
28	23.883 866	190.698 887	.005 244
29	26.749 930	214.582 754	.004 660
30	29.959 922	241.332 684	.004 144
31	33.555 113	271.292 606	.003 686
32	37.581 726	304.847 719	.003 280
33	42.091 533	342.429 446	.002 920
34	47.142 517	384.520 979	.002 601
35	52.799 620	431.663 496	.002 317
36	59.135 574	484.463 116	.002 064
37	66.231 843	543.598 690	.001 840
38	74.179 664	609.830 533	.001 640
39	83.081 224	684.010 197	.001 462
40	93.050 970	767.091 420	.001 304
41	104.217 087	860.142 391	.001 163
42	116.723 137	964.359 478	.001 037
43	130.729 914	1,081.082 615	.000 925
44	146.417 503	1,211.812 529	.000 825
45	163.987 604	1,358.230 032	.000 736
46	183.666 116	1,522.217 636	.000 657
47	205.706 050	1,705.883 752	.000 586
48	230.390 776	1,911.589 803	.000 523
49	258.037 669	2,141.980 579	.000 467
50	289.002 190	2,400.018 249	.000 417

RATE
12%

DISCOUNT FACTOR How much 1 at a future date is worth today	PRESENT WORTH OF AN ANNUITY FACTOR How much 1 received or paid annually for X years is worth today	CAPITAL RECOVERY FACTOR Annual payment that will repay a $1 loan in X years with compound interest on the unpaid balance	Year
.892 857	.892 857	1.120 000	1
.797 194	1.690 051	.591 698	2
.711 780	2.401 831	.416 349	3
.635 518	3.037 349	.329 234	4
.567 427	3.604 776	.277 410	5
.506 631	4.111 407	.243 226	6
.452 349	4.563 757	.219 118	7
.403 883	4.967 640	.201 303	8
.360 610	5.328 250	.187 679	9
.321 973	5.650 223	.176 984	10
.287 476	5.937 699	.168 415	11
.256 675	6.194 374	.161 437	12
.229 174	6.423 548	.155 677	13
.204 620	6.628 168	.150 871	14
.182 696	6.810 864	.146 824	15
.163 122	6.973 986	.143 390	16
.145 644	7.119 630	.140 457	17
.130 040	7.249 670	.137 937	18
.116 107	7.365 777	.135 763	19
.103 667	7.469 444	.133 879	20
.092 560	7.562 003	.132 240	21
.082 643	7.644 646	.130 811	22
.073 788	7.718 434	.129 560	23
.065 882	7.784 316	.128 463	24
.058 823	7.843 139	.127 500	25
.052 521	7.895 660	.126 652	26
.046 894	7.942 554	.125 904	27
.041 869	7.984 423	.125 244	28
.037 383	8.021 806	.124 660	29
.033 378	8.055 184	.124 144	30
.029 802	8.084 986	.123 686	31
.026 609	8.111 594	.123 280	32
.023 758	8.135 352	.122 920	33
.021 212	8.156 564	.122 601	34
.018 940	8.175 504	.122 317	35
.016 910	8.192 414	.122 064	36
.015 098	8.207 513	.121 840	37
.013 481	8.220 993	.121 640	38
.012 036	8.233 030	.121 462	39
.010 747	8.243 777	.121 304	40
.009 595	8.253 372	.121 163	41
.008 567	8.261 939	.121 037	42
.007 649	8.269 589	.120 925	43
.006 830	8.276 418	.120 825	44
.006 098	8.282 516	.120 736	45
.005 445	8.287 961	.120 657	46
.004 861	8.292 822	.120 586	47
.004 340	8.297 163	.120 523	48
.003 875	8.301 038	.120 467	49
.003 460	8.304 498	.120 417	50

RATE
13%

Year	COMPOUNDING FACTOR FOR 1 What an initial amount becomes when growing at compound interest	COMPOUNDING FACTOR FOR 1 PER ANNUM Growth of equal year-end deposits all growing at compound interest	SINKING FUND FACTOR Level deposit required each year to reach 1 by a given year
1	1.130 000	1.000 000	1.000 000
2	1.276 900	2.130 000	.469 484
3	1.442 897	3.406 900	.293 522
4	1.630 474	4.849 797	.206 194
5	1.842 435	6.480 271	.154 315
6	2.081 952	8.322 706	.120 153
7	2.352 605	10.404 658	.096 111
8	2.658 444	12.757 263	.078 387
9	3.004 042	15.415 707	.064 869
10	3.394 567	18.419 749	.054 290
11	3.835 861	21.814 317	.045 841
12	4.334 523	25.650 178	.038 986
13	4.898 011	29.984 701	.033 350
14	5.534 753	34.882 712	.028 667
15	6.254 270	40.417 464	.024 742
16	7.067 326	46.671 735	.021 426
17	7.986 078	53.739 060	.018 608
18	9.024 268	61.725 138	.016 201
19	10.197 423	70.749 406	.014 134
20	11.523 088	80.946 829	.012 354
21	13.021 089	92.469 917	.010 814
22	14.713 831	105.491 006	.009 479
23	16.626 629	120.204 837	.008 319
24	18.788 091	136.831 465	.007 308
25	21.230 542	155.619 556	.006 426
26	23.990 513	176.850 098	.005 655
27	27.109 279	200.840 611	.004 979
28	30.633 486	227.949 890	.004 387
29	34.615 839	258.583 376	.003 867
30	39.115 898	293.199 215	.003 411
31	44.200 965	332.315 113	.003 009
32	49.947 090	376.516 078	.002 656
33	56.440 212	426.463 168	.002 345
34	63.777 439	482.903 380	.002 071
35	72.068 506	546.680 819	.001 829
36	81.437 412	618.749 325	.001 616
37	92.024 276	700.186 738	.001 428
38	103.987 432	792.211 014	.001 262
39	117.505 798	896.198 445	.001 116
40	132.781 552	1,013.704 243	.000 986
41	150.043 153	1,146.485 795	.000 872
42	169.548 763	1,296.528 948	.000 771
43	191.590 103	1,466.077 712	.000 682
44	216.496 816	1,657.667 814	.000 603
45	244.641 402	1,874.164 630	.000 534
46	276.444 784	2,118.806 032	.000 472
47	312.382 606	2,395.250 816	.000 417
48	352.992 345	2,707.633 422	.000 369
49	398.881 350	3,060.625 767	.000 327
50	450.735 925	3,459.507 117	.000 289

RATE 13%

DISCOUNT FACTOR How much 1 at a future date is worth today	PRESENT WORTH OF AN ANNUITY FACTOR How much 1 received or paid annually for X years is worth today	CAPITAL RECOVERY FACTOR Annual payment that will repay a $1 loan in X years with compound interest on the unpaid balance	Year
.884 956	.884 956	1.130 000	1
.783 147	1.668 102	.599 484	2
.693 050	2.361 153	.423 522	3
.613 319	2.974 471	.336 194	4
.542 760	3.517 231	.284 315	5
.480 319	3.997 550	.250 153	6
.425 061	4.422 610	.226 111	7
.376 160	4.798 770	.208 387	8
.332 885	5.131 655	.194 869	9
.294 588	5.426 243	.184 290	10
.260 698	5.686 941	.175 841	11
.230 706	5.917 647	.168 986	12
.204 165	6.121 812	.163 350	13
.180 677	6.302 488	.158 667	14
.159 891	6.462 379	.154 742	15
.141 496	6.603 875	.151 426	16
.125 218	6.729 093	.148 608	17
.110 812	6.839 905	.146 201	18
.098 064	6.937 969	.144 134	19
.086 782	7.024 752	.142 354	20
.076 798	7.101 550	.140 814	21
.067 963	7.169 513	.139 479	22
.060 144	7.229 658	.138 319	23
.053 225	7.282 883	.137 308	24
.047 102	7.329 985	.136 426	25
.041 683	7.371 668	.135 655	26
.036 888	7.408 556	.134 979	27
.032 644	7.441 200	.134 387	28
.028 889	7.470 088	.133 867	29
.025 565	7.495 653	.133 411	30
.022 624	7.518 277	.133 009	31
.020 021	7.538 299	.132 656	32
.017 718	7.556 016	.132 345	33
.015 680	7.571 696	.132 071	34
.013 876	7.585 572	.131 829	35
.012 279	7.597 851	.131 616	36
.010 867	7.608 718	.131 428	37
.009 617	7.618 334	.131 262	38
.008 510	7.626 844	.131 116	39
.007 531	7.634 376	.130 986	40
.006 665	7.641 040	.130 872	41
.005 898	7.646 938	.130 771	42
.005 219	7.652 158	.130 682	43
.004 619	7.656 777	.130 603	44
.004 088	7.660 864	.130 534	45
.003 617	7.664 482	.130 472	46
.003 201	7.667 683	.130 417	47
.002 833	7.670 516	.130 369	48
.002 507	7.673 023	.130 327	49
.002 219	7.675 242	.130 289	50

RATE
14%

Year	COMPOUNDING FACTOR FOR 1 What an initial amount becomes when growing at compound interest	COMPOUNDING FACTOR FOR 1 PER ANNUM Growth of equal year-end deposits all growing at compound interest	SINKING FUND FACTOR Level deposit required each year to reach 1 by a given year
1	1.140 000	1.000 000	1.000 000
2	1.299 600	2.140 000	.467 290
3	1.481 544	3.439 600	.290 731
4	1.688 960	4.921 144	.203 205
5	1.925 415	6.610 104	.151 284
6	2.194 973	8.535 519	.117 157
7	2.502 269	10.730 491	.093 192
8	2.852 586	13.232 760	.075 570
9	3.251 949	16.085 347	.062 168
10	3.707 221	19.337 295	.051 714
11	4.226 232	23.044 516	.043 394
12	4.817 905	27.270 749	.036 669
13	5.492 411	32.088 654	.031 164
14	6.261 349	37.581 065	.026 609
15	7.137 938	43.842 414	.022 809
16	8.137 249	50.980 352	.019 615
17	9.276 464	59.117 601	.016 915
18	10.575 169	68.394 066	.014 621
19	12.055 693	78.969 235	.012 663
20	13.743 490	91.024 928	.010 986
21	15.667 578	104.768 418	.009 545
22	17.861 039	120.435 996	.008 303
23	20.361 585	138.297 035	.007 231
24	23.212 207	158.658 620	.006 303
25	26.461 916	181.870 827	.005 498
26	30.166 584	208.332 743	.004 800
27	34.389 906	238.499 327	.004 193
28	39.204 493	272.889 233	.003 664
29	44.693 122	312.093 725	.003 204
30	50.950 159	356.786 847	.002 803
31	58.083 181	407.737 006	.002 453
32	66.214 826	465.820 186	.002 147
33	75.484 902	532.035 012	.001 880
34	86.052 788	607.519 914	.001 646
35	98.100 178	693.572 702	.001 442
36	111.834 203	791.672 881	.001 263
37	127.490 992	903.507 084	.001 107
38	145.339 731	1,030.998 076	.000 970
39	165.687 293	1,176.337 806	.000 850
40	188.883 514	1,342.025 099	.000 745
41	215.327 206	1,530.908 613	.000 653
42	245.473 015	1,746.235 819	.000 573
43	279.839 237	1,991.708 833	.000 502
44	319.016 730	2,271.548 070	.000 440
45	363.679 072	2,590.564 800	.000 386
46	414.594 142	2,954.243 872	.000 338
47	472.637 322	3,368.838 014	.000 297
48	538.806 547	3,841.475 336	.000 260
49	614.239 464	4,380.281 883	.000 228
50	700.232 988	4,994.521 346	.000 200

RATE
14%

DISCOUNT FACTOR How much 1 at a future date is worth today	PRESENT WORTH OF AN ANNUITY FACTOR How much 1 received or paid annually for X years is worth today	CAPITAL RECOVERY FACTOR Annual payment that will repay a $1 loan in X years with compound interest on the unpaid balance	Year
.877 193	.877 193	1.140 000	1
.769 468	1.646 661	.607 290	2
.674 972	2.321 632	.430 731	3
.592 080	2.913 712	.343 205	4
.519 369	3.433 081	.291 284	5
.455 587	3.888 668	.257 157	6
.399 637	4.288 305	.233 192	7
.350 559	4.638 864	.215 570	8
.307 508	4.946 372	.202 168	9
.269 744	5.216 116	.191 714	10
.236 617	5.452 733	.183 394	11
.207 559	5.660 292	.176 669	12
.182 069	5.842 362	.171 164	13
.159 710	6.002 072	.166 609	14
.140 096	6.142 168	.162 809	15
.122 892	6.265 060	.159 615	16
.107 800	6.372 859	.156 915	17
.094 561	6.467 420	.154 621	18
.082 948	6.550 369	.152 663	19
.072 762	6.623 131	.150 986	20
.063 826	6.686 957	.149 545	21
.055 988	6.742 944	.148 303	22
.049 112	6.792 056	.147 231	23
.043 081	6.835 137	.146 303	24
.037 790	6.872 927	.145 498	25
.033 149	6.906 077	.144 800	26
.029 078	6.935 155	.144 193	27
.025 507	6.960 662	.143 664	28
.022 375	6.983 037	.143 204	29
.019 627	7.002 664	.142 803	30
.017 217	7.019 881	.142 453	31
.015 102	7.034 983	.142 147	32
.013 248	7.048 231	.141 880	33
.011 621	7.059 852	.141 646	34
.010 194	7.070 045	.141 442	35
.008 942	7.078 987	.141 263	36
.007 844	7.086 831	.141 107	37
.006 880	7.093 711	.140 970	38
.006 035	7.099 747	.140 850	39
.005 294	7.105 041	.140 745	40
.004 644	7.109 685	.140 653	41
.004 074	7.113 759	.140 573	42
.003 573	7.117 332	.140 502	43
.003 135	7.120 467	.140 440	44
.002 750	7.123 217	.140 386	45
.002 412	7.125 629	.140 338	46
.002 116	7.127 744	.140 297	47
.001 856	7.129 600	.140 260	48
.001 628	7.131 228	.140 228	49
.001 428	7.132 656	.140 200	50

RATE
15%

Year	COMPOUNDING FACTOR FOR 1 What an initial amount becomes when growing at compound interest	COMPOUNDING FACTOR FOR 1 PER ANNUM Growth of equal year-end deposits all growing at compound interest	SINKING FUND FACTOR Level deposit required each year to reach 1 by a given year
1	1.150 000	1.000 000	1.000 000
2	1.322 500	2.150 000	.465 116
3	1.520 875	3.472 500	.287 977
4	1.749 006	4.993 375	.200 265
5	2.011 357	6.742 381	.148 316
6	2.313 061	8.753 738	.114 237
7	2.660 020	11.066 799	.090 360
8	3.059 023	13.726 819	.072 850
9	3.517 876	16.785 842	.059 574
10	4.045 558	20.303 718	.049 252
11	4.652 391	24.349 276	.041 069
12	5.350 250	29.001 667	.034 481
13	6.152 788	34.351 917	.029 110
14	7.075 706	40.504 705	.024 688
15	8.137 062	47.580 411	.021 017
16	9.357 621	55.717 472	.017 948
17	10.761 264	65.075 093	.015 367
18	12.375 454	75.836 357	.013 186
19	14.231 772	88.211 811	.011 336
20	16.366 537	102.443 583	.009 761
21	18.821 518	118.810 120	.008 417
22	21.644 746	137.631 638	.007 266
23	24.891 458	159.276 384	.006 278
24	28.625 176	184.167 841	.005 430
25	32.918 953	212.793 017	.004 699
26	37.856 796	245.711 970	.004 070
27	43.535 315	283.568 766	.003 526
28	50.065 612	327.104 080	.003 057
29	57.575 454	377.169 693	.002 651
30	66.211 772	434.745 146	.002 300
31	76.143 538	500.956 918	.001 996
32	87.565 068	577.100 456	.001 733
33	100.699 829	664.665 524	.001 505
34	115.804 803	765.365 353	.001 307
35	133.175 523	881.170 156	.001 135
36	153.151 852	1,014.345 680	.000 986
37	176.124 630	1,167.497 532	.000 857
38	202.543 324	1,343.622 161	.000 744
39	232.924 823	1,546.165 485	.000 647
40	267.863 546	1,779.090 308	.000 562
41	308.043 078	2,046.953 854	.000 489
42	354.249 540	2,354.996 933	.000 425
43	407.386 971	2,709.246 473	.000 369
44	468.495 017	3,116.633 443	.000 321
45	538.769 269	3,585.128 460	.000 279
46	619.584 659	4,123.897 729	.000 242
47	712.522 358	4,743.482 388	.000 211
48	819.400 712	5,456.004 746	.000 183
49	942.310 819	6,275.405 458	.000 159
50	1,083.657 442	7,217.716 277	.000 139

RATE
15%

DISCOUNT FACTOR How much 1 at a future date is worth today	PRESENT WORTH OF AN ANNUITY FACTOR How much 1 received or paid annually for X years is worth today	CAPITAL RECOVERY FACTOR Annual payment that will repay a $1 loan in X years with compound interest on the unpaid balance	Year
.869 565	.869 565	1.150 000	1
.756 144	1.625 709	.615 116	2
.657 516	2.283 225	.437 977	3
.571 753	2.854 978	.350 265	4
.497 177	3.352 155	.298 316	5
.432 328	3.784 483	.264 237	6
.375 937	4.160 420	.240 360	7
.326 902	4.487 322	.222 850	8
.284 262	4.771 584	.209 574	9
.247 185	5.018 769	.199 252	10
.214 943	5.233 712	.191 069	11
.186 907	5.420 619	.184 481	12
.162 528	5.583 147	.179 110	13
.141 329	5.724 476	.174 688	14
.122 894	5.847 370	.171 017	15
.106 865	5.954 235	.167 948	16
.092 926	6.047 161	.165 367	17
.080 805	6.127 966	.163 186	18
.070 265	6.198 231	.161 336	19
.061 100	6.259 331	.159 761	20
.053 131	6.312 462	.158 417	21
.046 201	6.358 663	.157 266	22
.040 174	6.398 837	.156 278	23
.034 934	6.433 771	.155 430	24
.030 378	6.464 149	.154 699	25
.026 415	6.490 564	.154 070	26
.022 970	6.513 534	.153 526	27
.019 974	6.533 508	.153 057	28
.017 369	6.550 877	.152 651	29
.015 103	6.565 980	.152 300	30
.013 133	6.579 113	.151 996	31
.011 420	6.590 533	.151 733	32
.009 931	6.600 463	.151 505	33
.008 635	6.609 099	.151 307	34
.007 509	6.616 607	.151 135	35
.006 529	6.623 137	.150 986	36
.005 678	6.628 815	.150 857	37
.004 937	6.633 752	.150 744	38
.004 293	6.638 045	.150 647	39
.003 733	6.641 778	.150 562	40
.003 246	6.645 025	.150 489	41
.002 823	6.647 848	.150 425	42
.002 455	6.650 302	.150 369	43
.002 134	6.652 437	.150 321	44
.001 856	6.654 293	.150 279	45
.001 614	6.655 907	.150 242	46
.001 403	6.657 310	.150 211	47
.001 220	6.658 531	.150 183	48
.001 061	6.659 592	.150 159	49
.000 923	6.660 515	.150 139	50

RATE
16%

Year	COMPOUNDING FACTOR FOR 1 What an initial amount becomes when growing at compound interest	COMPOUNDING FACTOR FOR 1 PER ANNUM Growth of equal year-end deposits all growing at compound interest	SINKING FUND FACTOR Level deposit required each year to reach 1 by a given year
1	1.160 000	1.000 000	1.000 000
2	1.345 600	2.160 000	.462 963
3	1.560 896	3.505 600	.285 258
4	1.810 639	5.066 496	.197 375
5	2.100 342	6.877 135	.145 409
6	2.436 396	8.977 477	.111 390
7	2.826 220	11.413 873	.087 613
8	3.278 415	14.240 093	.070 224
9	3.802 961	17.518 508	.057 082
10	4.411 435	21.321 469	.046 901
11	5.117 265	25.732 904	.038 861
12	5.936 027	30.850 169	.032 415
13	6.885 791	36.786 196	.027 184
14	7.987 518	43.671 987	.022 898
15	9.265 521	51.659 505	.019 358
16	10.748 004	60.925 026	.016 414
17	12.467 685	71.673 030	.013 952
18	14.462 514	84.140 715	.011 885
19	16.776 517	98.603 230	.010 142
20	19.460 759	115.379 747	.008 667
21	22.574 481	134.840 506	.007 416
22	26.186 398	157.414 987	.006 353
23	30.376 222	183.601 385	.005 447
24	35.236 417	213.977 607	.004 673
25	40.874 244	249.214 024	.004 013
26	47.414 123	290.088 267	.003 447
27	55.000 382	337.502 390	.002 963
28	63.800 444	392.502 773	.002 548
29	74.008 515	456.303 216	.002 192
30	85.849 877	530.311 731	.001 886
31	99.585 857	616.161 608	.001 623
32	115.519 594	715.747 465	.001 397
33	134.002 729	831.267 059	.001 203
34	155.443 166	965.269 789	.001 036
35	180.314 073	1,120.712 955	.000 892
36	209.164 324	1,301.027 028	.000 769
37	242.630 616	1,510.191 352	.000 662
38	281.451 515	1,752.821 968	.000 571
39	326.483 757	2,034.273 483	.000 492
40	378.721 158	2,360.757 241	.000 424
41	439.316 544	2,739.478 399	.000 365
42	509.607 191	3,178.794 943	.000 315
43	591.144 341	3,688.402 134	.000 271
44	685.727 436	4,279.546 475	.000 234
45	795.443 826	4,965.273 911	.000 201
46	922.714 838	5,760.717 737	.000 174
47	1,070.349 212	6,683.432 575	.000 150
48	1,241.605 086	7,753.781 787	.000 129
49	1,440.261 900	8,995.386 873	.000 111
50	1,670.703 804	10,435.648 77	.000 096

RATE 16%

DISCOUNT FACTOR How much 1 at a future date is worth today	PRESENT WORTH OF AN ANNUITY FACTOR How much 1 received or paid annually for X years is worth today	CAPITAL RECOVERY FACTOR Annual payment that will repay a $1 loan in X years with compound interest on the unpaid balance	Year
.862 069	.862 069	1.160 000	1
.743 163	1.605 232	.622 963	2
.640 658	2.245 890	.445 258	3
.552 291	2.798 181	.357 375	4
.476 113	3.274 294	.305 409	5
.410 442	3.684 736	.271 390	6
.353 830	4.038 565	.247 613	7
.305 025	4.343 591	.230 224	8
.262 953	4.606 544	.217 082	9
.226 684	4.833 227	.206 901	10
.195 417	5.028 644	.198 861	11
.168 463	5.197 107	.192 415	12
.145 227	5.342 334	.187 184	13
.125 195	5.467 529	.182 898	14
.107 927	5.575 456	.179 358	15
.093 041	5.668 497	.176 414	16
.080 207	5.748 704	.173 952	17
.069 144	5.817 848	.171 885	18
.059 607	5.877 455	.170 142	19
.051 385	5.928 841	.168 667	20
.044 298	5.973 139	.167 416	21
.038 188	6.011 326	.166 353	22
.032 920	6.044 247	.165 447	23
.028 380	6.072 627	.164 673	24
.024 465	6.097 092	.164 013	25
.021 091	6.118 183	.163 447	26
.018 182	6.136 364	.162 963	27
.015 674	6.152 038	.162 548	28
.013 512	6.165 550	.162 192	29
.011 648	6.177 198	.161 886	30
.010 042	6.187 240	.161 623	31
.008 657	6.195 897	.161 397	32
.007 463	6.203 359	.161 203	33
.006 433	6.209 792	.161 036	34
.005 546	6.215 338	.160 892	35
.004 781	6.220 119	.160 769	36
.004 121	6.224 241	.160 662	37
.003 553	6.227 794	.160 571	38
.003 063	6.230 857	.160 492	39
.002 640	6.233 497	.160 424	40
.002 276	6.235 773	.160 365	41
.001 962	6.237 736	.160 315	42
.001 692	6.239 427	.160 271	43
.001 458	6.240 886	.160 234	44
.001 257	6.242 143	.160 201	45
.001 084	6.243 227	.160 174	46
.000 934	6.244 161	.160 150	47
.000 805	6.244 966	.160 129	48
.000 694	6.245 661	.160 111	49
.000 599	6.246 259	.160 096	50

RATE
17%

Year	COMPOUNDING FACTOR FOR 1 What an initial amount becomes when growing at compound interest	COMPOUNDING FACTOR FOR 1 PER ANNUM Growth of equal year-end deposits all growing at compound interest	SINKING FUND FACTOR Level deposit required each year to reach 1 by a given year
1	1.170 000	1.000 000	1.000 000
2	1.368 900	2.170 000	.460 829
3	1.601 613	3.538 900	.282 574
4	1.873 887	5.140 513	.194 533
5	2.192 448	7.014 400	.142 564
6	2.565 164	9.206 848	.108 615
7	3.001 242	11.772 012	.084 947
8	3.511 453	14.773 255	.067 690
9	4.108 400	18.284 708	.054 691
10	4.806 828	22.393 108	.044 657
11	5.623 989	27.199 937	.036 765
12	6.580 067	32.823 926	.030 466
13	7.698 679	39.403 993	.025 378
14	9.007 454	47.102 672	.021 230
15	10.538 721	56.110 126	.017 822
16	12.330 304	66.648 848	.015 004
17	14.426 456	78.979 152	.012 662
18	16.878 953	93.405 608	.010 706
19	19.748 375	110.284 561	.009 067
20	23.105 599	130.032 936	.007 690
21	27.033 551	153.138 535	.006 530
22	31.629 255	180.172 086	.005 550
23	37.006 228	211.801 341	.004 721
24	43.297 287	248.807 569	.004 019
25	50.657 826	292.104 856	.003 423
26	59.269 656	342.762 681	.002 917
27	69.345 497	402.032 337	.002 487
28	81.134 232	471.377 835	.002 121
29	94.927 051	552.512 066	.001 810
30	111.064 650	647.439 118	.001 545
31	129.945 641	758.503 768	.001 318
32	152.036 399	888.449 408	.001 126
33	177.882 587	1,040.485 808	.000 961
34	208.122 627	1,218.368 395	.000 821
35	243.503 474	1,426.491 022	.000 701
36	284.899 064	1,669.994 496	.000 599
37	333.331 905	1,954.893 560	.000 512
38	389.998 329	2,288.225 465	.000 437
39	456.298 045	2,678.223 794	.000 373
40	533.868 713	3,134.521 839	.000 319
41	624.626 394	3,668.390 552	.000 273
42	730.812 881	4,293.016 946	.000 233
43	855.051 071	5,023.829 827	.000 199
44	1,000.409 753	5,878.880 897	.000 170
45	1,170.479 411	6,879.290 650	.000 145
46	1,369.460 910	8,049.770 060	.000 124
47	1,602.269 265	9,419.230 971	.000 106
48	1,874.655 040	11,021.500 24	.000 091
49	2,193.346 397	12,896.155 28	.000 078
50	2,566.215 284	15,089.501 67	.000 066

RATE 17%

DISCOUNT FACTOR How much 1 at a future date is worth today	PRESENT WORTH OF AN ANNUITY FACTOR How much 1 received or paid annually for X years is worth today	CAPITAL RECOVERY FACTOR Annual payment that will repay a $1 loan in X years with compound interest on the unpaid balance	Year
.854 701	.854 701	1.170 000	1
.730 514	1.585 214	.630 829	2
.624 371	2.209 585	.452 574	3
.533 650	2.743 235	.364 533	4
.456 111	3.199 346	.312 564	5
.389 839	3.589 185	.278 615	6
.333 195	3.922 380	.254 947	7
.284 782	4.207 163	.237 690	8
.243 404	4.450 566	.224 691	9
.208 037	4.658 604	.214 657	10
.177 810	4.836 413	.206 765	11
.151 974	4.988 387	.200 466	12
.129 892	5.118 280	.195 378	13
.111 019	5.229 299	.191 230	14
.094 888	5.324 187	.187 822	15
.081 101	5.405 288	.185 004	16
.069 317	5.474 605	.182 662	17
.059 245	5.533 851	.180 706	18
.050 637	5.584 488	.179 067	19
.043 280	5.627 767	.177 690	20
.036 991	5.664 758	.176 530	21
.031 616	5.696 375	.175 550	22
.027 022	5.723 397	.174 721	23
.023 096	5.746 493	.174 019	24
.019 740	5.766 234	.173 423	25
.016 872	5.783 106	.172 917	26
.014 421	5.797 526	.172 487	27
.012 325	5.809 851	.172 121	28
.010 534	5.820 386	.171 810	29
.009 004	5.829 390	.171 545	30
.007 696	5.837 085	.171 318	31
.006 577	5.843 663	.171 126	32
.005 622	5.849 284	.170 961	33
.004 805	5.854 089	.170 821	34
.004 107	5.858 196	.170 701	35
.003 510	5.861 706	.170 599	36
.003 000	5.864 706	.170 512	37
.002 564	5.867 270	.170 437	38
.002 192	5.869 461	.170 373	39
.001 873	5.871 335	.170 319	40
.001 601	5.872 936	.170 273	41
.001 368	5.874 304	.170 233	42
.001 170	5.875 473	.170 199	43
.001 000	5.876 473	.170 170	44
.000 854	5.877 327	.170 145	45
.000 730	5.878 058	.170 124	46
.000 624	5.878 682	.170 106	47
.000 533	5.879 215	.170 091	48
.000 456	5.879 671	.170 078	49
.000 390	5.880 061	.170 066	50

RATE
18%

Year	COMPOUNDING FACTOR FOR 1 What an initial amount becomes when growing at compound interest	COMPOUNDING FACTOR FOR 1 PER ANNUM Growth of equal year-end deposits all growing at compound interest	SINKING FUND FACTOR Level deposit required each year to reach 1 by a given year
1	1.180 000	1.000 000	1.000 000
2	1.392 400	2.180 000	.458 716
3	1.643 032	3.572 400	.279 924
4	1.938 778	5.215 432	.191 739
5	2.287 758	7.154 210	.139 778
6	2.699 554	9.441 968	.105 910
7	3.185 474	12.141 522	.082 362
8	3.758 859	15.326 996	.065 244
9	4.435 454	19.085 855	.052 395
10	5.233 836	23.521 309	.042 515
11	6.175 926	28.755 144	.034 776
12	7.287 593	34.931 070	.028 628
13	8.599 359	42.218 663	.023 686
14	10.147 244	50.818 022	.019 678
15	11.973 748	60.965 266	.016 403
16	14.129 023	72.939 014	.013 710
17	16.672 247	87.068 036	.011 485
18	19.673 251	103.740 283	.009 639
19	23.214 436	123.413 534	.008 103
20	27.393 035	146.627 970	.006 820
21	32.323 781	174.021 005	.005 746
22	38.142 061	206.344 785	.004 846
23	45.007 632	244.486 847	.004 090
24	53.109 006	289.494 479	.003 454
25	62.668 627	342.603 486	.002 919
26	73.948 980	405.272 113	.002 467
27	87.259 797	479.221 093	.002 087
28	102.966 560	566.480 890	.001 765
29	121.500 541	669.447 450	.001 494
30	143.370 638	790.947 991	.001 264
31	169.177 353	934.318 630	.001 070
32	199.629 277	1,103.495 983	.000 906
33	235.562 547	1,303.125 260	.000 767
34	277.963 805	1,538.687 807	.000 650
35	327.997 290	1,816.651 612	.000 550
36	387.036 802	2,144.648 902	.000 466
37	456.703 427	2,531.685 705	.000 395
38	538.910 044	2,988.389 132	.000 335
39	635.913 852	3,527.299 175	.000 284
40	750.378 345	4,163.213 027	.000 240
41	885.446 447	4,913.591 372	.000 204
42	1,044.826 807	5,799.037 818	.000 172
43	1,232.895 633	6,843.864 626	.000 146
44	1,454.816 847	8,076.760 258	.000 124
45	1,716.683 879	9,531.577 105	.000 105
46	2,025.686 977	11,248.260 98	.000 089
47	2,390.310 633	13,273.947 96	.000 075
48	2,820.566 547	15,664.258 59	.000 064
49	3,328.268 525	18,484.825 14	.000 054
50	3,927.356 860	21,813.093 67	.000 046

RATE
18%

DISCOUNT FACTOR How much 1 at a future date is worth today	PRESENT WORTH OF AN ANNUITY FACTOR How much 1 received or paid annually for X years is worth today	CAPITAL RECOVERY FACTOR Annual payment that will repay a $1 loan in X years with compound interest on the unpaid balance	Year
.847 458	.847 458	1.180 000	1
.718 184	1.565 642	.638 716	2
.608 631	2.174 273	.459 924	3
.515 789	2.690 062	.371 739	4
.437 109	3.127 171	.319 778	5
.370 432	3.497 603	.285 910	6
.313 925	3.811 528	.262 362	7
.266 038	4.077 566	.245 244	8
.225 456	4.303 022	.232 395	9
.191 064	4.494 086	.222 515	10
.161 919	4.656 005	.214 776	11
.137 220	4.793 225	.208 628	12
.116 288	4.909 513	.203 686	13
.098 549	5.008 062	.199 678	14
.083 516	5.091 578	.196 403	15
.070 776	5.162 354	.193 710	16
.059 980	5.222 334	.191 485	17
.050 830	5.273 164	.189 639	18
.043 077	5.316 241	.188 103	19
.036 506	5.352 746	.186 820	20
.030 937	5.383 683	.185 746	21
.026 218	5.409 901	.184 846	22
.022 218	5.432 120	.184 090	23
.018 829	5.450 949	.183 454	24
.015 957	5.466 906	.182 919	25
.013 523	5.480 429	.182 467	26
.011 460	5.491 889	.182 087	27
.009 712	5.501 601	.181 765	28
.008 230	5.509 831	.181 494	29
.006 975	5.516 806	.181 264	30
.005 911	5.522 717	.181 070	31
.005 009	5.527 726	.180 906	32
.004 245	5.531 971	.180 767	33
.003 598	5.535 569	.180 650	34
.003 049	5.538 618	.180 550	35
.002 584	5.541 201	.180 466	36
.002 190	5.543 391	.180 395	37
.001 856	5.545 247	.180 335	38
.001 573	5.546 819	.180 284	39
.001 333	5.548 152	.180 240	40
.001 129	5.549 281	.180 204	41
.000 957	5.550 238	.180 172	42
.000 811	5.551 049	.180 146	43
.000 687	5.551 737	.180 124	44
.000 583	5.552 319	.180 105	45
.000 494	5.552 813	.180 089	46
.000 418	5.553 231	.180 075	47
.000 355	5.553 586	.180 064	48
.000 300	5.553 886	.180 054	49
.000 255	5.554 141	.180 046	50

RATE
19%

Year	COMPOUNDING FACTOR FOR 1 What an initial amount becomes when growing at compound interest	COMPOUNDING FACTOR FOR 1 PER ANNUM Growth of equal year-end deposits all growing at compound interest	SINKING FUND FACTOR Level deposit required each year to reach 1 by a given year
1	1.190 000	1.000 000	1.000 000
2	1.416 100	2.190 000	.456 621
3	1.685 159	3.606 100	.277 308
4	2.005 339	5.291 259	.188 991
5	2.386 354	7.296 598	.137 050
6	2.839 761	9.682 952	.103 274
7	3.379 315	12.522 713	.079 855
8	4.021 385	15.902 028	.062 885
9	4.785 449	19.923 413	.050 192
10	5.694 684	24.708 862	.040 471
11	6.776 674	30.403 546	.032 891
12	8.064 242	37.180 220	.026 896
13	9.596 448	45.244 461	.022 102
14	11.419 773	54.840 909	.018 235
15	13.589 530	66.260 682	.015 092
16	16.171 540	79.850 211	.012 523
17	19.244 133	96.021 751	.010 414
18	22.900 518	115.265 884	.008 676
19	27.251 616	138.166 402	.007 238
20	32.429 423	165.418 018	.006 045
21	38.591 014	197.847 442	.005 054
22	45.923 307	236.438 456	.004 229
23	54.648 735	282.361 762	.003 542
24	65.031 994	337.010 497	.002 967
25	77.388 073	402.042 491	.002 487
26	92.091 807	479.430 565	.002 086
27	109.589 251	571.522 372	.001 750
28	130.411 208	681.111 623	.001 468
29	155.189 338	811.522 831	.001 232
30	184.675 312	966.712 169	.001 034
31	219.763 621	1,151.387 481	.000 869
32	261.518 710	1,371.151 103	.000 729
33	311.207 264	1,632.669 812	.000 612
34	370.336 645	1,943.877 077	.000 514
35	440.700 607	2,314.213 721	.000 432
36	524.433 722	2,754.914 328	.000 363
37	624.076 130	3,279.348 051	.000 305
38	742.650 594	3,903.424 180	.000 256
39	883.754 207	4,646.074 775	.000 215
40	1,051.667 507	5,529.828 982	.000 181
41	1,251.484 333	6,581.496 488	.000 152
42	1,489.266 356	7,832.980 821	.000 128
43	1,772.226 964	9,322.247 177	.000 107
44	2,108.950 087	11,094.474 14	.000 090
45	2,509.650 603	13,203.424 23	.000 076
46	2,986.484 218	15,713.074 83	.000 064
47	3,553.916 219	18,699.559 05	.000 053
48	4,229.160 301	22,253.475 27	.000 045
49	5,032.700 758	26,482.635 57	.000 038
50	5,988.913 902	31,515.336 33	.000 032

RATE
19%

DISCOUNT FACTOR How much 1 at a future date is worth today	PRESENT WORTH OF AN ANNUITY FACTOR How much 1 received or paid annually for X years is worth today	CAPITAL RECOVERY FACTOR Annual payment that will repay a $1 loan in X years with compound interest on the unpaid balance	Year
.840 336	.840 336	1.190 000	1
.706 165	1.546 501	.646 621	2
.593 416	2.139 917	.467 308	3
.498 669	2.638 586	.378 991	4
.419 049	3.057 635	.327 050	5
.352 142	3.409 777	.293 274	6
.295 918	3.705 695	.269 855	7
.248 671	3.954 366	.252 885	8
.208 967	4.163 332	.240 192	9
.175 602	4.338 935	.230 471	10
.147 565	4.486 500	.222 891	11
.124 004	4.610 504	.216 896	12
.104 205	4.714 709	.212 102	13
.087 567	4.802 277	.208 235	14
.073 586	4.875 863	.205 092	15
.061 837	4.937 700	.202 523	16
.051 964	4.989 664	.200 414	17
.043 667	5.033 331	.198 676	18
.036 695	5.070 026	.197 238	19
.030 836	5.100 862	.196 045	20
.025 913	5.126 775	.195 054	21
.021 775	5.148 550	.194 229	22
.018 299	5.166 849	.193 542	23
.015 377	5.182 226	.192 967	24
.012 922	5.195 148	.192 487	25
.010 859	5.206 007	.192 086	26
.009 125	5.215 132	.191 750	27
.007 668	5.222 800	.191 468	28
.006 444	5.229 243	.191 232	29
.005 415	5.234 658	.191 034	30
.004 550	5.239 209	.190 869	31
.003 824	5.243 033	.190 729	32
.003 213	5.246 246	.190 612	33
.002 700	5.248 946	.190 514	34
.002 269	5.251 215	.190 432	35
.001 907	5.253 122	.190 363	36
.001 602	5.254 724	.190 305	37
.001 347	5.256 071	.190 256	38
.001 132	5.257 202	.190 215	39
.000 951	5.258 153	.190 181	40
.000 799	5.258 952	.190 152	41
.000 671	5.259 624	.190 128	42
.000 564	5.260 188	.190 107	43
.000 474	5.260 662	.190 090	44
.000 398	5.261 061	.190 076	45
.000 335	5.261 396	.190 064	46
.000 281	5.261 677	.190 053	47
.000 236	5,261 913	.190 045	48
.000 199	5.262 112	.190 038	49
.000 167	5.262 279	.190 032	50

RATE
20%

Year	COMPOUNDING FACTOR FOR 1 What an initial amount becomes when growing at compound interest	COMPOUNDING FACTOR FOR 1 PER ANNUM Growth of equal year-end deposits all growing at compound interest	SINKING FUND FACTOR Level deposit required each year to reach 1 by a given year
1	1.200 000	1.000 000	1.000 000
2	1.440 000	2.200 000	.454 545
3	1.728 000	3.640 000	.274 725
4	2.073 600	5.368 000	.186 289
5	2.488 320	7.441 600	.134 380
6	2.985 984	9.929 920	.100 706
7	3.583 181	12.915 904	.077 424
8	4.299 817	16.499 085	.060 609
9	5.159 780	20.798 902	.048 079
10	6.191 736	25.958 682	.038 523
11	7.430 084	32.150 419	.031 104
12	8.916 100	39.580 502	.025 265
13	10.699 321	48.496 603	.020 620
14	12.839 185	59.195 923	.016 893
15	15.407 022	72.035 108	.013 882
16	18.488 426	87.442 129	.011 436
17	22.186 111	105.930 555	.009 440
18	26.623 333	128.116 666	.007 805
19	31.948 000	154.740 000	.006 462
20	38.337 600	186.688 000	.005 357
21	46.005 120	225.025 600	.004 444
22	55.206 144	271.030 719	.003 690
23	66.247 373	326.236 863	.003 065
24	79.496 847	392.484 236	.002 548
25	95.396 217	471.981 083	.002 119
26	114.475 460	567.377 300	.001 762
27	137.370 552	681.852 760	.001 467
28	164.844 662	819.223 312	.001 221
29	197.813 595	984.067 974	.001 016
30	237.376 314	1,181.881 569	.000 846
31	284.851 577	1,419.257 883	.000 705
32	341.821 892	1,704.109 459	.000 587
33	410.186 270	2,045.931 351	.000 489
34	492.223 524	2,456.117 621	.000 407
35	590.668 229	2,948.341 146	.000 339
36	708.801 875	3,539.009 375	.000 283
37	850.562 250	4,247.811 250	.000 235
38	1,020.674 700	5,098.373 500	.000 196
39	1,224.809 640	6,119.048 200	.000 163
40	1,469.771 568	7,343.857 840	.000 136
41	1,763.725 882	8,813.629 408	.000 113
42	2,116.471 058	10,577.355 29	.000 095
43	2,539.765 269	12,693.826 35	.000 079
44	3,047.718 323	15,233.591 62	.000 066
45	3,657.261 988	18,281.309 94	.000 055
46	4,388.714 386	21,938.571 93	.000 046
47	5,266.457 263	26,327.286 31	.000 038
48	6,319.748 715	31,593.743 58	.000 032
49	7,583.698 458	37,913.492 29	.000 026
50	9,100.438 150	45,497.190 75	.000 022

RATE
20%

DISCOUNT FACTOR How much 1 at a future date is worth today	PRESENT WORTH OF AN ANNUITY FACTOR How much 1 received or paid annually for X years is worth today	CAPITAL RECOVERY FACTOR Annual payment that will repay a $1 loan in X years with compound interest on the unpaid balance	Year
.833 333	.833 333	1.200 000	1
.694 444	1.527 778	.654 545	2
.578 704	2.106 481	.474 725	3
.482 253	2.588 735	.386 289	4
.401 878	2.990 612	.334 380	5
.334 898	3.325 510	.300 706	6
.279 082	3.604 592	.277 424	7
.232 568	3.837 160	.260 609	8
.193 807	4.030 967	.248 079	9
.161 506	4.192 472	.238 523	10
.134 588	4.327 060	.231 104	11
.112 157	4.439 217	.225 265	12
.093 464	4.532 681	.220 620	13
.077 887	4.610 567	.216 893	14
.064 905	4.675 473	.213 882	15
.054 088	4.729 561	.211 436	16
.045 073	4.774 634	.209 440	17
.037 561	4.812 195	.207 805	18
.031 301	4.843 496	.206 462	19
.026 084	4.869 580	.205 357	20
.021 737	4.891 316	.204 444	21
.018 114	4.909 430	.203 690	22
.015 095	4.924 525	.203 065	23
.012 579	4.937 104	.202 548	24
.010 483	4.947 587	.202 119	25
.008 735	4.956 323	.201 762	26
.007 280	4.963 602	.201 467	27
.006 066	4.969 668	.201 221	28
.005 055	4.974 724	.201 016	29
.004 213	4.978 936	.200 846	30
.003 511	4.982 447	.200 705	31
.002 926	4.985 372	.200 587	32
.002 438	4.987 810	.200 489	33
.002 032	4.989 842	.200 407	34
.001 693	4.991 535	.200 339	35
.001 411	4.992 946	.200 283	36
.001 176	4.994 122	.200 235	37
.000 980	4.995 101	.200 196	38
.000 816	4.995 918	.200 163	39
.000 680	4.996 598	.200 136	40
.000 567	4.997 165	.200 113	41
.000 472	4.997 638	.200 095	42
.000 394	4.998 031	.200 079	43
.000 328	4.998 359	.200 066	44
.000 273	4.998 633	.200 055	45
.000 228	4.998 861	.200 046	46
.000 190	4.999 051	.200 038	47
.000 158	4.999 209	.200 032	48
.000 132	4.999 341	.200 026	49
.000 110	4.999 451	.200 022	50

RATE
21%

Year	COMPOUNDING FACTOR FOR 1 What an initial amount becomes when growing at compound interest	COMPOUNDING FACTOR FOR 1 PER ANNUM Growth of equal year-end deposits all growing at compound interest	SINKING FUND FACTOR Level deposit required each year to reach 1 by a given year
1	1.210 000	1.000 000	1.000 000
2	1.464 100	2.210 000	.452 489
3	1.771 561	3.674 100	.272 175
4	2.143 589	5.445 661	.183 632
5	2.593 742	7.589 250	.131 765
6	3.138 428	10.182 992	.098 203
7	3.797 498	13.321 421	.075 067
8	4.594 973	17.118 919	.058 415
9	5.559 917	21.713 892	.046 053
10	6.727 500	27.273 809	.036 665
11	8.140 275	34.001 309	.029 411
12	9.849 733	42.141 584	.023 730
13	11.918 177	51.991 317	.019 234
14	14.420 994	63.909 493	.015 647
15	17.449 402	78.330 487	.012 766
16	21.113 777	95.779 889	.010 441
17	25.547 670	116.893 666	.008 555
18	30.912 681	142.441 336	.007 020
19	37.404 343	173.354 016	.005 769
20	45.259 256	210.758 360	.004 745
21	54.763 699	256.017 615	.003 906
22	66.264 076	310.781 315	.003 218
23	80.179 532	377.045 391	.002 652
24	97.017 234	457.224 923	.002 187
25	117.390 853	554.242 157	.001 804
26	142.042 932	671.633 009	.001 489
27	171.871 948	813.675 941	.001 229
28	207.965 057	985.547 889	.001 015
29	251.637 719	1,193.512 946	.000 838
30	304.481 640	1,445.150 664	.000 692
31	368.422 784	1,749.632 304	.000 572
32	445.791 568	2,118.055 088	.000 472
33	539.407 798	2,563.846 656	.000 390
34	652.683 435	3,103.254 454	.000 322
35	789.746 957	3,755.937 890	.000 266
36	955.593 818	4,545.684 846	.000 220
37	1,156.268 519	5,501.278 664	.000 182
38	1,399.084 909	6,657.547 183	.000 150
39	1,692.892 739	8,056.632 092	.000 124
40	2,048.400 215	9,749.524 831	.000 103
41	2,478.564 260	11,797.925 05	.000 085
42	2,999.062 754	14,276.489 31	.000 070
43	3,628.865 933	17,275.552 06	.000 058
44	4,390.927 778	20,904.417 99	.000 048
45	5,313.022 612	25,295.345 77	.000 040
46	6,428.757 360	30,608.368 38	.000 033
47	7,778.796 406	37,037.125 74	.000 027
48	9,412.343 651	44,815.922 15	.000 022
49	11,388.935 82	54,228.265 80	.000 018
50	13,780.612 34	65,617.201 62	.000 015

RATE
21%

DISCOUNT FACTOR How much 1 at a future date is worth today	PRESENT WORTH OF AN ANNUITY FACTOR How much 1 received or paid annually for X years is worth today	CAPITAL RECOVERY FACTOR Annual payment that will repay a $1 loan in X years with compound interest on the unpaid balance	Year
.826 446	.826 446	1.210 000	1
.683 013	1.509 460	.662 489	2
.564 474	2.073 934	.482 175	3
.466 507	2.540 441	.393 632	4
.385 543	2.925 984	.341 765	5
.318 631	3.244 615	.308 203	6
.263 331	3.507 946	.285 067	7
.217 629	3.725 576	.268 415	8
.179 859	3.905 434	.256 053	9
.148 644	4.054 078	.246 665	10
.122 846	4.176 924	.239 411	11
.101 526	4.278 450	.233 730	12
.083 905	4.362 355	.229 234	13
.069 343	4.431 698	.225 647	14
.057 309	4.489 007	.222 766	15
.047 362	4.536 369	.220 441	16
.039 143	4.575 512	.218 555	17
.032 349	4.607 861	.217 020	18
.026 735	4.634 596	.215 769	19
.022 095	4.656 691	.214 745	20
.018 260	4.674 951	.213 906	21
.015 091	4.690 042	.213 218	22
.012 472	4.702 514	.212 652	23
.010 307	4.712 822	.212 187	24
.008 519	4.721 340	.211 804	25
.007 040	4.728 380	.211 489	26
.005 818	4.734 199	.211 229	27
.004 809	4.739 007	.211 015	28
.003 974	4.742 981	.210 838	29
.003 284	4.746 265	.210 692	30
.002 714	4.748 980	.210 572	31
.002 243	4.751 223	.210 472	32
.001 854	4.753 077	.210 390	33
.001 532	4.754 609	.210 322	34
.001 266	4.755 875	.210 266	35
.001 046	4.756 922	.210 220	36
.000 865	4.757 786	.210 182	37
.000 715	4.758 501	.210 150	38
.000 591	4.759 092	.210 124	39
.000 488	4.759 580	.210 103	40
.000 403	4.759 984	.210 085	41
.000 333	4.760 317	.210 070	42
.000 276	4.760 593	.210 058	43
.000 228	4.760 820	.210 048	44
.000 188	4.761 008	.210 040	45
.000 156	4.761 164	.210 033	46
.000 129	4.761 293	.210 027	47
.000 106	4.761 399	.210 022	48
.000 088	4.761 487	.210 018	49
.000 073	4.761 559	.210 015	50

RATE
22%

Year	COMPOUNDING FACTOR FOR 1 What an initial amount becomes when growing at compound interest	COMPOUNDING FACTOR FOR 1 PER ANNUM Growth of equal year-end deposits all growing at compound interest	SINKING FUND FACTOR Level deposit required each year to reach 1 by a given year
1	1.220 000	1.000 000	1.000 000
2	1.488 400	2.220 000	.450 450
3	1.815 848	3.708 400	.269 658
4	2.215 335	5.524 248	.181 020
5	2.702 708	7.739 583	.129 206
6	3.297 304	10.442 291	.095 764
7	4.022 711	13.739 595	.072 782
8	4.907 707	17.762 306	.056 299
9	5.987 403	22.670 013	.044 111
10	7.304 631	28.657 416	.034 895
11	8.911 650	35.962 047	.027 807
12	10.872 213	44.873 697	.022 285
13	13.264 100	55.745 911	.017 939
14	16.182 202	69.010 011	.014 491
15	19.742 287	85.192 213	.011 738
16	24.085 590	104.934 500	.009 530
17	29.384 420	129.020 090	.007 751
18	35.848 992	158.404 510	.006 313
19	43.735 771	194.253 503	.005 148
20	53.357 640	237.989 273	.004 202
21	65.096 321	291.346 913	.003 432
22	79.417 512	356.443 234	.002 805
23	96.889 364	435.860 746	.002 294
24	118.205 024	532.750 110	.001 877
25	144.210 130	650.955 134	.001 536
26	175.936 358	795.165 264	.001 258
27	214.642 357	971.101 622	.001 030
28	261.863 675	1,185.743 978	.000 843
29	319.473 684	1,447.607 654	.000 691
30	389.757 894	1,767.081 337	.000 566
31	475.504 631	2,156.839 232	.000 464
32	580.115 650	2,632.343 863	.000 380
33	707.741 093	3,212.459 512	.000 311
34	863.444 133	3,920.200 605	.000 255
35	1,053.401 842	4,783.644 738	.000 209
36	1,285.150 248	5,837.046 581	.000 171
37	1,567.883 302	7,122.196 828	.000 140
38	1,912.817 629	8,690.080 131	.000 115
39	2,333.637 507	10,602.897 76	.000 094
40	2,847.037 759	12,936.535 27	.000 077
41	3,473.386 066	15,783.573 03	.000 063
42	4,237.531 000	19,256.959 09	.000 052
43	5,169.787 820	23,494.490 09	.000 043
44	6,307.141 140	28,664.277 91	.000 035
45	7,694.712 191	34,971.419 05	.000 029
46	9,387.548 873	42,666.131 24	.000 023
47	11,452.809 63	52,053.680 12	.000 019
48	13,972.427 74	63,506.489 74	.000 016
49	17,046.361 85	77,478.917 48	.000 013
50	20,796.561 45	94,525.279 33	.000 011

RATE 22%

DISCOUNT FACTOR How much 1 at a future date is worth today	PRESENT WORTH OF AN ANNUITY FACTOR How much 1 received or paid annually for X years is worth today	CAPITAL RECOVERY FACTOR Annual payment that will repay a $1 loan in X years with compound interest on the unpaid balance	Year
.819 672	.819 672	1.220 000	1
.671 862	1.491 535	.670 450	2
.550 707	2.042 241	.489 658	3
.451 399	2.493 641	.401 020	4
.369 999	2.863 640	.349 206	5
.303 278	3.166 918	.315 764	6
.248 589	3.415 506	.292 782	7
.203 761	3.619 268	.276 299	8
.167 017	3.786 285	.264 111	9
.136 899	3.923 184	.254 895	10
.112 213	4.035 397	.247 807	11
.091 978	4.127 375	.242 285	12
.075 391	4.202 766	.237 939	13
.061 796	4.264 562	.234 491	14
.050 653	4.315 215	.231 738	15
.041 519	4.356 734	.229 530	16
.034 032	4.390 765	.227 751	17
.027 895	4.418 660	.226 313	18
.022 865	4.441 525	.225 148	19
.018 741	4.460 266	.224 202	20
.015 362	4.475 628	.223 432	21
.012 592	4.488 220	.222 805	22
.010 321	4.498 541	.222 294	23
.008 460	4.507 001	.221 877	24
.006 934	4.513 935	.221 536	25
.005 684	4.519 619	.221 258	26
.004 659	4.524 278	.221 030	27
.003 819	4.528 096	.220 843	28
.003 130	4.531 227	.220 691	29
.002 566	4.533 792	.220 566	30
.002 103	4.535 895	.220 464	31
.001 724	4.537 619	.220 380	32
.001 413	4.539 032	.220 311	33
.001 158	4.540 190	.220 255	34
.000 949	4.541 140	.220 209	35
.000 778	4.541 918	.220 171	36
.000 638	4.542 555	.220 140	37
.000 523	4.543 078	.220 115	38
.000 429	4.543 507	.220 094	39
.000 351	4.543 858	.220 077	40
.000 288	4.544 146	.220 063	41
.000 236	4.544 382	.220 052	42
.000 193	4.544 575	.220 043	43
.000 159	4.544 734	.220 035	44
.000 130	4.544 864	.220 029	45
.000 107	4.544 970	.220 023	46
.000 087	4.545 058	.220 019	47
.000 072	4.545 129	.220 016	48
.000 059	4.545 188	.220 013	49
.000 048	4.545 236	.220 011	50

RATE
23%

Year	COMPOUNDING FACTOR FOR 1 What an initial amount becomes when growing at compound interest	COMPOUNDING FACTOR FOR 1 PER ANNUM Growth of equal year-end deposits all growing at compound interest	SINKING FUND FACTOR Level deposit required each year to reach 1 by a given year
1	1.230 000	1.000 000	1.000 000
2	1.512 900	2.230 000	.448 430
3	1.860 867	3.742 900	.267 173
4	2.288 866	5.603 767	.178 451
5	2.815 306	7.892 633	.126 700
6	3.462 826	10.707 939	.093 389
7	4.259 276	14.170 765	.070 568
8	5.238 909	18.430 041	.054 259
9	6.443 859	23.668 950	.042 249
10	7.925 946	30.112 809	.033 208
11	9.748 914	38.038 755	.026 289
12	11.991 164	47.787 669	.020 926
13	14.749 132	59.778 833	.016 728
14	18.141 432	74.527 964	.013 418
15	22.313 961	92.669 396	.010 791
16	27.446 172	114.983 357	.008 697
17	33.758 792	142.429 529	.007 021
18	41.523 314	176.188 321	.005 676
19	51.073 676	217.711 635	.004 593
20	62.820 622	268.785 311	.003 720
21	77.269 364	331.605 932	.003 016
22	95.041 318	408.875 297	.002 446
23	116.900 822	503.916 615	.001 984
24	143.788 010	620.817 437	.001 611
25	176.859 253	764.605 447	.001 308
26	217.536 881	941.464 700	.001 062
27	267.570 364	1,159.001 581	.000 863
28	329.111 547	1,426.571 945	.000 701
29	404.807 203	1,755.683 492	.000 570
30	497.912 860	2,160.490 695	.000 463
31	612.432 818	2,658.403 555	.000 376
32	753.292 366	3,270.836 373	.000 306
33	926.549 610	4,024.128 738	.000 249
34	1,139.656 020	4,950.678 348	.000 202
35	1,401.776 905	6,090.334 368	.000 164
36	1,724.185 593	7,492.111 273	.000 133
37	2,120.748 279	9,216.296 866	.000 109
38	2,608.520 383	11,337.045 14	.000 088
39	3,208.480 071	13,945.565 53	.000 072
40	3,946.430 488	17,154.045 60	.000 058
41	4,854.109 500	21,100.476 09	.000 047
42	5,970.554 685	25,954.585 59	.000 039
43	7,343.782 263	31,925.140 27	.000 031
44	9,032.852 183	39,268.922 53	.000 025
45	11,110.408 19	48,301.774 72	.000 021
46	13,665.802 07	59,412.182 90	.000 017
47	16,808.936 54	73,077.984 97	.000 014
48	20,674.991 95	89,886.921 51	.000 011
49	25,430.240 10	110,561.913 5	.000 009
50	31,279.195 32	135,992.153 6	.000 007

RATE
23%

DISCOUNT FACTOR How much 1 at a future date is worth today	PRESENT WORTH OF AN ANNUITY FACTOR How much 1 received or paid annually for X years is worth today	CAPITAL RECOVERY FACTOR Annual payment that will repay a $1 loan in X years with compound interest on the unpaid balance	Year
.813 008	.813 008	1.230 000	1
.660 982	1.473 990	.678 430	2
.537 384	2.011 374	.497 173	3
.436 897	2.448 272	.408 451	4
.355 201	2.803 473	.356 700	5
.288 781	3.092 254	.323 389	6
.234 782	3.327 036	.300 568	7
.190 879	3.517 916	.284 259	8
.155 187	3.673 102	.272 249	9
.126 168	3.799 270	.263 208	10
.102 576	3.901 846	.256 289	11
.083 395	3.985 240	.250 926	12
.067 801	4.053 041	.246 728	13
.055 122	4.108 163	.243 418	14
.044 815	4.152 978	.240 791	15
.036 435	4.189 413	.238 697	16
.029 622	4.219 035	.237 021	17
.024 083	4.243 118	.235 676	18
.019 580	4.262 698	.234 593	19
.015 918	4.278 616	.233 720	20
.012 942	4.291 558	.233 016	21
.010 522	4.302 079	.232 446	22
.008 554	4.310 634	.231 984	23
.006 955	4.317 588	.231 611	24
.005 654	4.323 243	.231 308	25
.004 597	4.327 839	.231 062	26
.003 737	4.331 577	.230 863	27
.003 038	4.334 615	.230 701	28
.002 470	4.337 086	.230 570	29
.002 008	4.339 094	.230 463	30
.001 633	4.340 727	.230 376	31
.001 328	4.342 054	.230 306	32
.001 079	4.343 134	.230 249	33
.000 877	4.344 011	.230 202	34
.000 713	4.344 724	.230 164	35
.000 580	4.345 304	.230 133	36
.000 472	4.345 776	.230 109	37
.000 383	4.346 159	.230 088	38
.000 312	4.346 471	.230 072	39
.000 253	4.346 724	.230 058	40
.000 206	4.346 930	.230 047	41
.000 167	4.347 098	.230 039	42
.000 136	4.347 234	.230 031	43
.000 111	4.347 345	.230 025	44
.000 090	4.347 435	.230 021	45
.000 073	4.347 508	.230 017	46
.000 059	4.347 567	.230 014	47
.000 048	4.347 616	.230 011	48
.000 039	4.347 655	.230 009	49
.000 032	4.347 687	.230 007	50

RATE
24%

Year	COMPOUNDING FACTOR FOR 1 What an initial amount becomes when growing at compound interest	COMPOUNDING FACTOR FOR 1 PER ANNUM Growth of equal year-end deposits all growing at compound interest	SINKING FUND FACTOR Level deposit required each year to reach 1 by a given year
1	1.240 000	1.000 000	1.000 000
2	1.537 600	2.240 000	.446 429
3	1.906 624	3.777 600	.264 718
4	2.364 214	5.684 224	.175 926
5	2.931 625	8.048 438	.124 248
6	3.635 215	10.980 063	.091 074
7	4.507 667	14.615 278	.068 422
8	5.589 507	19.122 945	.052 293
9	6.930 988	24.712 451	.040 465
10	8.594 426	31.643 440	.031 602
11	10.657 088	40.237 865	.024 852
12	13.214 789	50.894 953	.019 648
13	16.386 338	64.109 741	.015 598
14	20.319 059	80.496 079	.012 423
15	25.195 633	100.815 138	.009 919
16	31.242 585	126.010 772	.007 936
17	38.740 806	157.253 357	.006 359
18	48.038 599	195.994 162	.005 102
19	59.567 863	244.032 761	.004 098
20	73.864 150	303.600 624	.003 294
21	91.591 546	377.464 774	.002 649
22	113.573 517	469.056 320	.002 132
23	140.831 161	582.629 836	.001 716
24	174.630 639	723.460 997	.001 382
25	216.541 993	898.091 636	.001 113
26	268.512 071	1,114.633 629	.000 897
27	332.954 968	1,383.145 700	.000 723
28	412.864 160	1,716.100 668	.000 583
29	511.951 559	2,128.964 828	.000 470
30	634.819 933	2,640.916 387	.000 379
31	787.176 717	3,275.736 320	.000 305
32	976.099 129	4,062.913 037	.000 246
33	1,210.362 920	5,039.012 166	.000 198
34	1,500.850 021	6,249.375 086	.000 160
35	1,861.054 026	7,750.225 106	.000 129
36	2,307.706 992	9,611.279 132	.000 104
37	2,861.556 670	11,918.986 12	.000 084
38	3,548.330 270	14,780.542 79	.000 068
39	4,399.929 535	18,328.873 06	.000 055
40	5,455.912 624	22,728.802 60	.000 044
41	6,765.331 653	28,184.715 22	.000 035
42	8,389.011 250	34,950.046 88	.000 029
43	10,402.373 95	43,339.058 13	.000 023
44	12,898.943 70	53,741.432 08	.000 019
45	15,994.690 19	66,640.375 77	.000 015
46	19,833.415 83	82,635.065 96	.000 012
47	24,593.435 63	102,468.481 8	.000 010
48	30,495.860 18	127,061.917 4	.000 008
49	37,814.866 62	157,557.777 6	.000 006
50	46,890.434 61	195,372.644 2	.000 005

RATE
24%

DISCOUNT FACTOR How much 1 at a future date is worth today	PRESENT WORTH OF AN ANNUITY FACTOR How much 1 received or paid annually for X years is worth today	CAPITAL RECOVERY FACTOR Annual payment that will repay a $1 loan in X years with compound interest on the unpaid balance	Year
.806 452	.806 452	1.240 000	1
.650 364	1.456 816	.686 429	2
.524 487	1.981 303	.504 718	3
.422 974	2.404 277	.415 926	4
.341 108	2.745 384	.364 248	5
.275 087	3.020 471	.331 074	6
.221 844	3.242 316	.308 422	7
.178 907	3.421 222	.292 293	8
.144 280	3.565 502	.280 465	9
.116 354	3.681 856	.271 602	10
.093 834	3.775 691	.264 852	11
.075 673	3.851 363	.259 648	12
.061 026	3.912 390	.255 598	13
.049 215	3.961 605	.252 423	14
.039 689	4.001 294	.249 919	15
.032 008	4.033 302	.247 936	16
.025 813	4.059 114	.246 359	17
.020 817	4.079 931	.245 102	18
.016 788	4.096 718	.244 098	19
.013 538	4.110 257	.243 294	20
.010 918	4.121 175	.242 649	21
.008 805	4.129 980	.242 132	22
.007 101	4.137 080	.241 716	23
.005 726	4.142 807	.241 382	24
.004 618	4.147 425	.241 113	25
.003 724	4.151 149	.240 897	26
.003 003	4.154 152	.240 723	27
.002 422	4.156 575	.240 583	28
.001 953	4.158 528	.240 470	29
.001 575	4.160 103	.240 379	30
.001 270	4.161 373	.240 305	31
.001 024	4.162 398	.240 246	32
.000 826	4.163 224	.240 198	33
.000 666	4.163 890	.240 160	34
.000 537	4.164 428	.240 129	35
.000 433	4.164 861	.240 104	36
.000 349	4.165 211	.240 084	37
.000 282	4.165 492	.240 068	38
.000 227	4.165 720	.240 055	39
.000 183	4.165 903	.240 044	40
.000 148	4.166 051	.240 035	41
.000 119	4.166 170	.240 029	42
.000 096	4.166 266	.240 023	43
.000 078	4.166 344	.240 019	44
.000 063	4.166 406	.240 015	45
.000 050	4.166 457	.240 012	46
.000 041	4.166 497	.240 010	47
.000 033	4.166 530	.240 008	48
.000 026	4.166 556	.240 006	49
.000 021	4.166 578	.240 005	50

RATE
25%

Year	COMPOUNDING FACTOR FOR 1 What an initial amount becomes when growing at compound interest	COMPOUNDING FACTOR FOR 1 PER ANNUM Growth of equal year-end deposits all growing at compound interest	SINKING FUND FACTOR Level deposit required each year to reach 1 by a given year
1	1.250 000	1.000 000	1.000 000
2	1.562 500	2.250 000	.444 444
3	1.953 125	3.812 500	.262 295
4	2.441 406	5.765 625	.173 442
5	3.051 758	8.207 031	.121 847
6	3.814 697	11.258 789	.088 819
7	4.768 372	15.073 486	.066 342
8	5.960 464	19.841 858	.050 399
9	7.450 581	25.802 322	.038 756
10	9.313 226	33.252 903	.030 073
11	11.641 532	42.566 129	.023 493
12	14.551 915	54.207 661	.018 448
13	18.189 894	68.759 576	.014 543
14	22.737 368	86.949 470	.011 501
15	28.421 709	109.686 838	.009 117
16	35.527 137	138.108 547	.007 241
17	44.408 921	173.635 684	.005 759
18	55.511 151	218.044 605	.004 586
19	69.388 939	273.555 756	.003 656
20	86.736 174	342.944 695	.002 916
21	108.420 217	429.680 869	.002 327
22	135.525 272	538.101 086	.001 858
23	169.406 589	673.626 358	.001 485
24	211.758 237	843.032 947	.001 186
25	264.697 796	1,054.791 184	.000 948
26	330.872 245	1,319.488 980	.000 758
27	413.590 306	1,650.361 225	.000 606
28	516.987 883	2,063.951 531	.000 485
29	646.234 854	2,580.939 414	.000 387
30	807.793 567	3,227.174 268	.000 310
31	1,009.741 959	4,034.967 835	.000 248
32	1,262.177 448	5,044.709 793	.000 198
33	1,577.721 810	6,306.887 242	.000 159
34	1,972.152 263	7,884.609 052	.000 127
35	2,465.190 329	9,856.761 315	.000 101
36	3,081.487 911	12,321.951 64	.000 081
37	3,851.859 889	15,403.439 56	.000 065
38	4,814.824 861	19,255.299 44	.000 052
39	6,018.531 076	24,070.124 30	.000 042
40	7,523.163 845	30,088.655 38	.000 033
41	9,403.954 807	37,611.819 23	.000 027
42	11,754.943 51	47,015.774 03	.000 021
43	14,693.679 39	58,770.717 54	.000 017
44	18,367.099 23	73,464.396 93	.000 014
45	22,958.874 04	91,831.496 16	.000 011
46	28,698.592 55	114,790.370 2	.000 009
47	35,873.240 69	143,488.962 7	.000 007
48	44,841.550 86	179,362.203 4	.000 006
49	56,051.938 57	224,203.754 3	.000 004
50	70,064.923 22	280,255.692 9	.000 004

RATE
25%

DISCOUNT FACTOR How much 1 at a future date is worth today	PRESENT WORTH OF AN ANNUITY FACTOR How much 1 received or paid annually for X years is worth today	CAPITAL RECOVERY FACTOR Annual payment that will repay a $1 loan in X years with compound interest on the unpaid balance	Year
.800 000	.800 000	1.250 000	1
.640 000	1.440 000	.694 444	2
.512 000	1.952 000	.512 295	3
.409 600	2.361 600	.423 442	4
.327 680	2.689 280	.371 847	5
.262 144	2.951 424	.338 819	6
.209 715	3.161 139	.316 342	7
.167 772	3.328 911	.300 399	8
.134 218	3.463 129	.288 756	9
.107 374	3.570 503	.280 073	10
.085 899	3.656 403	.273 493	11
.068 719	3.725 122	.268 448	12
.054 976	3.780 098	.264 543	13
.043 980	3.824 078	.261 501	14
.035 184	3.859 263	.259 117	15
.028 147	3.887 410	.257 241	16
.022 518	3.909 928	.255 759	17
.018 014	3.927 942	.254 586	18
.014 412	3.942 354	.253 656	19
.011 529	3.953 883	.252 916	20
.009 223	3.963 107	.252 327	21
.007 379	3.970 485	.251 858	22
.005 903	3.976 388	.251 485	23
.004 722	3.981 111	.251 186	24
.003 778	3.984 888	.250 948	25
.003 022	3.987 911	.250 758	26
.002 418	3.990 329	.250 606	27
.001 934	3.992 263	.250 485	28
.001 547	3.993 810	.250 387	29
.001 238	3.995 048	.250 310	30
.000 990	3.996 039	.250 248	31
.000 792	3.996 831	.250 198	32
.000 634	3.997 465	.250 159	33
.000 507	3.997 972	.250 127	34
.000 406	3.998 377	.250 101	35
.000 325	3.998 702	.250 081	36
.000 260	3.998 962	.250 065	37
.000 208	3.999 169	.250 052	38
.000 166	3.999 335	.250 042	39
.000 133	3.999 468	.250 033	40
.000 106	3.999 575	.250 027	41
.000 085	3.999 660	.250 021	42
.000 068	3.999 728	.250 017	43
.000 054	3.999 782	.250 014	44
.000 044	3.999 826	.250 011	45
.000 035	3.999 861	.250 009	46
.000 028	3.999 888	.250 007	47
.000 022	3.999 911	.250 006	48
.000 018	3.999 929	.250 004	49
.000 014	3.999 943	.250 004	50

RATE 26%

Year	COMPOUNDING FACTOR FOR 1 What an initial amount becomes when growing at compound interest	COMPOUNDING FACTOR FOR 1 PER ANNUM Growth of equal year-end deposits all growing at compound interest	SINKING FUND FACTOR Level deposit required each year to reach 1 by a given year
1	1.260 000	1.000 000	1.000 000
2	1.587 600	2.260 000	.442 478
3	2.000 376	3.847 600	.259 902
4	2.520 474	5.847 976	.170 999
5	3.175 797	8.368 450	.119 496
6	4.001 504	11.544 247	.086 623
7	5.041 895	15.545 751	.064 326
8	6.352 788	20.587 646	.048 573
9	8.004 513	26.940 434	.037 119
10	10.085 686	34.944 947	.028 616
11	12.707 965	45.030 633	.022 207
12	16.012 035	57.738 598	.017 319
13	20.175 165	73.750 633	.013 559
14	25.420 707	93.925 798	.010 647
15	32.030 091	119.346 505	.008 379
16	40.357 915	151.376 596	.006 606
17	50.850 973	191.734 511	.005 216
18	64.072 226	242.585 484	.004 122
19	80.731 005	306.657 710	.003 261
20	101.721 066	387.388 715	.002 581
21	128.168 543	489.109 781	.002 045
22	161.492 364	617.278 324	.001 620
23	203.480 379	778.770 688	.001 284
24	256.385 277	982.251 067	.001 018
25	323.045 450	1,238.636 345	.000 807
26	407.037 266	1,561.681 794	.000 640
27	512.866 956	1,968.719 061	.000 508
28	646.212 364	2,481.586 016	.000 403
29	814.227 579	3,127.798 381	.000 320
30	1,025.926 749	3,942.025 959	.000 254
31	1,292.667 704	4,967.952 709	.000 201
32	1,628.761 307	6,260.620 413	.000 160
33	2,052.239 247	7,889.381 721	.000 127
34	2,585.821 452	9,941.620 968	.000 101
35	3,258.135 029	12,527.442 42	.000 080
36	4,105.250 137	15,785.577 45	.000 063
37	5,172.615 172	19,890.827 59	.000 050
38	6,517.495 117	25,063.442 76	.000 040
39	8,212.043 847	31,580.937 88	.000 032
40	10,347.175 25	39,792.981 72	.000 025
41	13,037.440 81	50,140.156 97	.000 020
42	16,427.175 42	63,177.597 78	.000 016
43	20,698.241 03	79,604.773 21	.000 013
44	26,079.783 70	100,303.014 2	.000 010
45	32,860.527 46	126,382.797 9	.000 008
46	41,404.264 61	159,243.325 4	.000 006
47	52,169.373 40	200,647.590 0	.000 005
48	65,733.410 49	252,816.963 4	.000 004
49	82,824.097 22	318,550.373 9	.000 003
50	104,358.362 5	401,374.471 1	.000 002

RATE
26%

DISCOUNT FACTOR How much 1 at a future date is worth today	PRESENT WORTH OF AN ANNUITY FACTOR How much 1 received or paid annually for X years is worth today	CAPITAL RECOVERY FACTOR Annual payment that will repay a $1 loan in X years with compound interest on the unpaid balance	Year
.793 651	.793 651	1.260 000	1
.629 882	1.423 532	.702 478	2
.499 906	1.923 438	.519 902	3
.396 751	2.320 189	.430 999	4
.314 882	2.635 071	.379 496	5
.249 906	2.884 977	.346 623	6
.198 338	3.083 315	.324 326	7
.157 411	3.240 726	.308 573	8
.124 930	3.365 656	.297 119	9
.099 150	3.464 806	.288 616	10
.078 691	3.543 497	.282 207	11
.062 453	3.605 950	.277 319	12
.049 566	3.655 516	.273 559	13
.039 338	3.694 854	.270 647	14
.031 221	3.726 074	.268 379	15
.024 778	3.750 853	.266 606	16
.019 665	3.770 518	.265 216	17
.015 607	3.786 125	.264 122	18
.012 387	3.798 512	.263 261	19
.009 831	3.808 343	.262 581	20
.007 802	3.816 145	.262 045	21
.006 192	3.822 338	.261 620	22
.004 914	3.827 252	.261 284	23
.003 900	3.831 152	.261 018	24
.003 096	3.834 248	.260 807	25
.002 457	3.836 705	.260 640	26
.001 950	3.838 655	.260 508	27
.001 547	3.840 202	.260 403	28
.001 228	3.841 430	.260 320	29
.000 975	3.842 405	.260 254	30
.000 774	3.843 178	.260 201	31
.000 614	3.843 792	.260 160	32
.000 487	3.844 280	.260 127	33
.000 387	3.844 666	.260 101	34
.000 307	3.844 973	.260 080	35
.000 244	3.845 217	.260 063	36
.000 193	3.845 410	.260 050	37
.000 153	3.845 564	.260 040	38
.000 122	3.845 685	.260 032	39
.000 097	3.845 782	.260 025	40
.000 077	3.845 859	.260 020	41
.000 061	3.845 920	.260 016	42
.000 048	3.845 968	.260 013	43
.000 038	3.846 006	.260 010	44
.000 030	3.846 037	.260 008	45
.000 024	3.846 061	.260 006	46
.000 019	3.846 080	.260 005	47
.000 015	3.846 095	.260 004	48
.000 012	3.846 107	.260 003	49
.000 010	3.846 117	.260 002	50

RATE
27%

Year	COMPOUNDING FACTOR FOR 1 What an initial amount becomes when growing at compound interest	COMPOUNDING FACTOR FOR 1 PER ANNUM Growth of equal year-end deposits all growing at compound interest	SINKING FUND FACTOR Level deposit required each year to reach 1 by a given year
1	1.270 000	1.000 000	1.000 000
2	1.612 900	2.270 000	.440 529
3	2.048 383	3.882 900	.257 539
4	2.601 446	5.931 283	.168 598
5	3.303 837	8.532 729	.117 196
6	4.195 873	11.836 566	.084 484
7	5.328 759	16.032 439	.062 374
8	6.767 523	21.361 198	.046 814
9	8.594 755	28.128 721	.035 551
10	10.915 339	36.723 476	.027 231
11	13.862 480	47.638 815	.020 991
12	17.605 350	61.501 295	.016 260
13	22.358 794	79.106 644	.012 641
14	28.395 668	101.465 438	.009 856
15	36.062 499	129.861 106	.007 701
16	45.799 373	165.923 605	.006 027
17	58.165 204	211.722 978	.004 723
18	73.869 809	269.888 182	.003 705
19	93.814 658	343.757 991	.002 909
20	119.144 615	437.572 649	.002 285
21	151.313 661	556.717 264	.001 796
22	192.168 350	708.030 926	.001 412
23	244.053 804	900.199 276	.001 111
24	309.948 332	1,144.253 080	.000 874
25	393.634 381	1,454.201 412	.000 688
26	499.915 664	1,847.835 793	.000 541
27	634.892 893	2,347.751 457	.000 426
28	806.313 974	2,982.644 350	.000 335
29	1,024.018 748	3,788.958 324	.000 264
30	1,300.503 809	4,812.977 072	.000 208
31	1,651.639 838	6,113.480 881	.000 164
32	2,097.582 594	7,765.120 720	.000 129
33	2,663.929 895	9,862.703 314	.000 101
34	3,383.190 966	12,526.633 21	.000 080
35	4,296.652 527	15,909.824 17	.000 063
36	5,456.748 710	20,206.476 70	.000 049
37	6,930.070 861	25,663.225 41	.000 039
38	8,801.189 994	32,593.296 27	.000 031
39	11,177.511 29	41,394.486 27	.000 024
40	14,195.439 34	52,571.997 56	.000 019
41	18,028.207 96	66,767.436 90	.000 015
42	22,895.824 11	84,795.644 86	.000 012
43	29,077.696 62	107,691.469 0	.000 009
44	36,928.674 71	136,769.165 6	.000 007
45	46,899.416 88	173,697.840 3	.000 006
46	59,562.259 44	220,597.257 2	.000 005
47	75,644.069 49	280,159.516 6	.000 004
48	96,067.968 25	355,803.586 1	.000 003
49	122,006.319 7	451,871.554 4	.000 002
50	154,948.026 0	573,877.874 1	.000 002

RATE
27%

DISCOUNT FACTOR How much 1 at a future date is worth today	PRESENT WORTH OF AN ANNUITY FACTOR How much 1 received or paid annually for X years is worth today	CAPITAL RECOVERY FACTOR Annual payment that will repay a $1 loan in X years with compound interest on the unpaid balance	Year
.787 402	.787 402	1.270 000	1
.620 001	1.407 403	.710 529	2
.488 190	1.895 593	.527 539	3
.384 402	2.279 994	.438 598	4
.302 678	2.582 673	.387 196	5
.238 329	2.821 002	.354 484	6
.187 661	3.008 663	.332 374	7
.147 765	3.156 428	.316 814	8
.116 350	3.272 778	.305 551	9
.091 614	3.364 392	.297 231	10
.072 137	3.436 529	.290 991	11
.056 801	3.493 330	.286 260	12
.044 725	3.538 055	.282 641	13
.035 217	3.573 272	.279 856	14
.027 730	3.601 001	.277 701	15
.021 834	3.622 836	.276 027	16
.017 192	3.640 028	.274 723	17
.013 537	3.653 565	.273 705	18
.010 659	3.664 225	.272 909	19
.008 393	3.672 618	.272 285	20
.006 609	3.679 227	.271 796	21
.005 204	3.684 430	.271 412	22
.004 097	3.688 528	.271 111	23
.003 226	3.691 754	.270 874	24
.002 540	3.694 295	.270 688	25
.002 000	3.696 295	.270 541	26
.001 575	3.697 870	.270 426	27
.001 240	3.699 110	.270 335	28
.000 977	3.700 087	.270 264	29
.000 769	3.700 856	.270 208	30
.000 605	3.701 461	.270 164	31
.000 477	3.701 938	.270 129	32
.000 375	3.702 313	.270 101	33
.000 296	3.702 609	.270 080	34
.000 233	3.702 842	.270 063	35
.000 183	3.703 025	.270 049	36
.000 144	3.703 169	.270 039	37
.000 114	3.703 283	.270 031	38
.000 089	3.703 372	.270 024	39
.000 070	3.703 443	.270 019	40
.000 055	3.703 498	.270 015	41
.000 044	3.703 542	.270 012	42
.000 034	3.703 576	.270 009	43
.000 027	3.703 603	.270 007	44
.000 021	3.703 625	.270 006	45
.000 017	3.703 642	.270 005	46
.000 013	3.703 655	.270 004	47
.000 010	3.703 665	.270 003	48
.000 008	3.703 673	.270 002	49
.000 006	3.703 680	.270 002	5

RATE
28%

Year	COMPOUNDING FACTOR FOR 1 What an initial amount becomes when growing at compound interest	COMPOUNDING FACTOR FOR 1 PER ANNUM Growth of equal year-end deposits all growing at compound interest	SINKING FUND FACTOR Level deposit required each year to reach 1 by a given year
1	1.280 000	1.000 000	1.000 000
2	1.638 400	2.280 000	.438 596
3	2.097 152	3.918 400	.255 206
4	2.684 355	6.015 552	.166 236
5	3.435 974	8.699 907	.114 944
6	4.398 047	12.135 880	.082 400
7	5.629 500	16.533 927	.060 482
8	7.205 759	22.163 426	.045 119
9	9.223 372	29.369 186	.034 049
10	11.805 916	38.592 558	.025 912
11	15.111 573	50.398 474	.019 842
12	19.342 813	65.510 047	.015 265
13	24.758 801	84.852 860	.011 785
14	31.691 265	109.611 661	.009 123
15	40.564 819	141.302 926	.007 077
16	51.922 969	181.867 745	.005 499
17	66.461 400	233.790 714	.004 277
18	85.070 592	300.252 113	.003 331
19	108.890 357	385.322 705	.002 595
20	139.379 657	494.213 062	.002 023
21	178.405 962	633.592 720	.001 578
22	228.359 631	811.998 682	.001 232
23	292.300 327	1,040.358 312	.000 961
24	374.144 419	1,332.658 640	.000 750
25	478.904 857	1,706.803 059	.000 586
26	612.998 216	2,185.707 916	.000 458
27	784.637 717	2,798.706 132	.000 357
28	1,004.336 278	3,583.343 849	.000 279
29	1,285.550 435	4,587.680 126	.000 218
30	1,645.504 557	5,873.230 562	.000 170
31	2,106.245 833	7,518.735 119	.000 133
32	2,695.994 667	9,624.980 953	.000 104
33	3,450.873 173	12,320.975 62	.000 081
34	4,417.117 662	15,771.848 79	.000 063
35	5,653.910 607	20,188.966 45	.000 050
36	7,237.005 577	25,842.877 06	.000 039
37	9,263.367 139	33,079.882 64	.000 030
38	11,857.109 94	42,343.249 78	.000 024
39	15,177.100 72	54,200.359 72	.000 018
40	19,426.688 92	69,377.460 44	.000 014
41	24,866.161 82	88,804.149 36	.000 011
42	31,828.687 13	113,670.311 2	.000 009
43	40,740.719 53	145,498.998 3	.000 007
44	52,148.120 99	186,239.717 8	.000 005
45	[illegible]6,749.594 87	238,387.838 8	.000 004
[illegible]	[illegible]5,439.481 44	305,137.433 7	.000 003
[illegible]	[illegible]9,362.536 2	390,576.915 1	.000 003
[illegible]	[illegible]9,984.046 4	499,939.451 4	.000 002
[illegible]	[illegible],179.579 4	639,923.497 8	.000 002
[illegible]	[illegible],349.861 6	819,103.077 1	.000 001

RATE
28%

DISCOUNT FACTOR How much 1 at a future date is worth today	PRESENT WORTH OF AN ANNUITY FACTOR How much 1 received or paid annually for X years is worth today	CAPITAL RECOVERY FACTOR Annual payment that will repay a $1 loan in X years with compound interest on the unpaid balance	Year
.781 250	.781 250	1.280 000	1
.610 352	1.391 602	.718 596	2
.476 837	1.868 439	.535 206	3
.372 529	2.240 968	.446 236	4
.291 038	2.532 006	.394 944	5
.227 374	2.759 380	.362 400	6
.177 636	2.937 015	.340 482	7
.138 778	3.075 793	.325 119	8
.108 420	3.184 214	.314 049	9
.084 703	3.268 917	.305 912	10
.066 174	3.335 091	.299 842	11
.051 699	3.386 790	.295 265	12
.040 390	3.427 180	.291 785	13
.031 554	3.458 734	.289 123	14
.024 652	3.483 386	.287 077	15
.019 259	3.502 645	.285 499	16
.015 046	3.517 692	.284 277	17
.011 755	3.529 447	.283 331	18
.009 184	3.538 630	.282 595	19
.007 175	3.545 805	.282 023	20
.005 605	3.551 410	.281 578	21
.004 379	3.555 789	.281 232	22
.003 421	3.559 210	.280 961	23
.002 673	3.561 883	.280 750	24
.002 088	3.563 971	.280 586	25
.001 631	3.565 602	.280 458	26
.001 274	3.566 877	.280 357	27
.000 996	3.567 873	.280 279	28
.000 778	3.568 650	.280 218	29
.000 608	3.569 258	.280 170	30
.000 475	3.569 733	.280 133	31
.000 371	3.570 104	.280 104	32
.000 290	3.570 394	.280 081	33
.000 226	3.570 620	.280 063	34
.000 177	3.570 797	.280 050	35
.000 138	3.570 935	.280 039	36
.000 108	3.571 043	.280 030	37
.000 084	3.571 127	.280 024	38
.000 066	3.571 193	.280 018	39
.000 051	3.571 245	.280 014	40
.000 040	3.571 285	.280 011	41
.000 031	3.571 316	.280 009	42
.000 025	3.571 341	.280 007	43
.000 019	3.571 360	.280 005	44
.000 015	3.571 375	.280 004	45
.000 012	3.571 387	.280 003	46
.000 009	3.571 396	.280 003	47
.000 007	3.571 403	.280 002	48
.000 006	3.571 409	.280 002	49
.000 004	3.571 413	.280 001	50

RATE
29%

Year	COMPOUNDING FACTOR FOR 1 What an initial amount becomes when growing at compound interest	COMPOUNDING FACTOR FOR 1 PER ANNUM Growth of equal year-end deposits all growing at compound interest	SINKING FUND FACTOR Level deposit required each year to reach 1 by a given year
1	1.290 000	1.000 000	1.000 000
2	1.664 100	2.290 000	.436 681
3	2.146 689	3.954 100	.252 902
4	2.769 229	6.100 789	.163 913
5	3.572 305	8.870 018	.112 739
6	4.608 274	12.442 323	.080 371
7	5.944 673	17.050 597	.058 649
8	7.668 628	22.995 270	.043 487
9	9.892 530	30.663 898	.032 612
10	12.761 364	40.556 428	.024 657
11	16.462 160	53.317 792	.018 755
12	21.236 186	69.779 952	.014 331
13	27.394 680	91.016 138	.010 987
14	35.339 137	118.410 819	.008 445
15	45.587 487	153.749 956	.006 504
16	58.807 859	199.337 443	.005 017
17	75.862 137	258.145 302	.003 874
18	97.862 157	334.007 439	.002 994
19	126.242 183	431.869 596	.002 316
20	162.852 416	558.111 779	.001 792
21	210.079 617	720.964 195	.001 387
22	271.002 705	931.043 812	.001 074
23	349.593 490	1,202.046 518	.000 832
24	450.975 602	1,551.640 008	.000 644
25	581.758 527	2,002.615 610	.000 499
26	750.468 500	2,584.374 137	.000 387
27	968.104 365	3,334.842 636	.000 300
28	1,248.854 630	4,302.947 001	.000 232
29	1,611.022 473	5,551.801 631	.000 180
30	2,078.218 990	7,162.824 104	.000 140
31	2,680.902 497	9,241.043 094	.000 108
32	3,458.364 222	11,921.945 59	.000 084
33	4,461.289 846	15,380.309 81	.000 065
34	5,755.063 901	19,841.599 66	.000 050
35	7,424.032 433	25,596.663 56	.000 039
36	9,577.001 838	33,020.695 99	.000 030
37	12,354.332 37	42,597.697 83	.000 023
38	15,937.088 76	54,952.030 20	.000 018
39	20,558.844 50	70,889.118 96	.000 014
40	26,520.909 40	91,447.963 46	.000 011
41	34,211.973 13	117,968.872 9	.000 008
42	44,133.445 34	152,180.846 0	.000 007
43	56,932.144 49	196,314.291 3	.000 005
44	73,442.466 39	253,246.435 8	.000 004
45	94,740.781 64	326,688.902 2	.000 003
46	122,215.608 3	421,429.683 8	.000 002
47	157,658.134 7	543,645.292 2	.000 002
48	203,378.993 8	701,303.426 9	.000 001
49	262,358.902 0	904,682.420 7	.000 001
50	338,442.983 6	1,167,041.323	.000 001

RATE 29%

DISCOUNT FACTOR How much 1 at a future date is worth today	PRESENT WORTH OF AN ANNUITY FACTOR How much 1 received or paid annually for X years is worth today	CAPITAL RECOVERY FACTOR Annual payment that will repay a $1 loan in X years with compound interest on the unpaid balance	Year
.775 194	.775 194	1.290 000	1
.600 925	1.376 119	.726 681	2
.465 834	1.841 953	.542 902	3
.361 111	2.203 064	.453 913	4
.279 931	2.482 996	.402 739	5
.217 001	2.699 997	.370 371	6
.168 218	2.868 214	.348 649	7
.130 401	2.998 616	.333 487	8
.101 086	3.099 702	.322 612	9
.078 362	3.178 064	.314 657	10
.060 745	3.238 809	.308 755	11
.047 089	3.285 899	.304 331	12
.036 503	3.322 402	.300 987	13
.028 297	3.350 699	.298 445	14
.021 936	3.372 635	.296 504	15
.017 005	3.389 640	.295 017	16
.013 182	3.402 821	.293 874	17
.010 218	3.413 040	.292 994	18
.007 921	3.420 961	.292 316	19
.006 141	3.427 102	.291 792	20
.004 760	3.431 862	.291 387	21
.003 690	3.435 552	.291 071	22
.002 860	3.438 412	.290 832	23
.002 217	3.440 630	.290 644	24
.001 719	3.442 349	.290 499	25
.001 333	3.443 681	.290 387	26
.001 033	3.444 714	.290 300	27
.000 801	3.445 515	.290 232	28
.000 621	3.446 135	.290 180	29
.000 481	3.446 617	.290 140	30
.000 373	3.446 990	.290 108	31
.000 289	3.447 279	.290 084	32
.000 224	3.447 503	.290 065	33
.000 174	3.447 677	.290 050	34
.000 135	3.447 811	.290 039	35
.000 104	3.447 916	.290 030	36
.000 081	3.447 997	.290 023	37
.000 063	3.448 059	.290 018	38
.000 049	3.448 108	.290 014	39
.000 038	3.448 146	.290 011	40
.000 029	3.448 175	.290 008	41
.000 023	3.448 198	.290 007	42
.000 018	3.448 215	.290 005	43
.000 014	3.448 229	.290 004	44
.000 011	3.448 239	.290 003	45
.000 008	3.448 248	.290 002	46
.000 006	3.448 254	.290 002	47
.000 005	3.448 259	.290 001	48
.000 004	3.448 263	.290 001	49
.000 003	3.448 266	.290 001	50

RATE
30%

Year	COMPOUNDING FACTOR FOR 1 What an initial amount becomes when growing at compound interest	COMPOUNDING FACTOR FOR 1 PER ANNUM Growth of equal year-end deposits all growing at compound interest	SINKING FUND FACTOR Level deposit required each year to reach 1 by a given year
1	1.300 000	1.000 000	1.000 000
2	1.690 000	2.300 000	.434 783
3	2.197 000	3.990 000	.250 627
4	2.856 100	6.187 000	.161 629
5	3.712 930	9.043 100	.110 582
6	4.826 809	12.756 030	.078 394
7	6.274 852	17.582 839	.056 874
8	8.157 307	23.857 691	.041 915
9	10.604 499	32.014 998	.031 235
10	13.785 849	42.619 497	.023 463
11	17.921 604	56.405 346	.017 729
12	23.298 085	74.326 950	.013 454
13	30.287 511	97.625 036	.010 243
14	39.373 764	127.912 546	.007 818
15	51.185 893	167.286 310	.005 978
16	66.541 661	218.472 203	.004 577
17	86.504 159	285.013 864	.003 509
18	112.455 407	371.518 023	.002 692
19	146.192 029	483.973 430	.002 066
20	190.049 638	630.165 459	.001 587
21	247.064 529	820.215 097	.001 219
22	321.183 888	1,067.279 626	.000 937
23	417.539 054	1,388.463 514	.000 720
24	542.800 770	1,806.002 568	.000 554
25	705.641 001	2,348.803 338	.000 426
26	917.333 302	3,054.444 340	.000 327
27	1,192.533 293	3,971.777 642	.000 252
28	1,550.293 280	5,164.310 934	.000 194
29	2,015.381 264	6,714.604 214	.000 149
30	2,619.995 644	8,729.985 479	.000 115
31	3,405.994 337	11,349.981 12	.000 088
32	4,427.792 638	14,755.975 46	.000 068
33	5,756.130 429	19,183.768 10	.000 052
34	7,482.969 558	24,939.898 53	.000 040
35	9,727.860 425	32,422.868 08	.000 031
36	12,646.218 55	42,150.728 51	.000 024
37	16,440.084 12	54,796.947 06	.000 018
38	21,372.109 35	71,237.031 18	.000 014
39	27,783.742 16	92,609.140 53	.000 011
40	36,118.864 81	120,392.882 7	.000 008
41	46,954.524 25	156,511.747 5	.000 006
42	61,040.881 53	203,466.271 8	.000 005
43	79,353.145 98	264,507.153 3	.000 004
44	103,159.089 8	343,860.299 3	.000 003
45	134,106.816 7	447,019.389 0	.000 002
46	174,338.861 7	581,126.205 8	.000 002
47	226,640.520 2	755,465.067 5	.000 001
48	294,632.676 3	982,105.587 7	.000 001
49	383,022.479 2	1,276,738.264	.000 001
50	497,929.223 0	1,659,760.743	.000 001

RATE 30%

DISCOUNT FACTOR How much 1 at a future date is worth today	PRESENT WORTH OF AN ANNUITY FACTOR How much 1 received or paid annually for X years is worth today	CAPITAL RECOVERY FACTOR Annual payment that will repay a $1 loan in X years with compound interest on the unpaid balance	Year
.769 231	.769 231	1.300 000	1
.591 716	1.360 947	.734 783	2
.455 166	1.816 113	.550 627	3
.350 128	2.166 241	.461 629	4
.269 329	2.435 570	.410 582	5
.207 176	2.642 746	.378 394	6
.159 366	2.802 112	.356 874	7
.122 589	2.924 702	.341 915	8
.094 300	3.019 001	.331 235	9
.072 538	3.091 539	.323 463	10
.055 799	3.147 338	.317 729	11
.042 922	3.190 260	.313 454	12
.033 017	3.223 277	.310 243	13
.025 398	3.248 675	.307 818	14
.019 537	3.268 211	.305 978	15
.015 028	3.283 239	.304 577	16
.011 560	3.294 800	.303 509	17
.008 892	3.303 692	.302 692	18
.006 840	3.310 532	.302 066	19
.005 262	3.315 794	.301 587	20
.004 048	3.319 842	.301 219	21
.003 113	3.322 955	.300 937	22
.002 395	3.325 350	.300 720	23
.001 842	3.327 192	.300 554	24
.001 417	3.328 609	.300 426	25
.001 090	3.329 700	.300 327	26
.000 839	3.330 538	.300 252	27
.000 645	3.331 183	.300 194	28
.000 496	3.331 679	.300 149	29
.000 382	3.332 061	.300 115	30
.000 294	3.332 355	.300 088	31
.000 226	3.332 581	.300 068	32
.000 174	3.332 754	.300 052	33
.000 134	3.332 888	.300 040	34
.000 103	3.332 991	.300 031	35
.000 079	3.333 070	.300 024	36
.000 061	3.333 131	.300 018	37
.000 047	3.333 177	.300 014	38
.000 036	3.333 213	.300 011	39
.000 028	3.333 241	.300 008	40
.000 021	3.333 262	.300 006	41
.000 016	3.333 279	.300 005	42
.000 013	3.333 291	.300 004	43
.000 010	3.333 301	.300 003	44
.000 007	3.333 308	.300 002	45
.000 006	3.333 314	.300 002	46
.000 004	3.333 319	.300 001	47
.000 003	3.333 322	.300 001	48
.000 003	3.333 325	.300 001	49
.000 002	3.333 327	.300 001	50

RATE
31%

Year	COMPOUNDING FACTOR FOR 1 What an initial amount becomes when growing at compound interest	COMPOUNDING FACTOR FOR 1 PER ANNUM Growth of equal year-end deposits all growing at compound interest	SINKING FUND FACTOR Level deposit required each year to reach 1 by a given year
1	1.310 000	1.000 000	1.000 000
2	1.716 100	2.310 000	.432 900
3	2.248 091	4.026 100	.248 379
4	2.944 999	6.274 191	.159 383
5	3.857 949	9.219 190	.108 469
6	5.053 913	13.077 139	.076 469
7	6.620 626	18.131 052	.055 154
8	8.673 020	24.751 679	.040 401
9	11.361 657	33.424 699	.029 918
10	14.883 770	44.786 356	.022 328
11	19.497 739	59.670 126	.016 759
12	25.542 038	79.167 865	.012 631
13	33.460 070	104.709 903	.009 550
14	43.832 692	138.169 973	.007 237
15	57.420 826	182.002 664	.005 494
16	75.221 282	239.423 490	.004 177
17	98.539 879	314.644 772	.003 178
18	129.087 242	413.184 651	.002 420
19	169.104 287	542.271 893	.001 844
20	221.526 616	711.376 180	.001 406
21	290.199 867	932.902 796	.001 072
22	380.161 826	1,223.102 663	.000 818
23	498.011 991	1,603.264 488	.000 624
24	652.395 709	2,101.276 480	.000 476
25	854.638 378	2,753.672 189	.000 363
26	1,119.576 276	3,608.310 567	.000 277
27	1,466.644 921	4,727.886 843	.000 212
28	1,921.304 847	6,194.531 764	.000 161
29	2,516.909 349	8,115.836 611	.000 123
30	3,297.151 248	10,632.745 96	.000 094
31	4,319.268 135	13,929.897 21	.000 072
32	5,658.241 256	18,249.165 34	.000 055
33	7,412.296 046	23,907.406 60	.000 042
34	9,710.107 820	31,319.702 65	.000 032
35	12,720.241 24	41,029.810 46	.000 024
36	16,663.516 03	53,750.051 71	.000 019
37	21,829.206 00	70,413.567 74	.000 014
38	28,596.259 86	92,242.773 74	.000 011
39	37,461.100 42	120,839.033 6	.000 008
40	49,074.041 54	158,300.134 0	.000 006
41	64,286.994 42	207,374.175 6	.000 005
42	84,215.962 69	271,661.170 0	.000 004
43	110,322.911 1	355,877.132 7	.000 003
44	144,523.013 6	466,200.043 8	.000 002
45	189,325.147 8	610,723.057 4	.000 002
46	248,015.943 6	800,048.205 2	.000 001
47	324,900.886 1	1,048,064.149	.000 001
48	425,620.160 8	1,372,965.035	.000 001
49	557,562.410 7	1,798,585.196	.000 001
50	730,406.758 0	2,356,147.606	.000 000

RATE
31%

DISCOUNT FACTOR How much 1 at a future date is worth today	PRESENT WORTH OF AN ANNUITY FACTOR How much 1 received or paid annually for X years is worth today	CAPITAL RECOVERY FACTOR Annual payment that will repay a $1 loan in X years with compound interest on the unpaid balance	Year
.763 359	.763 359	1.310 000	1
.582 717	1.346 075	.742 900	2
.444 822	1.790 897	.558 379	3
.339 559	2.130 456	.469 383	4
.259 205	2.389 661	.418 469	5
.197 866	2.587 527	.386 469	6
.151 043	2.738 571	.365 154	7
.115 300	2.853 871	.350 401	8
.088 015	2.941 886	.339 918	9
.067 187	3.009 073	.332 328	10
.051 288	3.060 361	.326 759	11
.039 151	3.099 512	.322 631	12
.029 886	3.129 399	.319 550	13
.022 814	3.152 213	.317 237	14
.017 415	3.169 628	.315 494	15
.013 294	3.182 922	.314 177	16
.010 148	3.193 070	.313 178	17
.007 747	3.200 817	.312 420	18
.005 914	3.206 731	.311 844	19
.004 514	3.211 245	.311 406	20
.003 446	3.214 691	.311 072	21
.002 630	3.217 321	.310 818	22
.002 008	3.219 329	.310 624	23
.001 533	3.220 862	.310 476	24
.001 170	3.222 032	.310 363	25
.000 893	3.222 925	.310 277	26
.000 682	3.223 607	.310 212	27
.000 520	3.224 127	.310 161	28
.000 397	3.224 525	.310 123	29
.000 303	3.224 828	.310 094	30
.000 232	3.225 060	.310 072	31
.000 177	3.225 236	.310 055	32
.000 135	3.225 371	.310 042	33
.000 103	3.225 474	.310 032	34
.000 079	3.225 553	.310 024	35
.000 060	3.225 613	.310 019	36
.000 046	3.225 659	.310 014	37
.000 035	3.225 694	.310 011	38
.000 027	3.225 720	.310 008	39
.000 020	3.225 741	.310 006	40
.000 016	3.225 756	.310 005	41
.000 012	3.225 768	.310 004	42
.000 009	3.225 777	.310 003	43
.000 007	3.225 784	.310 002	44
.000 005	3.225 789	.310 002	45
.000 004	3.225 793	.310 001	46
.000 003	3.225 797	.310 001	47
.000 002	3.225 799	.310 001	48
.000 002	3.225 801	.310 001	49
.000 001	3.225 802	.310 000	50

RATE
32%

Year	COMPOUNDING FACTOR FOR 1 What an initial amount becomes when growing at compound interest	COMPOUNDING FACTOR FOR 1 PER ANNUM Growth of equal year-end deposits all growing at compound interest	SINKING FUND FACTOR Level deposit required each year to reach 1 by a given year
1	1.320 000	1.000 000	1.000 000
2	1.742 400	2.320 000	.431 034
3	2.299 968	4.062 400	.246 160
4	3.035 958	6.362 368	.157 174
5	4.007 464	9.398 326	.106 402
6	5.289 853	13.405 790	.074 595
7	6.982 606	18.695 643	.053 488
8	9.217 040	25.678 249	.038 943
9	12.166 492	34.895 288	.028 657
10	16.059 770	47.061 780	.021 249
11	21.198 896	63.121 550	.015 842
12	27.982 543	84.320 446	.011 860
13	36.936 956	112.302 988	.008 904
14	48.756 782	149.239 945	.006 701
15	64.358 953	197.996 727	.005 051
16	84.953 818	262.355 680	.003 812
17	112.139 039	347.309 497	.002 879
18	148.023 532	459.448 536	.002 177
19	195.391 062	607.472 068	.001 646
20	257.916 202	802.863 130	.001 246
21	340.449 386	1,060.779 331	.000 943
22	449.393 190	1,401.228 717	.000 714
23	593.199 010	1,850.621 907	.000 540
24	783.022 694	2,443.820 917	.000 409
25	1,033.589 955	3,226.843 611	.000 310
26	1,364.338 741	4,260.433 566	.000 235
27	1,800.927 138	5,624.772 307	.000 178
28	2,377.223 823	7,425.699 446	.000 135
29	3,137.935 446	9,802.923 268	.000 102
30	4,142.074 789	12,940.858 71	.000 077
31	5,467.538 721	17,082.933 50	.000 059
32	7,217.151 112	22,550.472 22	.000 044
33	9,526.639 467	29,767.623 34	.000 034
34	12,575.164 10	39,294.262 80	.000 025
35	16,599.216 61	51,869.426 90	.000 019
36	21,910.965 92	68,468.643 51	.000 015
37	28,922.475 02	90,379.609 43	.000 011
38	38,177.667 02	119,302.084 4	.000 008
39	50,394.520 47	157,479.751 5	.000 006
40	66,520.767 02	207,874.271 9	.000 005
41	87,807.412 47	274,395.039 0	.000 004
42	115,905.784 5	362,202.451 4	.000 003
43	152,995.635 5	478,108.235 9	.000 002
44	201,954.238 8	631,103.871 4	.000 002
45	266,579.595 3	833,058.110 2	.000 001
46	351,885.065 8	1,099,637.705	.000 001
47	464,488.286 8	1,451,522.771	.000 001
48	613,124.538 6	1,916,011.058	.000 001
49	809,324.390 9	2,529,135.597	.000 000
50	1,068,308.196	3,338,459.988	.000 000

RATE
32%

DISCOUNT FACTOR How much 1 at a future date is worth today	PRESENT WORTH OF AN ANNUITY FACTOR How much 1 received or paid annually for X years is worth today	CAPITAL RECOVERY FACTOR Annual payment that will repay a $1 loan in X years with compound interest on the unpaid balance	Year
.757 576	.757 576	1.320 000	1
.573 921	1.331 497	.751 034	2
.434 789	1.766 285	.566 160	3
.329 385	2.095 671	.477 174	4
.249 534	2.345 205	.426 402	5
.189 041	2.534 246	.394 595	6
.143 213	2.677 459	.373 488	7
.108 495	2.785 954	.358 943	8
.082 193	2.868 147	.348 657	9
.062 267	2.930 414	.341 249	10
.047 172	2.977 587	.335 842	11
.035 737	3.013 323	.331 860	12
.027 073	3.040 396	.328 904	13
.020 510	3.060 906	.326 701	14
.015 538	3.076 444	.325 051	15
.011 771	3.088 215	.323 812	16
.008 918	3.097 133	.322 879	17
.006 756	3.103 888	.322 177	18
.005 118	3.109 006	.321 646	19
.003 877	3.112 884	.321 246	20
.002 937	3.115 821	.320 943	21
.002 225	3.118 046	.320 714	22
.001 686	3.119 732	.320 540	23
.001 277	3.121 009	.320 409	24
.000 968	3.121 977	.320 310	25
.000 733	3.122 710	.320 235	26
.000 555	3.123 265	.320 178	27
.000 421	3.123 685	.320 135	28
.000 319	3.124 004	.320 102	29
.000 241	3.124 246	.320 077	30
.000 183	3.124 428	.320 059	31
.000 139	3.124 567	.320 044	32
.000 105	3.124 672	.320 034	33
.000 080	3.124 751	.320 025	34
.000 060	3.124 812	.320 019	35
.000 046	3.124 857	.320 015	36
.000 035	3.124 892	.320 011	37
.000 026	3.124 918	.320 008	38
.000 020	3.124 938	.320 006	39
.000 015	3.124 953	.320 005	40
.000 011	3.124 964	.320 004	41
.000 009	3.124 973	.320 003	42
.000 007	3.124 980	.320 002	43
.000 005	3.124 985	.320 002	44
.000 004	3.124 988	.320 001	45
.000 003	3.124 991	.320 001	46
.000 002	3.124 993	.320 001	47
.000 002	3.124 995	.320 001	48
.000 001	3.124 996	.320 000	49
.000 001	3.124 997	.320 000	50

RATE
33%

Year	COMPOUNDING FACTOR FOR 1 What an initial amount becomes when growing at compound interest	COMPOUNDING FACTOR FOR 1 PER ANNUM Growth of equal year-end deposits all growing at compound interest	SINKING FUND FACTOR Level deposit required each year to reach 1 by a given year
1	1.330 000	1.000 000	1.000 000
2	1.768 900	2.330 000	.429 185
3	2.352 637	4.098 900	.243 968
4	3.129 007	6.451 537	.155 002
5	4.161 580	9.580 544	.104 378
6	5.534 901	13.742 124	.072 769
7	7.361 418	19.277 025	.051 875
8	9.790 686	26.638 443	.037 540
9	13.021 613	36.429 129	.027 451
10	17.318 745	49.450 741	.020 222
11	23.033 930	66.769 486	.014 977
12	30.635 127	89.803 417	.011 135
13	40.744 720	120.438 544	.008 303
14	54.190 477	161.183 264	.006 204
15	72.073 334	215.373 740	.004 643
16	95.857 535	287.447 075	.003 479
17	127.490 521	383.304 610	.002 609
18	169.562 393	510.795 131	.001 958
19	225.517 983	680.357 524	.001 470
20	299.938 917	905.875 507	.001 104
21	398.918 760	1,205.814 424	.000 829
22	530.561 951	1,604.733 184	.000 623
23	705.647 394	2,135.295 135	.000 468
24	938.511 035	2,840.942 529	.000 352
25	1,248.219 676	3,779.453 564	.000 265
26	1,660.132 169	5,027.673 239	.000 199
27	2,207.975 785	6,687.805 408	.000 150
28	2,936.607 794	8,895.781 193	.000 112
29	3,905.688 366	11,832.388 99	.000 085
30	5,194.565 526	15,738.077 35	.000 064
31	6,908.772 150	20,932.642 88	.000 048
32	9,188.666 960	27,841.415 03	.000 036
33	12,220.927 06	37,030.081 99	.000 027
34	16,253.832 99	49,251.009 04	.000 020
35	21,617.597 87	65,504.842 03	.000 015
36	28,751.405 17	87,122.439 90	.000 011
37	38,239.368 87	115,873.845 1	.000 009
38	50,858.360 60	154,113.213 9	.000 006
39	67,641.619 60	204,971.574 5	.000 005
40	89,963.354 07	272,613.194 1	.000 004
41	119,651.260 9	362,576.548 2	.000 003
42	159,136.177 0	482,227.809 1	.000 002
43	211,651.115 4	641,363.986 1	.000 002
44	281,495.983 5	853,015.101 5	.000 001
45	374,389.658 1	1,134,511.085	.000 001
46	497,938.245 2	1,508,900.743	.000 001
47	662,257.866 2	2,006,838.988	.000 000
48	880,802.962 0	2,669,096.854	.000 000
49	1,171,467.939	3,549,899.816	.000 000
50	1,558,052.359	4,721,367.756	.000 000

RATE
33%

DISCOUNT FACTOR How much 1 at a future date is worth today	PRESENT WORTH OF AN ANNUITY FACTOR How much 1 received or paid annually for X years is worth today	CAPITAL RECOVERY FACTOR Annual payment that will repay a $1 loan in X years with compound interest on the unpaid balance	Year
.751 880	.751 880	1.330 000	1
.565 323	1.317 203	.759 185	2
.425 055	1.742 258	.573 968	3
.319 590	2.061 848	.485 002	4
.240 293	2.302 141	.434 378	5
.180 672	2.482 813	.402 769	6
.135 843	2.618 656	.381 875	7
.102 138	2.720 794	.367 540	8
.076 795	2.797 590	.357 451	9
.057 741	2.855 331	.350 222	10
.043 414	2.898 745	.344 977	11
.032 642	2.931 387	.341 135	12
.024 543	2.955 930	.338 303	13
.018 453	2.974 384	.336 204	14
.013 875	2.988 258	.334 643	15
.010 432	2.998 690	.333 479	16
.007 844	3.006 534	.332 609	17
.005 898	3.012 432	.331 958	18
.004 434	3.016 866	.331 470	19
.003 334	3.020 200	.331 104	20
.002 507	3.022 707	.330 829	21
.001 885	3.024 592	.330 623	22
.001 417	3.026 009	.330 468	23
.001 066	3.027 074	.330 352	24
.000 801	3.027 875	.330 265	25
.000 602	3.028 478	.330 199	26
.000 453	3.028 931	.330 150	27
.000 341	3.029 271	.330 112	28
.000 256	3.029 527	.330 085	29
.000 193	3.029 720	.330 064	30
.000 145	3.029 864	.330 048	31
.000 109	3.029 973	.330 036	32
.000 082	3.030 055	.330 027	33
.000 062	3.030 117	.330 020	34
.000 046	3.030 163	.330 015	35
.000 035	3.030 198	.330 011	36
.000 026	3.030 224	.330 009	37
.000 020	3.030 243	.330 006	38
.000 015	3.030 258	.330 005	39
.000 011	3.030 269	.330 004	40
.000 008	3.030 278	.330 003	41
.000 006	3.030 284	.330 002	42
.000 005	3.030 289	.330 002	43
.000 004	3.030 292	.330 001	44
.000 003	3.030 295	.330 001	45
.000 002	3.030 297	.330 001	46
.000 002	3.030 298	.330 000	47
.000 001	3.030 300	.330 000	48
.000 001	3.030 300	.330 000	49
.000 001	3.030 301	.330 000	50

RATE
34%

Year	COMPOUNDING FACTOR FOR 1 What an initial amount becomes when growing at compound interest	COMPOUNDING FACTOR FOR 1 PER ANNUM Growth of equal year-end deposits all growing at compound interest	SINKING FUND FACTOR Level deposit required each year to reach 1 by a given year
1	1.340 000	1.000 000	1.000 000
2	1.795 600	2.340 000	.427 350
3	2.406 104	4.135 600	.241 803
4	3.224 179	6.541 704	.152 865
5	4.320 400	9.765 883	.102 397
6	5.789 336	14.086 284	.070 991
7	7.757 711	19.875 620	.050 313
8	10.395 333	27.633 331	.036 188
9	13.929 746	38.028 664	.026 296
10	18.665 859	51.958 409	.019 246
11	25.012 251	70.624 268	.014 159
12	33.516 417	95.636 520	.010 456
13	44.911 998	129.152 936	.007 743
14	60.182 078	174.064 934	.005 745
15	80.643 984	234.247 012	.004 269
16	108.062 939	314.890 996	.003 176
17	144.804 338	422.953 935	.002 364
18	194.037 813	567.758 273	.001 761
19	260.010 669	761.796 086	.001 313
20	348.414 297	1,021.806 755	.000 979
21	466.875 157	1,370.221 051	.000 730
22	625.612 711	1,837.096 209	.000 544
23	838.321 033	2,462.708 920	.000 406
24	1,123.350 184	3,301.029 953	.000 303
25	1,505.289 246	4,424.380 137	.000 226
26	2,017.087 590	5,929.669 383	.000 169
27	2,702.897 371	7,946.756 973	.000 126
28	3,621.882 477	10,649.654 34	.000 094
29	4,853.322 519	14,271.536 82	.000 070
30	6,503.452 176	19,124.859 34	.000 052
31	8,714.625 916	25,628.311 52	.000 039
32	11,677.598 73	34,342.937 43	.000 029
33	15,647.982 29	46,020.536 16	.000 022
34	20,968.296 27	61,668.518 45	.000 016
35	28,097.517 01	82,636.814 73	.000 012
36	37,650.672 79	110,734.331 7	.000 009
37	50,451.901 54	148,385.004 5	.000 007
38	67,605.548 06	198,836.906 1	.000 005
39	90,591.434 40	266,442.454 1	.000 004
40	121,392.522 1	357,033.888 5	.000 003
41	162,665.979 6	478,426.410 6	.000 002
42	217,972.412 7	641,092.390 2	.000 002
43	292,083.033 0	859,064.802 9	.000 001
44	391,391.264 2	1,151,147.836	.000 001
45	524,464.294 0	1,542,539.100	.000 001
46	702,782.154 0	2,067,003.394	.000 000
47	941,728.086 4	2,769,785.548	.000 000
48	1,261,915.636	3,711,513.635	.000 000
49	1,690,966.952	4,973,429.270	.000 000
50	2,265,895.716	6,664,396.222	.000 000

RATE
34%

DISCOUNT FACTOR How much 1 at a future date is worth today	PRESENT WORTH OF AN ANNUITY FACTOR How much 1 received or paid annually for X years is worth today	CAPITAL RECOVERY FACTOR Annual payment that will repay a $1 loan in X years with compound interest on the unpaid balance	Year
.746 269	.746 269	1.340 000	1
.556 917	1.303 186	.767 350	2
.415 610	1.718 795	.581 803	3
.310 156	2.028 952	.492 865	4
.231 460	2.260 412	.442 397	5
.172 731	2.433 143	.410 991	6
.128 904	2.562 047	.390 313	7
.096 197	2.658 244	.376 188	8
.071 789	2.730 033	.366 296	9
.053 574	2.783 607	.359 246	10
.039 980	2.823 587	.354 159	11
.029 836	2.853 423	.350 456	12
.022 266	2.875 689	.347 743	13
.016 616	2.892 305	.345 745	14
.012 400	2.904 705	.344 269	15
.009 254	2.913 959	.343 176	16
.006 906	2.920 865	.342 364	17
.005 154	2.926 019	.341 761	18
.003 846	2.929 865	.341 313	19
.002 870	2.932 735	.340 979	20
.002 142	2.934 877	.340 730	21
.001 598	2.936 475	.340 544	22
.001 193	2.937 668	.340 406	23
.000 890	2.938 558	.340 303	24
.000 664	2.939 223	.340 226	25
.000 496	2.939 718	.340 169	26
.000 370	2.940 088	.340 126	27
.000 276	2.940 364	.340 094	28
.000 206	2.940 570	.340 070	29
.000 154	2.940 724	.340 052	30
.000 115	2.940 839	.340 039	31
.000 086	2.940 925	.340 029	32
.000 064	2.940 989	.340 022	33
.000 048	2.941 036	.340 016	34
.000 036	2.941 072	.340 012	35
.000 027	2.941 098	.340 009	36
.000 020	2.941 118	.340 007	37
.000 015	2.941 133	.340 005	38
.000 011	2.941 144	.340 004	39
.000 008	2.941 152	.340 003	40
.000 006	2.941 158	.340 002	41
.000 005	2.941 163	.340 002	42
.000 003	2.941 166	.340 001	43
.000 003	2.941 169	.340 001	44
.000 002	2.941 171	.340 001	45
.000 001	2.941 172	.340 000	46
.000 001	2.941 173	.340 000	47
.000 001	2.941 174	.340 000	48
.000 001	2.941 175	.340 000	49
.000 000	2.941 175	.340 000	50

RATE
35%

Year	COMPOUNDING FACTOR FOR 1 What an initial amount becomes when growing at compound interest	COMPOUNDING FACTOR FOR 1 PER ANNUM Growth of equal year-end deposits all growing at compound interest	SINKING FUND FACTOR Level deposit required each year to reach 1 by a given year
1	1.350 000	1.000 000	1.000 000
2	1.822 500	2.350 000	.425 532
3	2.460 375	4.172 500	.239 664
4	3.321 506	6.632 875	.150 764
5	4.484 033	9.954 381	.100 458
6	6.053 445	14.438 415	.069 260
7	8.172 151	20.491 860	.048 800
8	11.032 404	28.664 011	.034 887
9	14.893 745	39.696 415	.025 191
10	20.106 556	54.590 160	.018 318
11	27.143 850	74.696 715	.013 387
12	36.644 198	101.840 566	.009 819
13	49.469 667	138.484 764	.007 221
14	66.784 051	187.954 431	.005 320
15	90.158 469	254.738 482	.003 926
16	121.713 933	344.896 951	.002 899
17	164.313 809	466.610 884	.002 143
18	221.823 643	630.924 694	.001 585
19	299.461 918	852.748 336	.001 173
20	404.273 589	1,152.210 254	.000 868
21	545.769 345	1,556.483 843	.000 642
22	736.788 616	2,102.253 188	.000 476
23	994.664 631	2,839.041 804	.000 352
24	1,342.797 252	3,833.706 435	.000 261
25	1,812.776 291	5,176.503 687	.000 193
26	2,447.247 992	6,989.279 978	.000 143
27	3,303.784 789	9,436.527 970	.000 106
28	4,460.109 466	12,740.312 76	.000 078
29	6,021.147 779	17,200.422 23	.000 058
30	8,128.549 501	23,221.570 00	.000 043
31	10,973.541 83	31,350.119 51	.000 032
32	14,814.281 47	42,323.661 33	.000 024
33	19,999.279 98	57,137.942 80	.000 018
34	26,999.027 97	77,137.222 78	.000 013
35	36,448.687 76	104,136.250 8	.000 010
36	49,205.728 48	140,584.938 5	.000 007
37	66,427.733 45	189,790.667 0	.000 005
38	89,677.440 15	256,218.400 4	.000 004
39	121,064.544 2	345,895.840 6	.000 003
40	163,437.134 7	466,960.384 8	.000 002
41	220,640.131 8	630,397.519 5	.000 002
42	297,864.178 0	851,037.651 3	.000 001
43	402,116.640 2	1,148,901.829	.000 001
44	542,857.464 3	1,551,018.470	.000 001
45	732,857.576 8	2,093,875.934	.000 000
46	989,357.728 7	2,826,733.511	.000 000
47	1,335,632.934	3,816,091.239	.000 000
48	1,803,104.461	5,151,724.173	.000 000
49	2,434,191.022	6,954,828.634	.000 000
50	3,286,157.879	9,389,019.656	.000 000

RATE
35%

DISCOUNT FACTOR How much 1 at a future date is worth today	PRESENT WORTH OF AN ANNUITY FACTOR How much 1 received or paid annually for X years is worth today	CAPITAL RECOVERY FACTOR Annual payment that will repay a $1 loan in X years with compound interest on the unpaid balance	Year
.740 741	.740 741	1.350 000	1
.548 697	1.289 438	.775 532	2
.406 442	1.695 880	.589 664	3
.301 068	1.996 948	.500 764	4
.223 014	2.219 961	.450 458	5
.165 195	2.385 157	.419 260	6
.122 367	2.507 523	.398 800	7
.090 642	2.598 165	.384 887	8
.067 142	2.665 308	.375 191	9
.049 735	2.715 043	.368 318	10
.036 841	2.751 884	.363 387	11
.027 289	2.779 173	.359 819	12
.020 214	2.799 387	.357 221	13
.014 974	2.814 361	.355 320	14
.011 092	2.825 453	.353 926	15
.008 216	2.833 669	.352 899	16
.006 086	2.839 755	.352 143	17
.004 508	2.844 263	.351 585	18
.003 339	2.847 602	.351 173	19
.002 474	2.850 076	.350 868	20
.001 832	2.851 908	.350 642	21
.001 357	2.853 265	.350 476	22
.001 005	2.854 270	.350 352	23
.000 745	2.855 015	.350 261	24
.000 552	2.855 567	.350 193	25
.000 409	2.855 975	.350 143	26
.000 303	2.856 278	.350 106	27
.000 224	2.856 502	.350 078	28
.000 166	2.856 668	.350 058	29
.000 123	2.856 791	.350 043	30
.000 091	2.856 882	.350 032	31
.000 068	2.856 950	.350 024	32
.000 050	2.857 000	.350 018	33
.000 037	2.857 037	.350 013	34
.000 027	2.857 064	.350 010	35
.000 020	2.857 085	.350 007	36
.000 015	2.857 100	.350 005	37
.000 011	2.857 111	.350 004	38
.000 008	2.857 119	.350 003	39
.000 006	2.857 125	.350 002	40
.000 005	2.857 130	.350 002	41
.000 003	2.857 133	.350 001	42
.000 002	2.857 136	.350 001	43
.000 002	2.857 138	.350 001	44
.000 001	2.857 139	.350 000	45
.000 001	2.857 140	.350 000	46
.000 001	2.857 141	.350 000	47
.000 001	2.857 141	.350 000	48
.000 000	2.857 142	.350 000	49
.000 000	2.857 142	.350 000	50

RATE
36%

Year	COMPOUNDING FACTOR FOR 1 What an initial amount becomes when growing at compound interest	COMPOUNDING FACTOR FOR 1 PER ANNUM Growth of equal year-end deposits all growing at compound interest	SINKING FUND FACTOR Level deposit required each year to reach 1 by a given year
1	1.360 000	1.000 000	1.000 000
2	1.849 600	2.360 000	.423 729
3	2.515 456	4.209 600	.237 552
4	3.421 020	6.725 056	.148 698
5	4.652 587	10.146 076	.098 560
6	6.327 519	14.798 664	.067 574
7	8.605 426	21.126 182	.047 335
8	11.703 379	29.731 608	.033 634
9	15.916 595	41.434 987	.024 134
10	21.646 570	57.351 582	.017 436
11	29.439 335	78.998 152	.012 659
12	40.037 495	108.437 487	.009 222
13	54.450 994	148.474 982	.006 735
14	74.053 351	202.925 976	.004 928
15	100.712 558	276.979 327	.003 610
16	136.969 078	377.691 885	.002 648
17	186.277 947	514.660 963	.001 943
18	253.338 008	700.938 910	.001 427
19	344.539 690	954.276 918	.001 048
20	468.573 979	1,298.816 608	.000 770
21	637.260 611	1,767.390 587	.000 566
22	866.674 431	2,404.651 198	.000 416
23	1,178.677 227	3,271.325 629	.000 306
24	1,603.001 028	4,450.002 856	.000 225
25	2,180.081 398	6,053.003 884	.000 165
26	2,964.910 702	8,233.085 282	.000 121
27	4,032.278 554	11,197.995 98	.000 089
28	5,483.898 833	15,230.274 54	.000 066
29	7,458.102 414	20,714.173 37	.000 048
30	10,143.019 28	28,172.275 78	.000 035
31	13,794.506 22	38,315.295 07	.000 026
32	18,760.528 46	52,109.801 29	.000 019
33	25,514.318 71	70,870.329 76	.000 014
34	34,699.473 45	96,384.648 47	.000 010
35	47,191.283 89	131,084.121 9	.000 008
36	64,180.146 09	178,275.405 8	.000 006
37	87,284.998 68	242,455.551 9	.000 004
38	118,707.598 2	329,740.550 6	.000 003
39	161,442.333 6	448,448.148 8	.000 002
40	219,561.573 6	609,890.482 4	.000 002
41	298,603.740 2	829,452.056 0	.000 001
42	406,101.086 6	1,128,055.796	.000 001
43	552,297.477 8	1,534,156.883	.000 001
44	751,124.569 8	2,086,454.361	.000 000
45	1,021,529.415	2,837,578.930	.000 000
46	1,389,280.004	3,859,108.345	.000 000
47	1,889,420.806	5,248,388.350	.000 000
48	2,569,612.296	7,137,809.156	.000 000
49	3,494,672.723	9,707,421.452	.000 000
50	4,752,754.903	13,202,094.17	.000 000

RATE
36%

DISCOUNT FACTOR How much 1 at a future date is worth today	PRESENT WORTH OF AN ANNUITY FACTOR How much 1 received or paid annually for X years is worth today	CAPITAL RECOVERY FACTOR Annual payment that will repay a $1 loan in X years with compound interest on the unpaid balance	Year
.735 294	.735 294	1.360 000	1
.540 657	1.275 952	.783 729	2
.397 542	1.673 494	.597 552	3
.292 310	1.965 804	.508 698	4
.214 934	2.180 738	.458 560	5
.158 040	2.338 778	.427 574	6
.116 206	2.454 984	.407 335	7
.085 445	2.540 429	.393 634	8
.062 828	2.603 257	.384 134	9
.046 197	2.649 454	.377 436	10
.033 968	2.683 422	.372 659	11
.024 977	2.708 398	.369 222	12
.018 365	2.726 764	.366 735	13
.013 504	2.740 267	.364 928	14
.009 929	2.750 197	.363 610	15
.007 301	2.757 497	.362 648	16
.005 368	2.762 866	.361 943	17
.003 947	2.766 813	.361 427	18
.002 902	2.769 715	.361 048	19
.002 134	2.771 850	.360 770	20
.001 569	2.773 419	.360 566	21
.001 154	2.774 573	.360 416	22
.000 848	2.775 421	.360 306	23
.000 624	2.776 045	.360 225	24
.000 459	2.776 504	.360 165	25
.000 337	2.776 841	.360 121	26
.000 248	2.777 089	.360 089	27
.000 182	2.777 271	.360 066	28
.000 134	2.777 405	.360 048	29
.000 099	2.777 504	.360 035	30
.000 072	2.777 576	.360 026	31
.000 053	2.777 630	.360 019	32
.000 039	2.777 669	.360 014	33
.000 029	2.777 698	.360 010	34
.000 021	2.777 719	.360 008	35
.000 016	2.777 734	.360 006	36
.000 011	2.777 746	.360 004	37
.000 008	2.777 754	.360 003	38
.000 006	2.777 761	.360 002	39
.000 005	2.777 765	.360 002	40
.000 003	2.777 768	.360 001	41
.000 002	2.777 771	.360 001	42
.000 002	2.777 773	.360 001	43
.000 001	2.777 774	.360 000	44
.000 001	2.777 775	.360 000	45
.000 001	2.777 776	.360 000	46
.000 001	2.777 776	.360 000	47
.000 000	2.777 777	.360 000	48
.000 000	2.777 777	.360 000	49
.000 000	2.777 777	.360 000	50

RATE
37%

Year	COMPOUNDING FACTOR FOR 1 What an initial amount becomes when growing at compound interest	COMPOUNDING FACTOR FOR 1 PER ANNUM Growth of equal year-end deposits all growing at compound interest	SINKING FUND FACTOR Level deposit required each year to reach 1 by a given year
1	1.370 000	1.000 000	1.000 000
2	1.876 900	2.370 000	.421 941
3	2.571 353	4.246 900	.235 466
4	3.522 754	6.818 253	.146 665
5	4.826 172	10.341 007	.096 702
6	6.611 856	15.167 179	.065 932
7	9.058 243	21.779 035	.045 916
8	12.409 793	30.837 278	.032 428
9	17.001 416	43.247 071	.023 123
10	23.291 940	60.248 488	.016 598
11	31.909 958	83.540 428	.011 970
12	43.716 643	115.450 387	.008 662
13	59.891 801	159.167 030	.006 283
14	82.051 767	219.058 831	.004 565
15	112.410 921	301.110 598	.003 321
16	154.002 962	413.521 520	.002 418
17	210.984 058	567.524 482	.001 762
18	289.048 160	778.508 540	.001 285
19	395.995 979	1,067.556 700	.000 937
20	542.514 491	1,463.552 679	.000 683
21	743.244 853	2,006.067 170	.000 498
22	1,018.245 448	2,749.312 023	.000 364
23	1,394.996 264	3,767.557 471	.000 265
24	1,911.144 882	5,162.553 735	.000 194
25	2,618.268 488	7,073.698 617	.000 141
26	3,587.027 829	9,691.967 106	.000 103
27	4,914.228 126	13,278.994 94	.000 075
28	6,732.492 533	18,193.223 06	.000 055
29	9,223.514 770	24,925.715 59	.000 040
30	12,636.215 23	34,149.230 36	.000 029
31	17,311.614 87	46,785.445 60	.000 021
32	23,716.912 37	64,097.060 47	.000 016
33	32,492.169 95	87,813.972 84	.000 011
34	44,514.272 83	120,306.142 8	.000 008
35	60,984.553 78	164,820.415 6	.000 006
36	83,548.838 68	225,804.969 4	.000 004
37	114,461.909 0	309,353.808 1	.000 003
38	156,812.815 3	423,815.717 1	.000 002
39	214,833.557 0	580,628.532 4	.000 002
40	294,321.973 1	795,462.089 4	.000 001
41	403,221.103 1	1,089,784.062	.000 001
42	552,412.911 3	1,493,005.166	.000 001
43	756,805.688 4	2,045,418.077	.000 000
44	1,036,823.793	2,802,223.765	.000 000
45	1,420,448.597	3,839,047.558	.000 000
46	1,946,014.577	5,259,496.155	.000 000
47	2,666,039.971	7,205,510.732	.000 000
48	3,652,474.760	9,871,550.703	.000 000
49	5,003,890.422	13,524,025.46	.000 000
50	6,855,329.878	18,527,915.89	.000 000

RATE 37%

DISCOUNT FACTOR How much 1 at a future date is worth today	PRESENT WORTH OF AN ANNUITY FACTOR How much 1 received or paid annually for X years is worth today	CAPITAL RECOVERY FACTOR Annual payment that will repay a $1 loan in X years with compound interest on the unpaid balance	Year
.729 927	.729 927	1.370 000	1
.532 793	1.262 720	.791 941	2
.388 900	1.651 621	.605 466	3
.283 869	1.935 490	.516 665	4
.207 204	2.142 693	.466 702	5
.151 243	2.293 937	.435 932	6
.110 397	2.404 333	.415 916	7
.080 582	2.484 915	.402 428	8
.058 819	2.543 733	.393 123	9
.042 933	2.586 667	.386 598	10
.031 338	2.618 005	.381 970	11
.022 875	2.640 880	.378 662	12
.016 697	2.657 576	.376 283	13
.012 187	2.669 764	.374 565	14
.008 896	2.678 660	.373 321	15
.006 493	2.685 153	.372 418	16
.004 740	2.689 893	.371 762	17
.003 460	2.693 352	.371 285	18
.002 525	2.695 878	.370 937	19
.001 843	2.697 721	.370 683	20
.001 345	2.699 066	.370 498	21
.000 982	2.700 048	.370 364	22
.000 717	2.700 765	.370 265	23
.000 523	2.701 289	.370 194	24
.000 382	2.701 670	.370 141	25
.000 279	2.701 949	.370 103	26
.000 203	2.702 153	.370 075	27
.000 149	2.702 301	.370 055	28
.000 108	2.702 410	.370 040	29
.000 079	2.702 489	.370 029	30
.000 058	2.702 547	.370 021	31
.000 042	2.702 589	.370 016	32
.000 031	2.702 620	.370 011	33
.000 022	2.702 642	.370 008	34
.000 016	2.702 658	.370 006	35
.000 012	2.702 670	.370 004	36
.000 009	2.702 679	.370 003	37
.000 006	2.702 685	.370 002	38
.000 005	2.702 690	.370 002	39
.000 003	2.702 694	.370 001	40
.000 002	2.702 696	.370 001	41
.000 002	2.702 698	.370 001	42
.000 001	2.702 699	.370 000	43
.000 001	2.702 700	.370 000	44
.000 001	2.702 701	.370 000	45
.000 001	2.702 701	.370 000	46
.000 000	2.702 702	.370 000	47
.000 000	2.702 702	.370 000	48
.000 000	2.702 702	.370 000	49
.000 000	2.702 702	.370 000	50

RATE
38%

Year	COMPOUNDING FACTOR FOR 1 What an initial amount becomes when growing at compound interest	COMPOUNDING FACTOR FOR 1 PER ANNUM Growth of equal year-end deposits all growing at compound interest	SINKING FUND FACTOR Level deposit required each year to reach 1 by a given year
1	1.380 000	1.000 000	1.000 000
2	1.904 400	2.380 000	.420 168
3	2.628 072	4.284 400	.233 405
4	3.626 739	6.912 472	.144 666
5	5.004 900	10.539 211	.094 884
6	6.906 762	15.544 112	.064 333
7	9.531 332	22.450 874	.044 542
8	13.153 238	31.982 206	.031 267
9	18.151 469	45.135 445	.022 156
10	25.049 027	63.286 914	.015 801
11	34.567 658	88.335 941	.011 320
12	47.703 367	122.903 598	.008 136
13	65.830 647	170.606 966	.005 861
14	90.846 293	236.437 613	.004 229
15	125.367 884	327.283 905	.003 055
16	173.007 680	452.651 790	.002 209
17	238.750 598	625.659 470	.001 598
18	329.475 826	864.410 068	.001 157
19	454.676 640	1,193.885 894	.000 838
20	627.453 763	1,648.562 533	.000 607
21	865.886 193	2,276.016 296	.000 439
22	1,194.922 946	3,141.902 489	.000 318
23	1,648.993 665	4,336.825 434	.000 231
24	2,275.611 258	5,985.819 100	.000 167
25	3,140.343 536	8,261.430 357	.000 121
26	4,333.674 079	11,401.773 89	.000 088
27	5,980.470 230	15,735.447 97	.000 064
28	8,253.048 917	21,715.918 20	.000 046
29	11,389.207 51	29,968.967 12	.000 033
30	15,717.106 36	41,358.174 62	.000 024
31	21,689.606 77	57,075.280 98	.000 018
32	29,931.657 35	78,764.887 75	.000 013
33	41,305.687 14	108,696.545 1	.000 009
34	57,001.848 25	150,002.232 2	.000 007
35	78,662.550 59	207,004.080 5	.000 005
36	108,554.319 8	285,666.631 1	.000 004
37	149,804.961 3	394,220.950 9	.000 003
38	206,730.846 6	544,025.912 2	.000 002
39	285,288.568 4	750,756.758 9	.000 001
40	393,698.224 4	1,036,045.327	.000 001
41	543,303.549 6	1,429,743.552	.000 001
42	749,758.898 5	1,973,047.101	.000 001
43	1,034,667.280	2,722,806.000	.000 000
44	1,427,840.846	3,757,473.280	.000 000
45	1,970,420.368	5,185,314.126	.000 000
46	2,719,180.108	7,155,734.493	.000 000
47	3,752,468.548	9,874,914.601	.000 000
48	5,178,406.597	13,627,383.15	.000 000
49	7,146,201.104	18,805,789.75	.000 000
50	9,861,757.523	25,951,990.85	.000 000

RATE
38%

DISCOUNT FACTOR How much 1 at a future date is worth today	PRESENT WORTH OF AN ANNUITY FACTOR How much 1 received or paid annually for X years is worth today	CAPITAL RECOVERY FACTOR Annual payment that will repay a $1 loan in X years with compound interest on the unpaid balance	Year
.724 638	.724 638	1.380 000	1
.525 100	1.249 737	.800 168	2
.380 507	1.630 245	.613 405	3
.275 730	1.905 974	.524 666	4
.199 804	2.105 778	.474 884	5
.144 786	2.250 564	.444 333	6
.104 917	2.355 481	.424 542	7
.076 027	2.431 508	.411 267	8
.055 092	2.486 600	.402 156	9
.039 922	2.526 522	.395 801	10
.028 929	2.555 451	.391 320	11
.020 963	2.576 413	.388 136	12
.015 190	2.591 604	.385 861	13
.011 008	2.602 612	.384 229	14
.007 977	2.610 588	.383 055	15
.005 780	2.616 368	.382 209	16
.004 188	2.620 557	.381 598	17
.003 035	2.623 592	.381 157	18
.002 199	2.625 791	.380 838	19
.001 594	2.627 385	.380 607	20
.001 155	2.628 540	.380 439	21
.000 837	2.629 377	.380 318	22
.000 606	2.629 983	.380 231	23
.000 439	2.630 423	.380 167	24
.000 318	2.630 741	.380 121	25
.000 231	2.630 972	.380 088	26
.000 167	2.631 139	.380 064	27
.000 121	2.631 260	.380 046	28
.000 088	2.631 348	.380 033	29
.000 064	2.631 412	.380 024	30
.000 046	2.631 458	.380 018	31
.000 033	2.631 491	.380 013	32
.000 024	2.631 515	.380 009	33
.000 018	2.631 533	.380 007	34
.000 013	2.631 545	.380 005	35
.000 009	2.631 555	.380 004	36
.000 007	2.631 561	.380 003	37
.000 005	2.631 566	.380 002	38
.000 004	2.631 570	.380 001	39
.000 003	2.631 572	.380 001	40
.000 002	2.631 574	.380 001	41
.000 001	2.631 575	.380 001	42
.000 001	2.631 576	.380 000	43
.000 001	2.631 577	.380 000	44
.000 001	2.631 578	.380 000	45
.000 000	2.631 578	.380 000	46
.000 000	2.631 578	.380 000	47
.000 000	2.631 578	.380 000	48
.000 000	2.631 579	.380 000	49
.000 000	2.631 579	.380 000	50

RATE
39%

Year	COMPOUNDING FACTOR FOR 1 What an initial amount becomes when growing at compound interest	COMPOUNDING FACTOR FOR 1 PER ANNUM Growth of equal year-end deposits all growing at compound interest	SINKING FUND FACTOR Level deposit required each year to reach 1 by a given year
1	1.390 000	1.000 000	1.000 000
2	1.932 100	2.390 000	.418 410
3	2.685 619	4.322 100	.231 369
4	3.733 010	7.007 719	.142 700
5	5.188 884	10.740 729	.093 104
6	7.212 549	15.929 614	.062 776
7	10.025 444	23.142 163	.043 211
8	13.935 367	33.167 607	.030 150
9	19.370 160	47.102 974	.021 230
10	26.924 522	66.473 133	.015 044
11	37.425 086	93.397 655	.010 707
12	52.020 869	130.822 741	.007 644
13	72.309 008	182.843 610	.005 469
14	100.509 521	255.152 618	.003 919
15	139.708 234	355.662 139	.002 812
16	194.194 446	495.370 373	.002 019
17	269.930 279	689.564 819	.001 450
18	375.203 088	959.495 099	.001 042
19	521.532 293	1,334.698 187	.000 749
20	724.929 887	1,856.230 480	.000 539
21	1,007.652 543	2,581.160 367	.000 387
22	1,400.637 035	3,588.812 910	.000 279
23	1,946.885 479	4,989.449 945	.000 200
24	2,706.170 815	6,936.335 424	.000 144
25	3,761.577 433	9,642.506 240	.000 104
26	5,228.592 632	13,404.083 67	.000 075
27	7,267.743 759	18,632.676 31	.000 054
28	10,102.163 83	25,900.420 06	.000 039
29	14,042.007 72	36,002.583 89	.000 028
30	19,518.390 73	50,044.591 61	.000 020
31	27,130.563 11	69,562.982 33	.000 014
32	37,711.482 72	96,693.545 44	.000 010
33	52,418.960 98	134,405.028 2	.000 007
34	72,862.355 77	186,823.989 2	.000 005
35	101,278.674 5	259,686.344 9	.000 004
36	140,777.357 6	360,965.019 4	.000 003
37	195,680.527 0	501,742.377 0	.000 002
38	271,995.932 6	697,422.904 1	.000 001
39	378,074.346 3	969,418.836 6	.000 001
40	525,523.341 3	1,347,493.183	.000 001
41	730,477.444 5	1,873,016.524	.000 001
42	1,015,363.648	2,603,493.969	.000 000
43	1,411,355.470	3,618,857.617	.000 000
44	1,961,784.104	5,030,213.087	.000 000
45	2,726,879.904	6,991,997.191	.000 000
46	3,790,363.067	9,718,877.095	.000 000
47	5,268,604.663	13,509,240.16	.000 000
48	7,323,360.482	18,777,844.83	.000 000
49	10,179,471.07	26,101,205.31	.000 000
50	14,149,464.79	36,280,676.38	.000 000

RATE
39%

DISCOUNT FACTOR How much 1 at a future date is worth today	PRESENT WORTH OF AN ANNUITY FACTOR How much 1 received or paid annually for X years is worth today	CAPITAL RECOVERY FACTOR Annual payment that will repay a $1 loan in X years with compound interest on the unpaid balance	Year
.719 424	.719 424	1.390 000	1
.517 572	1.236 996	.808 410	2
.372 354	1.609 350	.621 369	3
.267 880	1.877 230	.532 700	4
.192 720	2.069 950	.483 104	5
.138 647	2.208 597	.452 776	6
.099 746	2.308 343	.433 211	7
.071 760	2.380 103	.420 150	8
.051 626	2.431 729	.411 230	9
.037 141	2.468 870	.405 044	10
.026 720	2.495 590	.400 707	11
.019 223	2.514 813	.397 644	12
.013 830	2.528 642	.395 469	13
.009 949	2.538 592	.393 919	14
.007 158	2.545 749	.392 812	15
.005 149	2.550 899	.392 019	16
.003 705	2.554 603	.391 450	17
.002 665	2.557 269	.391 042	18
.001 917	2.559 186	.390 749	19
.001 379	2.560 566	.390 539	20
.000 992	2.561 558	.390 387	21
.000 714	2.562 272	.390 279	22
.000 514	2.562 786	.390 200	23
.000 370	2.563 155	.390 144	24
.000 266	2.563 421	.390 104	25
.000 191	2.563 612	.390 075	26
.000 138	2.563 750	.390 054	27
.000 099	2.563 849	.390 039	28
.000 071	2.563 920	.390 028	29
.000 051	2.563 971	.390 020	30
.000 037	2.564 008	.390 014	31
.000 027	2.564 035	.390 010	32
.000 019	2.564 054	.390 007	33
.000 014	2.564 067	.390 005	34
.000 010	2.564 077	.390 004	35
.000 007	2.564 084	.390 003	36
.000 005	2.564 089	.390 002	37
.000 004	2.564 093	.390 001	38
.000 003	2.564 096	.390 001	39
.000 002	2.564 098	.390 001	40
.000 001	2.564 099	.390 001	41
.000 001	2.564 100	.390 000	42
.000 001	2.564 101	.390 000	43
.000 001	2.564 101	.390 000	44
.000 000	2.564 102	.390 000	45
.000 000	2.564 102	.390 000	46
.000 000	2.564 102	.390 000	47
.000 000	2.564 102	.390 000	48
.000 000	2.564 102	.390 000	49
.000 000	2.564 102	.390 000	50

RATE
40%

Year	COMPOUNDING FACTOR FOR 1 What an initial amount becomes when growing at compound interest	COMPOUNDING FACTOR FOR 1 PER ANNUM Growth of equal year-end deposits all growing at compound interest	SINKING FUND FACTOR Level deposit required each year to reach 1 by a given year
1	1.400 000	1.000 000	1.000 000
2	1.960 000	2.400 000	.416 667
3	2.744 000	4.360 000	.229 358
4	3.841 600	7.104 000	.140 766
5	5.378 240	10.945 600	.091 361
6	7.529 536	16.323 840	.061 260
7	10.541 350	23.853 376	.041 923
8	14.757 891	34.394 726	.029 074
9	20.661 047	49.152 617	.020 345
10	28.925 465	69.813 664	.014 324
11	40.495 652	98.739 129	.010 128
12	56.693 912	139.234 781	.007 182
13	79.371 477	195.928 693	.005 104
14	111.120 068	275.300 171	.003 632
15	155.568 096	386.420 239	.002 588
16	217.795 334	541.988 334	.001 845
17	304.913 467	759.783 668	.001 316
18	426.878 854	1,064.697 136	.000 939
19	597.630 396	1,491.575 990	.000 670
20	836.682 554	2,089.206 386	.000 479
21	1,171.355 576	2,925.888 940	.000 342
22	1,639.897 806	4,097.244 516	.000 244
23	2,295.856 929	5,737.142 322	.000 174
24	3,214.199 700	8,032.999 251	.000 124
25	4,499.879 581	11,247.198 95	.000 089
26	6,299.831 413	15,747.078 53	.000 064
27	8,819.763 978	22,046.909 94	.000 045
28	12,347.669 57	30,866.673 92	.000 032
29	17,286.737 40	43,214.343 49	.000 023
30	24,201.432 36	60,501.080 89	.000 017
31	33,882.005 30	84,702.513 24	.000 012
32	47,434.807 42	118,584.518 5	.000 008
33	66,408.730 38	166,019.326 0	.000 006
34	92,972.222 54	232,428.056 3	.000 004
35	130,161.111 6	325,400.278 9	.000 003
36	182,225.556 2	455,561.390 4	.000 002
37	255,115.778 6	637,786.946 6	.000 002
38	357,162.090 1	892,902.725 2	.000 001
39	500,026.926 1	1,250,064.815	.000 001
40	700,037.696 6	1,750,091.741	.000 001
41	980,052.775 2	2,450,129.438	.000 000
42	1,372,073.885	3,430,182.213	.000 000
43	1,920,903.439	4,802,256.099	.000 000
44	2,689,264.815	6,723,159.538	.000 000
45	3,764,970.741	9,412,424.353	.000 000
46	5,270,959.038	13,177,395.09	.000 000
47	7,379,342.653	18,448,354.13	.000 000
48	10,331,079.71	25,827,696.79	.000 000
49	14,463,511.60	36,158,776.50	.000 000
50	20,248,916.24	50,622,288.10	.000 000

RATE 40%

DISCOUNT FACTOR How much 1 at a future date is worth today	PRESENT WORTH OF AN ANNUITY FACTOR How much 1 received or paid annually for X years is worth today	CAPITAL RECOVERY FACTOR Annual payment that will repay a $1 loan in X years with compound interest on the unpaid balance	Year
.714 286	.714 286	1.400 000	1
.510 204	1.224 490	.816 667	2
.364 431	1.588 921	.629 358	3
.260 308	1.849 229	.540 766	4
.185 934	2.035 164	.491 361	5
.132 810	2.167 974	.461 260	6
.094 865	2.262 839	.441 923	7
.067 760	2.330 599	.429 074	8
.048 400	2.378 999	.420 345	9
.034 572	2.413 571	.414 324	10
.024 694	2.438 265	.410 128	11
.017 639	2.455 904	.407 182	12
.012 599	2.468 503	.405 104	13
.008 999	2.477 502	.403 632	14
.006 428	2.483 930	.402 588	15
.004 591	2.488 521	.401 845	16
.003 280	2.491 801	.401 316	17
.002 343	2.494 144	.400 939	18
.001 673	2.495 817	.400 670	19
.001 195	2.497 012	.400 479	20
.000 854	2.497 866	.400 342	21
.000 610	2.498 476	.400 244	22
.000 436	2.498 911	.400 174	23
.000 311	2.499 222	.400 124	24
.000 222	2.499 444	.400 089	25
.000 159	2.499 603	.400 064	26
.000 113	2.499 717	.400 045	27
.000 081	2.499 798	.400 032	28
.000 058	2.499 855	.400 023	29
.000 041	2.499 897	.400 017	30
.000 030	2.499 926	.400 012	31
.000 021	2.499 947	.400 008	32
.000 015	2.499 962	.400 006	33
.000 011	2.499 973	.400 004	34
.000 008	2.499 981	.400 003	35
.000 005	2.499 986	.400 002	36
.000 004	2.499 990	.400 002	37
.000 003	2.499 993	.400 001	38
.000 002	2.499 995	.400 001	39
.000 001	2.499 996	.400 001	40
.000 001	2.499 997	.400 000	41
.000 001	2.499 998	.400 000	42
.000 001	2.499 999	.400 000	43
.000 000	2.499 999	.400 000	44
.000 000	2.499 999	.400 000	45
.000 000	2.500 000	.400 000	46
.000 000	2.500 000	.400 000	47
.000 000	2.500 000	.400 000	48
.000 000	2.500 000	.400 000	49
.000 000	2.500 000	.400 000	50

RATE
41%

Year	COMPOUNDING FACTOR FOR 1 What an initial amount becomes when growing at compound interest	COMPOUNDING FACTOR FOR 1 PER ANNUM Growth of equal year-end deposits all growing at compound interest	SINKING FUND FACTOR Level deposit required each year to reach 1 by a given year
1	1.410 000	1.000 000	1.000 000
2	1.988 100	2.410 000	.414 938
3	2.803 221	4.398 100	.227 371
4	3.952 542	7.201 321	.138 863
5	5.573 084	11.153 863	.089 655
6	7.858 048	16.726 946	.059 784
7	11.079 848	24.584 994	.040 675
8	15.622 585	35.664 842	.028 039
9	22.027 845	51.287 427	.019 498
10	31.059 262	73.315 272	.013 640
11	43.793 559	104.374 534	.009 581
12	61.748 918	148.168 093	.006 749
13	87.065 974	209.917 011	.004 764
14	122.763 024	296.982 985	.003 367
15	173.095 864	419.746 009	.002 382
16	244.065 168	592.841 872	.001 687
17	344.131 886	836.907 040	.001 195
18	485.225 960	1,181.038 926	.000 847
19	684.168 603	1,666.264 886	.000 600
20	964.677 731	2,350.433 490	.000 425
21	1,360.195 600	3,315.111 220	.000 302
22	1,917.875 797	4,675.306 821	.000 214
23	2,704.204 873	6,593.182 617	.000 152
24	3,812.928 871	9,297.387 490	.000 108
25	5,376.229 708	13,110.316 36	.000 076
26	7,580.483 889	18,486.546 07	.000 054
27	10,688.482 28	26,067.029 96	.000 038
28	15,070.760 02	36,755.512 24	.000 027
29	21,249.771 63	51,826.272 26	.000 019
30	29,962.177 99	73,076.043 89	.000 014
31	42,246.670 97	103,038.221 9	.000 010
32	59,567.806 07	145,284.892 9	.000 007
33	83,990.606 56	204,852.698 9	.000 005
34	118,426.755 2	288,843.305 5	.000 003
35	166,981.724 9	407,270.060 7	.000 002
36	235,444.232 1	574,251.785 6	.000 002
37	331,976.367 3	809,696.017 7	.000 001
38	468,086.677 8	1,141,672.385	.000 001
39	660,002.215 8	1,609,759.063	.000 001
40	930,603.124 2	2,269,761.279	.000 000
41	1,312,150.405	3,200,364.403	.000 000
42	1,850,132.071	4,512,514.808	.000 000
43	2,608,686.220	6,362,646.879	.000 000
44	3,678,247.571	8,971,333.100	.000 000
45	5,186,329.075	12,649,580.67	.000 000
46	7,312,723.996	17,835,909.75	.000 000
47	10,310,940.83	25,148,633.74	.000 000
48	14,538,426.58	35,459,574.58	.000 000
49	20,499,181.47	49,998,001.15	.000 000
50	28,903,845.88	70,497,182.62	.000 000

RATE
41%

DISCOUNT FACTOR How much 1 at a future date is worth today	PRESENT WORTH OF AN ANNUITY FACTOR How much 1 received or paid annually for X years is worth today	CAPITAL RECOVERY FACTOR Annual payment that will repay a $1 loan in X years with compound interest on the unpaid balance	Year
.709 220	.709 220	1.410 000	1
.502 993	1.212 213	.824 938	2
.356 732	1.568 945	.637 371	3
.253 002	1.821 947	.548 863	4
.179 434	2.001 381	.499 655	5
.127 258	2.128 639	.469 784	6
.090 254	2.218 893	.450 675	7
.064 010	2.282 903	.438 039	8
.045 397	2.328 300	.429 498	9
.032 197	2.360 496	.423 640	10
.022 834	2.383 331	.419 581	11
.016 195	2.399 525	.416 749	12
.011 486	2.411 011	.414 764	13
.008 146	2.419 157	.413 367	14
.005 777	2.424 934	.412 382	15
.004 097	2.429 031	.411 687	16
.002 906	2.431 937	.411 195	17
.002 061	2.433 998	.410 847	18
.001 462	2.435 459	.410 600	19
.001 037	2.436 496	.410 425	20
.000 735	2.437 231	.410 302	21
.000 521	2.437 753	.410 214	22
.000 370	2.438 122	.410 152	23
.000 262	2.438 385	.410 108	24
.000 186	2.438 571	.410 076	25
.000 132	2.438 703	.410 054	26
.000 094	2.438 796	.410 038	27
.000 066	2.438 863	.410 027	28
.000 047	2.438 910	.410 019	29
.000 033	2.438 943	.410 014	30
.000 024	2.438 967	.410 010	31
.000 017	2.438 983	.410 007	32
.000 012	2.438 995	.410 005	33
.000 008	2.439 004	.410 003	34
.000 006	2.439 010	.410 002	35
.000 004	2.439 014	.410 002	36
.000 003	2.439 017	.410 001	37
.000 002	2.439 019	.410 001	38
.000 002	2.439 021	.410 001	39
.000 001	2.439 022	.410 000	40
.000 001	2.439 023	.410 000	41
.000 001	2.439 023	.410 000	42
.000 000	2.439 023	.410 000	43
.000 000	2.439 024	.410 000	44
.000 000	2.439 024	.410 000	45
.000 000	2.439 024	.410 000	46
.000 000	2.439 024	.410 000	47
.000 000	2.439 024	.410 000	48
.000 000	2.439 024	.410 000	49
.000 000	2.439 024	.410 000	50

RATE
42%

Year	COMPOUNDING FACTOR FOR 1 What an initial amount becomes when growing at compound interest	COMPOUNDING FACTOR FOR 1 PER ANNUM Growth of equal year-end deposits all growing at compound interest	SINKING FUND FACTOR Level deposit required each year to reach 1 by a given year
1	1.420 000	1.000 000	1.000 000
2	2.016 400	2.420 000	.413 223
3	2.863 288	4.436 400	.225 408
4	4.065 869	7.299 688	.136 992
5	5.773 534	11.365 557	.087 985
6	8.198 418	17.139 091	.058 346
7	11.641 754	25.337 509	.039 467
8	16.531 290	36.979 263	.027 042
9	23.474 432	53.510 553	.018 688
10	33.333 694	76.984 986	.012 990
11	47.333 845	110.318 680	.009 065
12	67.214 061	157.652 525	.006 343
13	95.443 966	224.866 586	.004 447
14	135.530 432	320.310 551	.003 122
15	192.453 213	455.840 983	.002 194
16	273.283 562	648.294 196	.001 543
17	388.062 658	921.577 758	.001 085
18	551.048 975	1,309.640 417	.000 764
19	782.489 544	1,860.689 392	.000 537
20	1,111.135 153	2,643.178 936	.000 378
21	1,577.811 918	3,754.314 089	.000 266
22	2,240.492 923	5,332.126 007	.000 188
23	3,181.499 950	7,572.618 930	.000 132
24	4,517.729 930	10,754.118 88	.000 093
25	6,415.176 500	15,271.848 81	.000 065
26	9,109.550 630	21,687.025 31	.000 046
27	12,935.561 89	30,796.575 94	.000 032
28	18,368.497 89	43,732.137 83	.000 023
29	26,083.267 00	62,100.635 73	.000 016
30	37,038.239 15	88,183.902 73	.000 011
31	52,594.299 59	125,222.141 9	.000 008
32	74,683.905 41	177,816.441 5	.000 006
33	106,051.145 7	252,500.346 9	.000 004
34	150,592.626 9	358,551.492 6	.000 003
35	213,841.530 2	509,144.119 4	.000 002
36	303,654.972 8	722,985.649 6	.000 001
37	431,190.061 4	1,026,640.622	.000 001
38	612,289.887 2	1,457,830.684	.000 001
39	869,451.639 9	2,070,120.571	.000 000
40	1,234,621.329	2,939,572.211	.000 000
41	1,753,162.287	4,174,193.540	.000 000
42	2,489,490.447	5,927,355.826	.000 000
43	3,535,076.435	8,416,846.273	.000 000
44	5,019,808.537	11,951,922.71	.000 000
45	7,128,128.123	16,971,731.25	.000 000
46	10,121,941.93	24,099,859.37	.000 000
47	14,373,157.55	34,221,801.30	.000 000
48	20,409,883.72	48,594,958.85	.000 000
49	28,982,034.88	69,004,842.57	.000 000
50	41,154,489.53	97,986,877.45	.000 000

RATE 42%

DISCOUNT FACTOR How much 1 at a future date is worth today	PRESENT WORTH OF AN ANNUITY FACTOR How much 1 received or paid annually for X years is worth today	CAPITAL RECOVERY FACTOR Annual payment that will repay a $1 loan in X years with compound interest on the unpaid balance	Year
.704 225	.704 225	1.420 000	1
.495 933	1.200 159	.833 223	2
.349 249	1.549 408	.645 408	3
.245 950	1.795 357	.556 992	4
.173 204	1.968 562	.507 985	5
.121 975	2.090 536	.478 346	6
.085 898	2.176 434	.459 467	7
.060 491	2.236 925	.447 042	8
.042 600	2.279 525	.438 688	9
.030 000	2.309 525	.432 990	10
.021 127	2.330 651	.429 065	11
.014 878	2.345 529	.426 343	12
.010 477	2.356 006	.424 447	13
.007 378	2.363 385	.423 122	14
.005 196	2.368 581	.422 194	15
.003 659	2.372 240	.421 543	16
.002 577	2.374 817	.421 085	17
.001 815	2.376 632	.420 764	18
.001 278	2.377 910	.420 537	19
.000 900	2.378 810	.420 378	20
.000 634	2.379 443	.420 266	21
.000 446	2.379 890	.420 188	22
.000 314	2.380 204	.420 132	23
.000 221	2.380 425	.420 093	24
.000 156	2.380 581	.420 065	25
.000 110	2.380 691	.420 046	26
.000 077	2.380 768	.420 032	27
.000 054	2.380 823	.420 023	28
.000 038	2.380 861	.420 016	29
.000 027	2.380 888	.420 011	30
.000 019	2.380 907	.420 008	31
.000 013	2.380 921	.420 006	32
.000 009	2.380 930	.420 004	33
.000 007	2.380 937	.420 003	34
.000 005	2.380 941	.420 002	35
.000 003	2.380 945	.420 001	36
.000 002	2.380 947	.420 001	37
.000 002	2.380 948	.420 001	38
.000 001	2.380 950	.420 000	39
.000 001	2.380 950	.420 000	40
.000 001	2.380 951	.420 000	41
.000 000	2.380 951	.420 000	42
.000 000	2.380 952	.420 000	43
.000 000	2.380 952	.420 000	44
.000 000	2.380 952	.420 000	45
.000 000	2.380 952	.420 000	46
.000 000	2.380 952	.420 000	47
.000 000	2.380 952	.420 000	48
.000 000	2.380 952	.420 000	49
.000 000	2.380 952	.420 000	50

RATE
43%

Year	COMPOUNDING FACTOR FOR 1 What an initial amount becomes when growing at compound interest	COMPOUNDING FACTOR FOR 1 PER ANNUM Growth of equal year-end deposits all growing at compound interest	SINKING FUND FACTOR Level deposit required each year to reach 1 by a given year
1	1.430 000	1.000 000	1.000 000
2	2.044 900	2.430 000	.411 523
3	2.924 207	4.474 900	.223 469
4	4.181 616	7.399 107	.135 151
5	5.979 711	11.580 723	.086 350
6	8.550 987	17.560 434	.056 946
7	12.227 911	26.111 420	.038 297
8	17.485 912	38.339 331	.026 083
9	25.004 855	55.825 244	.017 913
10	35.756 942	80.830 099	.012 372
11	51.132 428	116.587 041	.008 577
12	73.119 371	167.719 469	.005 962
13	104.560 701	240.838 840	.004 152
14	149.521 803	345.399 541	.002 895
15	213.816 178	494.921 344	.002 021
16	305.757 134	708.737 522	.001 411
17	437.232 702	1,014.494 656	.000 986
18	625.242 764	1,451.727 358	.000 689
19	894.097 153	2,076.970 123	.000 481
20	1,278.558 928	2,971.067 275	.000 337
21	1,828.339 268	4,249.626 203	.000 235
22	2,614.525 153	6,077.965 471	.000 165
23	3,738.770 968	8,692.490 624	.000 115
24	5,346.442 484	12,431.261 59	.000 080
25	7,645.412 753	17,777.704 08	.000 056
26	10,932.940 24	25,423.116 83	.000 039
27	15,634.104 54	36,356.057 06	.000 028
28	22,356.769 49	51,990.161 60	.000 019
29	31,970.180 37	74,346.931 09	.000 013
30	45,717.357 93	106,317.111 5	.000 009
31	65,375.821 84	152,034.469 4	.000 007
32	93,487.425 23	217,410.291 2	.000 005
33	133,687.018 1	310,897.716 5	.000 003
34	191,172.435 9	444,584.734 5	.000 002
35	273,376.583 3	635,757.170 4	.000 002
36	390,928.514 1	909,133.753 7	.000 001
37	559,027.775 1	1,300,062.268	.000 001
38	799,409.718 4	1,859,090.043	.000 001
39	1,143,155.897	2,658,499.761	.000 000
40	1,634,712.933	3,801,655.659	.000 000
41	2,337,639.494	5,436,368.592	.000 000
42	3,342,824.477	7,774,008.086	.000 000
43	4,780,239.002	11,116,832.56	.000 000
44	6,835,741.773	15,897,071.57	.000 000
45	9,775,110.736	22,732,813.34	.000 000
46	13,978,408.35	32,507,924.07	.000 000
47	19,989,123.94	46,486,332.43	.000 000
48	28,584,447.24	66,475,456.37	.000 000
49	40,875,759.55	95,059,903.61	.000 000
50	58,452,336.16	135,935,663.2	.000 000

RATE
43%

DISCOUNT FACTOR How much 1 at a future date is worth today	PRESENT WORTH OF AN ANNUITY FACTOR How much 1 received or paid annually for X years is worth today	CAPITAL RECOVERY FACTOR Annual payment that will repay a $1 loan in X years with compound interest on the unpaid balance	Year
.699 301	.699 301	1.430 000	1
.489 021	1.188 322	.841 523	2
.341 973	1.530 295	.653 469	3
.239 142	1.769 437	.565 151	4
.167 232	1.936 669	.516 350	5
.116 946	2.053 615	.486 946	6
.081 780	2.135 395	.468 297	7
.057 189	2.192 584	.456 083	8
.039 992	2.232 576	.447 913	9
.027 967	2.260 543	.442 372	10
.019 557	2.280 100	.438 577	11
.013 676	2.293 776	.435 962	12
.009 564	2.303 340	.434 152	13
.006 688	2.310 028	.432 895	14
.004 677	2.314 705	.432 021	15
.003 271	2.317 975	.431 411	16
.002 287	2.320 263	.430 986	17
.001 599	2.321 862	.430 689	18
.001 118	2.322 980	.430 481	19
.000 782	2.323 762	.430 337	20
.000 547	2.324 309	.430 235	21
.000 382	2.324 692	.430 165	22
.000 267	2.324 959	.430 115	23
.000 187	2.325 146	.430 080	24
.000 131	2.325 277	.430 056	25
.000 091	2.325 369	.430 039	26
.000 064	2.325 433	.430 028	27
.000 045	2.325 477	.430 019	28
.000 031	2.325 509	.430 013	29
.000 022	2.325 531	.430 009	30
.000 015	2.325 546	.430 007	31
.000 011	2.325 557	.430 005	32
.000 007	2.325 564	.430 003	33
.000 005	2.325 569	.430 002	34
.000 004	2.325 573	.430 002	35
.000 003	2.325 575	.430 001	36
.000 002	2.325 577	.430 001	37
.000 001	2.325 578	.430 001	38
.000 001	2.325 579	.430 000	39
.000 001	2.325 580	.430 000	40
.000 000	2.325 580	.430 000	41
.000 000	2.325 581	.430 000	42
.000 000	2.325 581	.430 000	43
.000 000	2.325 581	.430 000	44
.000 000	2.325 581	.430 000	45
.000 000	2.325 581	.430 000	46
.000 000	2.325 581	.430 000	47
.000 000	2.325 581	.430 000	48
.000 000	2.325 581	.430 000	49
.000 000	2.325 581	.430 000	50

RATE
44%

Year	COMPOUNDING FACTOR FOR 1 What an initial amount becomes when growing at compound interest	COMPOUNDING FACTOR FOR 1 PER ANNUM Growth of equal year-end deposits all growing at compound interest	SINKING FUND FACTOR Level deposit required each year to reach 1 by a given year
1	1.440 000	1.000 000	1.000 000
2	2.073 600	2.440 000	.409 836
3	2.985 984	4.513 600	.221 553
4	4.299 817	7.499 584	.133 341
5	6.191 736	11.799 401	.084 750
6	8.916 100	17.991 137	.055 583
7	12.839 185	26.907 238	.037 165
8	18.488 426	39.746 422	.025 159
9	26.623 333	58.234 848	.017 172
10	38.337 600	84.858 182	.011 784
11	55.206 144	123.195 782	.008 117
12	79.496 847	178.401 925	.005 605
13	114.475 460	257.898 773	.003 877
14	164.844 662	372.374 233	.002 685
15	237.376 314	537.218 895	.001 861
16	341.821 892	774.595 209	.001 291
17	492.223 524	1,116.417 101	.000 896
18	708.801 875	1,608.640 625	.000 622
19	1,020.674 700	2,317.442 500	.000 432
20	1,469.771 568	3,338.117 200	.000 300
21	2,116.471 058	4,807.888 768	.000 208
22	3,047.718 323	6,924.359 826	.000 144
23	4,388.714 386	9,972.078 149	.000 100
24	6,319.748 715	14,360.792 53	.000 070
25	9,100.438 150	20,680.541 25	.000 048
26	13,104.630 94	29,780.979 40	.000 034
27	18,870.668 55	42,885.610 34	.000 023
28	27,173.762 71	61,756.278 88	.000 016
29	39,130.218 30	88,930.041 59	.000 011
30	56,347.514 35	128,060.259 9	.000 008
31	81,140.420 67	184,407.774 2	.000 005
32	116,842.205 8	265,548.194 9	.000 004
33	168,252.776 3	382,390.400 7	.000 003
34	242,283.997 9	550,643.177 0	.000 002
35	348,888.956 9	792,927.174 8	.000 001
36	502,400.098 0	1,141,816.132	.000 001
37	723,456.141 1	1,644,216.230	.000 001
38	1,041,776.843	2,367,672.371	.000 000
39	1,500,158.654	3,409,449.214	.000 000
40	2,160,228.462	4,909,607.868	.000 000
41	3,110,728.985	7,069,836.330	.000 000
42	4,479,449.739	10,180,565.32	.000 000
43	6,450,407.624	14,660,015.05	.000 000
44	9,288,586.978	21,110,422.68	.000 000
45	13,375,565.25	30,399,009.66	.000 000
46	19,260,813.96	43,774,574.91	.000 000
47	27,735,572.10	63,035,388.86	.000 000
48	39,939,223.82	90,770,960.96	.000 000
49	57,512,482.31	130,710,184.8	.000 000
50	82,817,974.52	188,222,667.1	.000 000

RATE
44%

DISCOUNT FACTOR How much 1 at a future date is worth today	PRESENT WORTH OF AN ANNUITY FACTOR How much 1 received or paid annually for X years is worth today	CAPITAL RECOVERY FACTOR Annual payment that will repay a $1 loan in X years with compound interest on the unpaid balance	Year
.694 444	.694 444	1.440 000	1
.482 253	1.176 698	.849 836	2
.334 898	1.511 596	.661 553	3
.232 568	1.744 164	.573 341	4
.161 506	1.905 669	.524 750	5
.112 157	2.017 826	.495 583	6
.077 887	2.095 712	.477 165	7
.054 088	2.149 800	.465 159	8
.037 561	2.187 361	.457 172	9
.026 084	2.213 445	.451 784	10
.018 114	2.231 559	.448 117	11
.012 579	2.244 138	.445 605	12
.008 735	2.252 874	.443 877	13
.006 066	2.258 940	.442 685	14
.004 213	2.263 153	.441 861	15
.002 926	2.266 078	.441 291	16
.002 032	2.268 110	.440 896	17
.001 411	2.269 521	.440 622	18
000 980	2.270 501	.440 432	19
.000 680	2.271 181	.440 300	20
.000 472	2.271 653	.440 208	21
.000 328	2.271 982	.440 144	22
.000 228	2.272 209	.440 100	23
.000 158	2.272 368	.440 070	24
.000 110	2.272 478	.440 048	25
.000 076	2.272 554	.440 034	26
.000 053	2.272 607	.440 023	27
.000 037	2.272 644	.440 016	28
.000 026	2.272 669	.440 011	29
.000 018	2.272 687	.440 008	30
.000 012	2.272 699	.440 005	31
.000 009	2.272 708	.440 004	32
.000 006	2.272 714	.440 003	33
.000 004	2.272 718	.440 002	34
.000 003	2.272 721	.440 001	35
.000 002	2.272 723	.440 001	36
.000 001	2.272 724	.440 001	37
.000 001	2.272 725	.440 000	38
.000 001	2.272 726	.440 000	39
.000 000	2.272 726	.440 000	40
.000 000	2.272 727	.440 000	41
.000 000	2.272 727	.440 000	42
.000 000	2.272 727	.440 000	43
.000 000	2.272 727	.440 000	44
.000 000	2.272 727	.440 000	45
.000 000	2.272 727	.440 000	46
.000 000	2.272 727	.440 000	47
.000 000	2.272 727	.440 000	48
.000 000	2.272 727	.440 000	49
.000 000	2.272 727	.440 000	50

RATE
45%

Year	COMPOUNDING FACTOR FOR 1 What an initial amount becomes when growing at compound interest	COMPOUNDING FACTOR FOR 1 PER ANNUM Growth of equal year-end deposits all growing at compound interest	SINKING FUND FACTOR Level deposit required each year to reach 1 by a given year
1	1.450 000	1.000 000	1.000 000
2	2.102 500	2.450 000	.408 163
3	3.048 625	4.552 500	.219 660
4	4.420 506	7.601 125	.131 559
5	6.409 734	12.021 631	.083 183
6	9.294 114	18.431 365	.054 255
7	13.476 466	27.725 480	.036 068
8	19.540 876	41.201 946	.024 271
9	28.334 269	60.742 821	.016 463
10	41.084 691	89.077 091	.011 226
11	59.572 802	130.161 781	.007 683
12	86.380 562	189.734 583	.005 271
13	125.251 815	276.115 145	.003 622
14	181.615 132	401.366 961	.002 491
15	263.341 942	582.982 093	.001 715
16	381.845 816	846.324 035	.001 182
17	553.676 433	1,228.169 850	.000 814
18	802.830 827	1,781.846 283	.000 561
19	1,164.104 699	2,584.677 110	.000 387
20	1,687.951 814	3,748.781 809	.000 267
21	2,447.530 131	5,436.733 623	.000 184
22	3,548.918 689	7,884.263 754	.000 127
23	5,145.932 099	11,433.182 44	.000 087
24	7,461.601 544	16,579.114 54	.000 060
25	10,819.322 24	24,040.716 09	.000 042
26	15,688.017 25	34,860.038 33	.000 029
27	22,747.625 01	50,548.055 57	.000 020
28	32,984.056 26	73,295.680 58	.000 014
29	47,826.881 58	106,279.736 8	.000 009
30	69,348.978 29	154,106.618 4	.000 006
31	100,556.018 5	223,455.596 7	.000 004
32	145,806.226 9	324,011.615 2	.000 003
33	211,419.028 9	469,817.842 1	.000 002
34	306,557.592 0	681,236.871 0	.000 001
35	444,508.508 3	987,794.463 0	.000 001
36	644,537.337 1	1,432,302.971	.000 001
37	934,579.138 8	2,076,840.308	.000 000
38	1,355,139.751	3,011,419.447	.000 000
39	1,964,952.639	4,366,559.198	.000 000
40	2,849,181.327	6,331,511.838	.000 000
41	4,131,312.924	9,180,693.165	.000 000
42	5,990,403.740	13,312,006.09	.000 000
43	8,686,085.423	19,302,409.83	.000 000
44	12,594,823.86	27,988,495.25	.000 000
45	18,262,494.60	40,583,319.12	.000 000
46	26,480,617.17	58,845,813.72	.000 000
47	38,396,894.90	85,326,430.89	.000 000
48	55,675,497.61	123,723,325.8	.000 000
49	80,729,471.53	179,398,823.4	.000 000
50	117,057,733.7	260,128,294.9	.000 000

RATE
45%

DISCOUNT FACTOR How much 1 at a future date is worth today	PRESENT WORTH OF AN ANNUITY FACTOR How much 1 received or paid annually for X years is worth today	CAPITAL RECOVERY FACTOR Annual payment that will repay a $1 loan in X years with compound interest on the unpaid balance	Year
.689 655	.689 655	1.450 000	1
.475 624	1.165 279	.858 163	2
.328 017	1.493 296	.669 660	3
.226 218	1.719 515	.581 559	4
.156 013	1.875 527	.533 183	5
.107 595	1.983 122	.504 255	6
.074 203	2.057 326	.486 068	7
.051 175	2.108 500	.474 271	8
.035 293	2.143 793	.466 463	9
.024 340	2.168 133	.461 226	10
.016 786	2.184 920	.457 683	11
.011 577	2.196 496	.455 271	12
.007 984	2.204 480	.453 622	13
.005 506	2.209 986	.452 491	14
.003 797	2.213 784	.451 715	15
.002 619	2.216 403	.451 182	16
.001 806	2.218 209	.450 814	17
.001 246	2.219 454	.450 561	18
.000 859	2.220 313	.450 387	19
.000 592	2.220 906	.450 267	20
.000 409	2.221 314	.450 184	21
.000 282	2.221 596	.450 127	22
.000 194	2.221 790	.450 087	23
.000 134	2.221 924	.450 060	24
.000 092	2.222 017	.450 042	25
.000 064	2.222 081	.450 029	26
.000 044	2.222 125	.450 020	27
.000 030	2.222 155	.450 014	28
.000 021	2.222 176	.450 009	29
.000 014	2.222 190	.450 006	30
.000 010	2.222 200	.450 004	31
.000 007	2.222 207	.450 003	32
.000 005	2.222 212	.450 002	33
.000 003	2.222 215	.450 001	34
.000 002	2.222 217	.450 001	35
.000 002	2.222 219	.450 001	36
.000 001	2.222 220	.450 000	37
.000 001	2.222 221	.450 000	38
.000 001	2.222 221	.450 000	39
.000 000	2.222 221	.450 000	40
.000 000	2.222 222	.450 000	41
.000 000	2.222 222	.450 000	42
.000 000	2.222 222	.450 000	43
.000 000	2.222 222	.450 000	44
.000 000	2.222 222	.450 000	45
.000 000	2.222 222	.450 000	46
.000 000	2.222 222	.450 000	47
.000 000	2.222 222	.450 000	48
.000 000	2.222 222	.450 000	49
.000 000	2.222 222	.450 000	50

RATE
46%

Year	COMPOUNDING FACTOR FOR 1 What an initial amount becomes when growing at compound interest	COMPOUNDING FACTOR FOR 1 PER ANNUM Growth of equal year-end deposits all growing at compound interest	SINKING FUND FACTOR Level deposit required each year to reach 1 by a given year
1	1.460 000	1.000 000	1.000 000
2	2.131 600	2.460 000	.406 504
3	3.112 136	4.591 600	.217 789
4	4.543 719	7.703 736	.129 807
5	6.633 829	12.247 455	.081 650
6	9.685 390	18.881 284	.052 963
7	14.140 670	28.566 674	.035 006
8	20.645 378	42.707 344	.023 415
9	30.142 252	63.352 723	.015 785
10	44.007 688	93.494 975	.010 696
11	64.251 225	137.502 663	.007 273
12	93.806 789	201.753 889	.004 957
13	136.957 912	295.560 677	.003 383
14	199.958 551	432.518 589	.002 312
15	291.939 484	632.477 140	.001 581
16	426.231 647	924.416 625	.001 082
17	622.298 205	1,350.648 272	.000 740
18	908.555 379	1,972.946 477	.000 507
19	1,326.490 854	2,881.501 856	.000 347
20	1,936.676 647	4,207.992 710	.000 238
21	2,827.547 904	6,144.669 357	.000 163
22	4,128.219 940	8,972.217 261	.000 111
23	6,027.201 113	13,100.437 20	.000 076
24	8,799.713 625	19,127.638 31	.000 052
25	12,847.581 89	27,927.351 94	.000 036
26	18,757.469 56	40,774.933 83	.000 025
27	27,385.905 56	59,532.403 39	.000 017
28	39,983.422 12	86,918.308 95	.000 012
29	58,375.796 29	126,901.731 1	.000 008
30	85,228.662 59	185,277.527 4	.000 005
31	124,433.847 4	270,506.190 0	.000 004
32	181,673.417 2	394,940.037 3	.000 003
33	265,243.189 1	576,613.454 5	.000 002
34	387,255.056 0	841,856.643 6	.000 001
35	565,392.381 8	1,229,111.700	.000 001
36	825,472.877 5	1,794,504.081	.000 001
37	1,205,190.401	2,619,976.959	.000 000
38	1,759,577.986	3,825,167.360	.000 000
39	2,568,983.859	5,584,745.346	.000 000
40	3,750,716.434	8,153,729.205	.000 000
41	5,476,045.994	11,904,445.64	.000 000
42	7,995,027.151	17,380,491.63	.000 000
43	11,672,739.64	25,375,518.78	.000 000
44	17,042,199.87	37,048,258.42	.000 000
45	24,881,611.82	54,090,458.30	.000 000
46	36,327,153.25	78,972,070.12	.000 000
47	53,037,643.75	115,299,223.4	.000 000
48	77,434,959.88	168,336,867.1	.000 000
49	113,055,041.4	245,771,827.0	.000 000
50	165,060,360.5	358,826,868.4	.000 000

RATE
46%

DISCOUNT FACTOR How much 1 at a future date is worth today	PRESENT WORTH OF AN ANNUITY FACTOR How much 1 received or paid annually for X years is worth today	CAPITAL RECOVERY FACTOR Annual payment that will repay a $1 loan in X years with compound interest on the unpaid balance	Year
.684 932	.684 932	1.460 000	1
.469 131	1.154 063	.866 504	2
.321 323	1.475 385	.677 789	3
.220 084	1.695 469	.589 807	4
.150 743	1.846 212	.541 650	5
.103 248	1.949 460	.512 963	6
.070 718	2.020 178	.495 006	7
.048 437	2.068 615	.483 415	8
.033 176	2.101 791	.475 785	9
.022 723	2.124 515	.470 696	10
.015 564	2.140 078	.467 273	11
.010 660	2.150 739	.464 957	12
.007 302	2.158 040	.463 383	13
.005 001	2.163 041	.462 312	14
.003 425	2.166 467	.461 581	15
.002 346	2.168 813	.461 082	16
.001 607	2.170 420	.460 740	17
.001 101	2.171 520	.460 507	18
.000 754	2.172 274	.460 347	19
.000 516	2.172 791	.460 238	20
.000 354	2.173 144	.460 163	21
.000 242	2.173 386	.460 111	22
.000 166	2.173 552	.460 076	23
.000 114	2.173 666	.460 052	24
.000 078	2.173 744	.460 036	25
.000 053	2.173 797	.460 025	26
.000 037	2.173 834	.460 017	27
.000 025	2.173 859	.460 012	28
.000 017	2.173 876	.460 008	29
.000 012	2.173 888	.460 005	30
.000 008	2.173 896	.460 004	31
.000 006	2.173 901	.460 003	32
.000 004	2.173 905	.460 002	33
.000 003	2.173 907	.460 001	34
.000 002	2.173 909	.460 001	35
.000 001	2.173 910	.460 001	36
.000 001	2.173 911	.460 000	37
.000 001	2.173 912	.460 000	38
.000 000	2.173 912	.460 000	39
.000 000	2.173 912	.460 000	40
.000 000	2.173 913	.460 000	41
.000 000	2.173 913	.460 000	42
.000 000	2.173 913	.460 000	43
.000 000	2.173 913	.460 000	44
.000 000	2.173 913	.460 000	45
.000 000	2.173 913	.460 000	46
.000 000	2.173 913	.460 000	47
.000 000	2.173 913	.460 000	48
.000 000	2.173 913	.460 000	49
.000 000	2.173 913	.460 000	50

RATE
47%

Year	COMPOUNDING FACTOR FOR 1 What an initial amount becomes when growing at compound interest	COMPOUNDING FACTOR FOR 1 PER ANNUM Growth of equal year-end deposits all growing at compound interest	SINKING FUND FACTOR Level deposit required each year to reach 1 by a given year
1	1.470 000	1.000 000	1.000 000
2	2.160 900	2.470 000	.404 858
3	3.176 523	4.630 900	.215 941
4	4.669 489	7.807 423	.128 083
5	6.864 149	12.476 912	.080 148
6	10.090 298	19.341 060	.051 703
7	14.832 739	29.431 359	.033 977
8	21.804 126	44.264 097	.022 592
9	32.052 065	66.068 223	.015 136
10	47.116 535	98.120 288	.010 192
11	69.261 307	145.236 823	.006 885
12	101.814 121	214.498 130	.004 662
13	149.666 758	316.312 251	.003 161
14	220.010 134	465.979 010	.002 146
15	323.414 898	685.989 144	.001 458
16	475.419 900	1,009.404 042	.000 991
17	698.867 252	1,484.823 941	.000 673
18	1,027.334 861	2,183.691 194	.000 458
19	1,510.182 246	3,211.026 055	.000 311
20	2,219.967 901	4,721.208 300	.000 212
21	3,263.352 815	6,941.176 201	.000 144
22	4,797.128 638	10,204.529 02	.000 098
23	7,051.779 097	15,001.657 65	.000 067
24	10,366.115 27	22,053.436 75	.000 045
25	15,238.189 45	32,419.552 02	.000 031
26	22,400.138 49	47,657.741 47	.000 021
27	32,928.203 58	70,057.879 97	.000 014
28	48,404.459 27	102,986.083 6	.000 010
29	71,154.555 13	151,390.542 8	.000 007
30	104,597.196 0	222,545.098 0	.000 004
31	153,757.878 2	327,142.294 0	.000 003
32	226,024.080 9	480,900.172 2	.000 002
33	332,255.398 9	706,924.253 1	.000 001
34	488,415.436 4	1,039,179.652	.000 001
35	717,970.691 6	1,527,595.088	.000 001
36	1,055,416.917	2,245,565.780	.000 000
37	1,551,462.867	3,300,982.697	.000 000
38	2,280,650.415	4,852,445.564	.000 000
39	3,352,556.110	7,133,095.979	.000 000
40	4,928,257.482	10,485,652.09	.000 000
41	7,244,538.499	15,413,909.57	.000 000
42	10,649,471.59	22,658,448.07	.000 000
43	15,654,723.24	33,307,919.66	.000 000
44	23,012,443.17	48,962,642.90	.000 000
45	33,828,291.45	71,975,086.07	.000 000
46	49,727,588.44	105,803,377.5	.000 000
47	73,099,555.00	155,530,966.0	.000 000
48	107,456,345.9	228,630,521.0	.000 000
49	157,960,828.4	336,086,866.8	.000 000
50	232,202,417.7	494,047,695.2	.000 000

RATE
47%

DISCOUNT FACTOR How much 1 at a future date is worth today	PRESENT WORTH OF AN ANNUITY FACTOR How much 1 received or paid annually for X years is worth today	CAPITAL RECOVERY FACTOR Annual payment that will repay a $1 loan in X years with compound interest on the unpaid balance	Year
.680 272	.680 272	1.470 000	1
.462 770	1.143 042	.874 858	2
.314 810	1.457 852	.685 941	3
.214 156	1.672 008	.598 083	4
.145 684	1.817 693	.550 148	5
.099 105	1.916 798	.521 703	6
.067 418	1.984 216	.503 977	7
.045 863	2.030 079	.492 592	8
.031 199	2.061 278	.485 136	9
.021 224	2.082 502	.480 192	10
.014 438	2.096 940	.476 885	11
.009 822	2.106 762	.474 662	12
.006 682	2.113 444	.473 161	13
.004 545	2.117 989	.472 146	14
.003 092	2.121 081	.471 458	15
.002 103	2.123 184	.470 991	16
.001 431	2.124 615	.470 673	17
.000 973	2.125 589	.470 458	18
.000 662	2.126 251	.470 311	19
.000 450	2.126 701	.470 212	20
.000 306	2.127 008	.470 144	21
.000 208	2.127 216	.470 098	22
.000 142	2.127 358	.470 067	23
.000 096	2.127 454	.470 045	24
.000 066	2.127 520	.470 031	25
.000 045	2.127 565	.470 021	26
.000 030	2.127 595	.470 014	27
.000 021	2.127 616	.470 010	28
.000 014	2.127 630	.470 007	29
.000 010	2.127 639	.470 004	30
.000 007	2.127 646	.470 003	31
.000 004	2.127 650	.470 002	32
.000 003	2.127 653	.470 001	33
.000 002	2.127 655	.470 001	34
.000 001	2.127 657	.470 001	35
.000 001	2.127 658	.470 000	36
.000 001	2.127 658	.470 000	37
.000 000	2.127 659	.470 000	38
.000 000	2.127 659	.470 000	39
.000 000	2.127 659	.470 000	40
.000 000	2.127 659	.470 000	41
.000 000	2.127 659	.470 000	42
.000 000	2.127 659	.470 000	43
.000 000	2.127 659	.470 000	44
.000 000	2.127 660	.470 000	45
.000 000	2.127 660	.470 000	46
.000 000	2.127 660	.470 000	47
.000 000	2.127 660	.470 000	48
.000 000	2.127 660	.470 000	49
.000 000	2.127 660	.470 000	50

RATE
48%

Year	COMPOUNDING FACTOR FOR 1 What an initial amount becomes when growing at compound interest	COMPOUNDING FACTOR FOR 1 PER ANNUM Growth of equal year-end deposits all growing at compound interest	SINKING FUND FACTOR Level deposit required each year to reach 1 by a given year
1	1.480 000	1.000 000	1.000 000
2	2.190 400	2.480 000	.403 226
3	3.241 792	4.670 400	.214 114
4	4.797 852	7.912 192	.126 387
5	7.100 821	12.710 044	.078 678
6	10.509 215	19.810 865	.050 477
7	15.553 639	30.320 081	.032 981
8	23.019 385	45.873 719	.021 799
9	34.068 690	68.893 105	.014 515
10	50.421 662	102.961 795	.009 712
11	74.624 059	153.383 457	.006 520
12	110.443 608	228.007 516	.004 386
13	163.456 539	338.451 124	.002 955
14	241.915 678	501.907 663	.001 992
15	358.035 204	743.823 342	.001 344
16	529.892 102	1,101.858 546	.000 908
17	784.240 311	1,631.750 647	.000 613
18	1,160.675 660	2,415.990 958	.000 414
19	1,717.799 977	3,576.666 618	.000 280
20	2,542.343 965	5,294.466 595	.000 189
21	3,762.669 069	7,836.810 560	.000 128
22	5,568.750 222	11,599.479 63	.000 086
23	8,241.750 328	17,168.229 85	.000 058
24	12,197.790 49	25,409.980 18	.000 039
25	18,052.729 92	37,607.770 67	.000 027
26	26,718.040 28	55,660.500 58	.000 018
27	39,542.699 62	82,378.540 87	.000 012
28	58,523.195 43	121,921.240 5	.000 008
29	86,614.329 24	180,444.435 9	.000 006
30	128,189.207 3	267,058.765 1	.000 004
31	189,720.026 8	395,247.972 4	.000 003
32	280,785.639 6	584,967.999 2	.000 002
33	415,562.746 6	865,753.638 8	.000 001
34	615,032.865 0	1,281,316.385	.000 001
35	910,248.640 2	1,896,349.250	.000 001
36	1,347,167.988	2,806,597.891	.000 000
37	1,993,808.621	4,153,765.878	.000 000
38	2,950,836.760	6,147,574.500	.000 000
39	4,367,238.405	9,098,411.259	.000 000
40	6,463,512.839	13,465,649.66	.000 000
41	9,565,999.001	19,929,162.50	.000 000
42	14,157,678.52	29,495,161.50	.000 000
43	20,953,364.21	43,652,840.03	.000 000
44	31,010,979.03	64,606,204.24	.000 000
45	45,896,248.97	95,617,183.27	.000 000
46	67,926,448.48	141,513,432.2	.000 000
47	100,531,143.7	209,439,880.7	.000 000
48	148,786,092.7	309,971,024.5	.000 000
49	220,203,417.3	458,757,117.2	.000 000
50	325,901,057.5	678,960,534.5	.000 000

RATE
48%

DISCOUNT FACTOR How much 1 at a future date is worth today	PRESENT WORTH OF AN ANNUITY FACTOR How much 1 received or paid annually for X years is worth today	CAPITAL RECOVERY FACTOR Annual payment that will repay a $1 loan in X years with compound interest on the unpaid balance	Year
.675 676	.675 676	1.480 000	1
.456 538	1.132 213	.883 226	2
.308 471	1.440 685	.694 114	3
.208 427	1.649 111	.606 387	4
.140 829	1.789 940	.558 678	5
.095 155	1.885 095	.530 477	6
.064 294	1.949 388	.512 981	7
.043 442	1.992 830	.501 799	8
.029 352	2.022 182	.494 515	9
.019 833	2.042 015	.489 712	10
.013 401	2.055 416	.486 520	11
.009 054	2.064 470	.484 386	12
.006 118	2.070 588	.482 955	13
.004 134	2.074 722	.481 992	14
.002 793	2.077 515	.481 344	15
.001 887	2.079 402	.480 908	16
.001 275	2.080 677	.480 613	17
.000 862	2.081 538	.480 414	18
.000 582	2.082 121	.480 280	19
.000 393	2.082 514	.480 189	20
.000 266	2.082 780	.480 128	21
.000 180	2.082 959	.480 086	22
.000 121	2.083 081	.480 058	23
.000 082	2.083 163	.480 039	24
.000 055	2.083 218	.480 027	25
.000 037	2.083 255	.480 018	26
.000 025	2.083 281	.480 012	27
.000 017	2.083 298	.480 008	28
.000 012	2.083 309	.480 006	29
.000 008	2.083 317	.480 004	30
.000 005	2.083 322	.480 003	31
.000 004	2.083 326	.480 002	32
.000 002	2.083 328	.480 001	33
.000 002	2.083 330	.480 001	34
.000 001	2.083 331	.480 001	35
.000 001	2.083 332	.480 000	36
.000 001	2.083 332	.480 000	37
.000 000	2.083 333	.480 000	38
.000 000	2.083 333	.480 000	39
.000 000	2.083 333	.480 000	40
.000 000	2.083 333	.480 000	41
.000 000	2.083 333	.480 000	42
.000 000	2.083 333	.480 000	43
.000 000	2.083 333	.480 000	44
.000 000	2.083 333	.480 000	45
.000 000	2.083 333	.480 000	46
.000 000	2.083 333	.480 000	47
.000 000	2.083 333	.480 000	48
.000 000	2.083 333	.480 000	49
.000 000	2.083 333	.480 000	50

RATE
49%

Year	COMPOUNDING FACTOR FOR 1 What an initial amount becomes when growing at compound interest	COMPOUNDING FACTOR FOR 1 PER ANNUM Growth of equal year-end deposits all growing at compound interest	SINKING FUND FACTOR Level deposit required each year to reach 1 by a given year
1	1.490 000	1.000 000	1.000 000
2	2.220 100	2.490 000	.401 606
3	3.307 949	4.710 100	.212 310
4	4.928 844	8.018 049	.124 719
5	7.343 978	12.946 893	.077 239
6	10.942 527	20.290 871	.049 283
7	16.304 365	31.233 397	.032 017
8	24.293 503	47.537 762	.021 036
9	36.197 320	71.831 265	.013 922
10	53.934 007	108.028 585	.009 257
11	80.361 670	161.962 592	.006 174
12	119.738 888	242.324 261	.004 127
13	178.410 943	362.063 150	.002 762
14	265.832 305	540.474 093	.001 850
15	396.090 135	806.306 398	.001 240
16	590.174 301	1,202.396 533	.000 832
17	879.359 709	1,792.570 835	.000 558
18	1,310.245 966	2,671.930 544	.000 374
19	1,952.266 490	3,982.176 510	.000 251
20	2,908.877 070	5,934.443 000	.000 169
21	4,334.226 834	8,843.320 070	.000 113
22	6,457.997 983	13,177.546 91	.000 076
23	9,622.416 995	19,635.544 89	.000 051
24	14,337.401 32	29,257.961 88	.000 034
25	21,362.727 97	43,595.363 21	.000 023
26	31,830.464 68	64,958.091 18	.000 015
27	47,427.392 37	96,788.555 86	.000 010
28	70,666.814 63	144,215.948 2	.000 007
29	105,293.553 8	214,882.762 9	.000 005
30	156,887.395 2	320,176.316 7	.000 003
31	233,762.218 8	477,063.711 8	.000 002
32	348,305.706 0	710,825.930 6	.000 001
33	518,975.501 9	1,059,131.637	.000 001
34	773,273.497 9	1,578,107.139	.000 001
35	1,152,177.512	2,351,380.636	.000 000
36	1,716,744.493	3,503,558.148	.000 000
37	2,557,949.294	5,220,302.641	.000 000
38	3,811,344.448	7,778,251.935	.000 000
39	5,678,903.228	11,589,596.38	.000 000
40	8,461,565.809	17,268,499.61	.000 000
41	12,607,733.06	25,730,065.42	.000 000
42	18,785,522.25	38,337,798.48	.000 000
43	27,990,428.16	57,123,320.73	.000 000
44	41,705,737.95	85,113,748.89	.000 000
45	62,141,549.55	126,819,486.8	.000 000
46	92,590,908.83	188,961,036.4	.000 000
47	137,960,454.2	281,551,945.2	.000 000
48	205,561,076.7	419,512,399.4	.000 000
49	306,286,004.3	625,073,476.1	.000 000
50	456,366,146.4	931,359,480.4	.000 000

RATE
49%

DISCOUNT FACTOR How much 1 at a future date is worth today	PRESENT WORTH OF AN ANNUITY FACTOR How much 1 received or paid annually for X years is worth today	CAPITAL RECOVERY FACTOR Annual payment that will repay a $1 loan in X years with compound interest on the unpaid balance	Year
.671 141	.671 141	1.490 000	1
.450 430	1.121 571	.891 606	2
.302 302	1.423 873	.702 310	3
.202 887	1.626 761	.614 719	4
.136 166	1.762 927	.567 239	5
.091 387	1.854 313	.539 283	6
.061 333	1.915 646	.522 017	7
.041 163	1.956 810	.511 036	8
.027 626	1.984 436	.503 922	9
.018 541	2.002 977	.499 257	10
.012 444	2.015 421	.496 174	11
.008 352	2.023 772	.494 127	12
.005 605	2.029 377	.492 762	13
.003 762	2.033 139	.491 850	14
.002 525	2.035 664	.491 240	15
.001 694	2.037 358	.490 832	16
.001 137	2.038 496	.490 558	17
.000 763	2.039 259	.490 374	18
.000 512	2.039 771	.490 251	19
.000 344	2.040 115	.490 169	20
.000 231	2.040 345	.490 113	21
.000 155	2.040 500	.490 076	22
.000 104	2.040 604	.490 051	23
.000 070	2.040 674	.490 034	24
.000 047	2.040 721	.490 023	25
.000 031	2.040 752	.490 015	26
.000 021	2.040 773	.490 010	27
.000 014	2.040 787	.490 007	28
.000 009	2.040 797	.490 005	29
.000 006	2.040 803	.490 003	30
.000 004	2.040 808	.490 002	31
.000 003	2.040 810	.490 001	32
.000 002	2.040 812	.490 001	33
.000 001	2.040 814	.490 001	34
.000 001	2.040 815	.490 000	35
.000 001	2.040 815	.490 000	36
.000 000	2.040 816	.490 000	37
.000 000	2.040 816	.490 000	38
.000 000	2.040 816	.490 000	39
.000 000	2.040 816	.490 000	40
.000 000	2.040 816	.490 000	41
.000 000	2.040 816	.490 000	42
.000 000	2.040 816	.490 000	43
.000 000	2.040 816	.490 000	44
.000 000	2.040 816	.490 000	45
.000 000	2.040 816	.490 000	46
.000 000	2.040 816	.490 000	47
.000 000	2.040 816	.490 000	48
.000 000	2.040 816	.490 000	49
.000 000	2.040 816	.490 000	50

RATE
50%

Year	COMPOUNDING FACTOR FOR 1 What an initial amount becomes when growing at compound interest	COMPOUNDING FACTOR FOR 1 PER ANNUM Growth of equal year-end deposits all growing at compound interest	SINKING FUND FACTOR Level deposit required each year to reach 1 by a given year
1	1.500 000	1.000 000	1.000 000
2	2.250 000	2.500 000	.400 000
3	3.375 000	4.750 000	.210 526
4	5.062 500	8.125 000	.123 077
5	7.593 750	13.187 500	.075 829
6	11.390 625	20.781 250	.048 120
7	17.085 938	32.171 875	.031 083
8	25.628 906	49.257 812	.020 301
9	38.443 359	74.886 719	.013 354
10	57.665 039	113.330 078	.008 824
11	86.497 559	170.995 117	.005 848
12	129.746 338	257.492 676	.003 884
13	194.619 507	387.239 014	.002 582
14	291.929 260	581.858 521	.001 719
15	437.893 890	873.787 781	.001 144
16	656.840 836	1,311.681 671	.000 762
17	985.261 253	1,968.522 507	.000 508
18	1,477.891 880	2,953.783 760	.000 339
19	2,216.837 820	4,431.675 640	.000 226
20	3,325.256 730	6,648.513 460	.000 150
21	4,987.885 095	9,973.770 190	.000 100
22	7,481.827 643	14,961.655 29	.000 067
23	11,222.741 46	22,443.482 93	.000 045
24	16,834.112 20	33,666.224 39	.000 030
25	25,251.168 29	50,500.336 59	.000 020
26	37,876.752 44	75,751.504 88	.000 013
27	56,815.128 66	113,628.257 3	.000 009
28	85,222.692 99	170,443.386 0	.000 006
29	127,834.039 5	255,666.079 0	.000 004
30	191,751.059 2	383,500.118 5	.000 003
31	287,626.588 8	575,251.177 7	.000 002
32	431,439.883 3	862,877.766 6	.000 001
33	647,159.824 9	1,294,317.650	.000 001
34	970,739.737 4	1,941,477.475	.000 001
35	1,456,109.606	2,912,217.212	.000 000
36	2,184,164.409	4,368,326.818	.000 000
37	3,276,246.614	6,552,491.227	.000 000
38	4,914,369.920	9,828,737.841	.000 000
39	7,371,554.881	14,743,107.76	.000 000
40	11,057,332.32	22,114,662.64	.000 000
41	16,585,998.48	33,171,994.96	.000 000
42	24,878,997.72	49,757,993.44	.000 000
43	37,318,496.58	74,636,991.17	.000 000
44	55,977,744.87	111,955,487.8	.000 000
45	83,966,617.31	167,933,232.6	.000 000
46	125,949,926.0	251,899,849.9	.000 000
47	188,924,889.0	377,849,775.9	.000 000
48	283,387,333.4	566,774,664.9	.000 000
49	425,081,000.1	850,161,998.3	.000 000
50	637,621,500.2	1,275,242,998.	.000 000

RATE
50%

DISCOUNT FACTOR How much 1 at a future date is worth today	PRESENT WORTH OF AN ANNUITY FACTOR How much 1 received or paid annually for X years is worth today	CAPITAL RECOVERY FACTOR Annual payment that will repay a $1 loan in X years with compound interest on the unpaid balance	Year
.666 667	.666 667	1.500 000	1
.444 444	1.111 111	.900 000	2
.296 296	1.407 407	.710 526	3
.197 531	1.604 938	.623 077	4
.131 687	1.736 626	.575 829	5
.087 791	1.824 417	.548 120	6
.058 528	1.882 945	.531 083	7
.039 018	1.921 963	.520 301	8
.026 012	1.947 975	.513 354	9
.017 342	1.965 317	.508 824	10
.011 561	1.976 878	.505 848	11
.007 707	1.984 585	.503 884	12
.005 138	1.989 724	.502 582	13
.003 425	1.993 149	.501 719	14
.002 284	1.995 433	.501 144	15
.001 522	1.996 955	.500 762	16
.001 015	1.997 970	.500 508	17
.000 677	1.998 647	.500 339	18
.000 451	1.999 098	.500 226	19
.000 301	1.999 399	.500 150	20
.000 200	1.999 599	.500 100	21
.000 134	1.999 733	.500 067	22
.000 089	1.999 822	.500 045	23
.000 059	1.999 881	.500 030	24
.000 040	1.999 921	.500 020	25
.000 026	1.999 947	.500 013	26
.000 018	1.999 965	.500 009	27
.000 012	1.999 977	.500 006	28
.000 008	1.999 984	.500 004	29
.000 005	1.999 990	.500 003	30
.000 003	1.999 993	.500 002	31
.000 002	1.999 995	.500 001	32
.000 002	1.999 997	.500 001	33
.000 001	1.999 998	.500 001	34
.000 001	1.999 999	.500 000	35
.000 000	1.999 999	.500 000	36
.000 000	1.999 999	.500 000	37
.000 000	2.000 000	.500 000	38
.000 000	2.000 000	.500 000	39
.000 000	2.000 000	.500 000	40
.000 000	2.000 000	.500 000	41
.000 000	2.000 000	.500 000	42
.000 000	2.000 000	.500 000	43
.000 000	2.000 000	.500 000	44
.000 000	2.000 000	.500 000	45
.000 000	2.000 000	.500 000	46
.000 000	2.000 000	.500 000	47
.000 000	2.000 000	.500 000	48
.000 000	2.000 000	.500 000	49
.000 000	2.000 000	.500 000	50

DISCOUNT FACTOR—How much 1 at a future date is worth today.

Year	1%	3%	5%	6%	8%	10%	12%	14%	15%	16%	18%
1	.990	.971	.952	.943	.926	.909	.893	.877	.870	.862	.847
2	.980	.943	.907	.890	.857	.826	.797	.769	.756	.743	.718
3	.971	.915	.864	.840	.794	.751	.712	.675	.658	.641	.609
4	.961	.888	.823	.792	.735	.683	.636	.592	.572	.552	.516
5	.951	.863	.784	.747	.681	.621	.567	.519	.497	.476	.437
6	.942	.837	.746	.705	.630	.564	.507	.456	.432	.410	.370
7	.933	.813	.711	.665	.583	.513	.452	.400	.376	.354	.314
8	.923	.789	.677	.627	.540	.467	.404	.351	.327	.305	.266
9	.914	.766	.645	.592	.500	.424	.361	.308	.284	.263	.225
10	.905	.744	.614	.558	.463	.386	.322	.270	.247	.227	.191
11	.896	.722	.585	.527	.429	.350	.287	.237	.215	.195	.162
12	.887	.701	.557	.497	.397	.319	.257	.208	.187	.168	.137
13	.879	.681	.530	.469	.368	.290	.229	.182	.163	.145	.116
14	.870	.661	.505	.442	.340	.263	.205	.160	.141	.125	.099
15	.861	.642	.481	.417	.315	.239	.183	.140	.123	.108	.084
16	.853	.623	.458	.394	.292	.218	.163	.123	.107	.093	.071
17	.844	.605	.436	.371	.270	.198	.146	.108	.093	.080	.060
18	.836	.587	.416	.350	.250	.180	.130	.095	.081	.069	.051
19	.828	.570	.396	.331	.232	.164	.116	.083	.070	.060	.043
20	.820	.554	.377	.312	.215	.149	.104	.073	.061	.051	.037
21	.811	.538	.359	.294	.199	.135	.093	.064	.053	.044	.031
22	.803	.522	.342	.278	.184	.123	.083	.056	.046	.038	.026
23	.795	.507	.326	.262	.170	.112	.074	.049	.040	.033	.022
24	.788	.492	.310	.247	.158	.102	.066	.043	.035	.028	.019
25	.780	.478	.295	.233	.146	.092	.059	.038	.030	.024	.016
26	.772	.464	.281	.220	.135	.084	.053	.033	.026	.021	.014
27	.764	.450	.268	.207	.125	.076	.047	.029	.023	.018	.011
28	.757	.437	.255	.196	.116	.069	.042	.026	.020	.016	.010
29	.749	.424	.243	.185	.107	.063	.037	.022	.017	.014	.008
30	.742	.412	.231	.174	.099	.057	.033	.020	.015	.012	.007
35	.706	.355	.181	.130	.068	.036	.019	.010	.008	.006	.003
40	.672	.307	.142	.097	.046	.022	.011	.005	.004	.003	.001
45	.639	.264	.111	.073	.031	.014	.006	.003	.002	.001	.001
50	.608	.228	.087	.054	.021	.009	.003	.001	.001	.001	.000

DISCOUNT FACTOR—How much 1 at a future date is worth today.

20%	22%	24%	25%	26%	28%	30%	35%	40%	45%	50%	Year
.833	.820	.806	.800	.794	.781	.769	.741	.714	.690	.667	1
.694	.672	.650	.640	.630	.610	.592	.549	.510	.476	.444	2
.579	.551	.524	.512	.500	.477	.455	.406	.364	.328	.296	3
.482	.451	.423	.410	.397	.373	.350	.301	.260	.226	.198	4
.402	.370	.341	.328	.315	.291	.269	.223	.186	.156	.132	5
.335	.303	.275	.262	.250	.227	.207	.165	.133	.108	.088	6
.279	.249	.222	.210	.198	.178	.159	.122	.095	.074	.059	7
.233	.204	.179	.168	.157	.139	.123	.091	.068	.051	.039	8
.194	.167	.144	.134	.125	.108	.094	.067	.048	.035	.026	9
.162	.137	.116	.107	.099	.085	.073	.050	.035	.024	.017	10
.135	.112	.094	.086	.079	.066	.056	.037	.025	.017	.012	11
.112	.092	.076	.069	.062	.052	.043	.027	.018	.012	.008	12
.093	.075	.061	.055	.050	.040	.033	.020	.013	.008	.005	13
.078	.062	.049	.044	.039	.032	.025	.015	.009	.006	.003	14
.065	.051	.040	.035	.031	.025	.020	.011	.006	.004	.002	15
.054	.042	.032	.028	.025	.019	.015	.008	.005	.003	.002	16
.045	.034	.026	.023	.020	.015	.012	.006	.003	.002	.001	17
.038	.028	.021	.018	.016	.012	.009	.005	.002	.001	.001	18
.031	.023	.017	.014	.012	.009	.007	.003	.002	.001	.000	19
.026	.019	.014	.012	.010	.007	.005	.002	.001	.001	.000	20
.022	.015	.011	.009	.008	.006	.004	.002	.001	.000	.000	21
.018	.013	.009	.007	.006	.004	.003	.001	.001	.000	.000	22
.015	.010	.007	.006	.005	.003	.002	.001	.000	.000	.000	23
.013	.008	.006	.005	.004	.003	.002	.001	.000	.000	.000	24
.010	.007	.005	.004	.003	.002	.001	.001	.000	.000	.000	25
.009	.006	.004	.003	.002	.002	.001	.000	.000	.000	.000	26
.007	.005	.003	.002	.002	.001	.001	.000	.000	.000	.000	27
.006	.004	.002	.002	.002	.001	.001	.000	.000	.000	.000	28
.005	.003	.002	.002	.001	.001	.000	.000	.000	.000	.000	29
.004	.003	.002	.001	.001	.001	.000	.000	.000	.000	.000	30
.002	.001	.001	.000	.000	.000	.000	.000	.000	.000	.000	35
.001	.000	.000	.000	.000	.000	.000	.000	.000	.000	.000	40
.000	.000	.000	.000	.000	.000	.000	.000	.000	.000	.000	45
.000	.000	.000	.000	.000	.000	.000	.000	.000	.000	.000	50

PRESENT WORTH OF AN ANNUITY FACTOR—
How much 1 received or paid annually for X years is worth today.

Year	1%	3%	5%	6%	8%	10%	12%	14%	15%	16%	18%
1	.990	.971	.952	.943	.926	.909	.893	.877	.870	.862	.847
2	1.970	1.913	1.859	1.833	1.783	1.736	1.690	1.647	1.626	1.605	1.566
3	2.941	2.829	2.723	2.673	2.577	2.487	2.402	2.322	2.283	2.246	2.174
4	3.902	3.717	3.546	3.465	3.312	3.170	3.037	2.914	2.855	2.798	2.690
5	4.853	4.580	4.329	4.212	3.993	3.791	3.605	3.433	3.352	3.274	3.127
6	5.795	5.417	5.076	4.917	4.623	4.355	4.111	3.889	3.784	3.685	3.498
7	6.728	6.230	5.786	5.582	5.206	4.868	4.564	4.288	4.160	4.039	3.812
8	7.652	7.020	6.463	6.210	5.747	5.335	4.968	4.639	4.487	4.344	4.078
9	8.566	7.786	7.108	6.802	6.247	5.759	5.328	4.946	4.772	4.607	4.303
10	9.471	8.530	7.722	7.360	6.710	6.145	5.650	5.216	5.019	4.833	4.494
11	10.368	9.253	8.306	7.887	7.139	6.495	5.938	5.453	5.234	5.029	4.656
12	11.255	9.954	8.863	8.384	7.536	6.814	6.194	5.660	5.421	5.197	4.793
13	12.134	10.635	9.394	8.853	7.904	7.103	6.424	5.842	5.583	5.342	4.910
14	13.004	11.296	9.899	9.295	8.244	7.367	6.628	6.002	5.724	5.468	5.008
15	13.865	11.938	10.380	9.712	8.559	7.606	6.811	6.142	5.847	5.575	5.092
16	14.718	12.561	10.838	10.106	8.851	7.824	6.974	6.265	5.954	5.668	5.162
17	15.562	13.166	11.274	10.477	9.122	8.022	7.120	6.373	6.047	5.749	5.222
18	16.398	13.754	11.690	10.828	9.372	8.201	7.250	6.467	6.128	5.818	5.273
19	17.226	14.324	12.085	11.158	9.604	8.365	7.366	6.550	6.198	5.877	5.316
20	18.046	14.877	12.462	11.470	9.818	8.514	7.469	6.623	6.259	5.929	5.353
21	18.857	15.415	12.821	11.764	10.017	8.649	7.562	6.687	6.312	5.973	5.384
22	19.660	15.937	13.163	12.042	10.201	8.772	7.645	6.743	6.359	6.011	5.410
23	20.456	16.444	13.489	12.303	10.371	8.883	7.718	6.792	6.399	6.044	5.432
24	21.243	16.936	13.799	12.550	10.529	8.985	7.784	6.835	6.434	6.073	5.451
25	22.023	17.413	14.094	12.783	10.675	9.077	7.843	6.873	6.464	6.097	5.467
26	22.795	17.877	14.375	13.003	10.810	9.161	7.896	6.906	6.491	6.118	5.480
27	23.560	18.327	14.643	13.211	10.935	9.237	7.943	6.935	6.514	6.136	5.492
28	24.316	18.764	14.898	13.406	11.051	9.307	7.984	6.961	6.534	6.152	5.502
29	25.066	19.188	15.141	13.591	11.158	9.370	8.022	6.983	6.551	6.166	5.510
30	25.808	19.600	15.372	13.765	11.258	9.427	8.055	7.003	6.566	6.177	5.517
35	29.409	21.487	16.374	14.498	11.655	9.644	8.176	7.070	6.617	6.215	5.539
40	32.835	23.115	17.159	15.046	11.925	9.779	8.244	7.105	6.642	6.233	5.548
45	36.095	24.519	17.774	15.456	12.108	9.863	8.283	7.123	6.654	6.242	5.552
50	39.196	25.730	18.256	15.762	12.233	9.915	8.304	7.133	6.661	6.246	5.554

PRESENT WORTH OF AN ANNUITY FACTOR—
How much 1 received or paid annually for X years is worth today.

20%	22%	24%	25%	26%	28%	30%	35%	40%	45%	50%	Year
.833	.820	.806	.800	.794	.781	.769	.741	.714	.690	.667	1
1.528	1.492	1.457	1.440	1.424	1.392	1.361	1.289	1.224	1.165	1.111	2
2.106	2.042	1.981	1.952	1.923	1.868	1.816	1.696	1.589	1.493	1.407	3
2.589	2.494	2.404	2.362	2.320	2.241	2.166	1.997	1.849	1.720	1.605	4
2.991	2.864	2.745	2.689	2.635	2.532	2.436	2.220	2.035	1.876	1.737	5
3.326	3.167	3.020	2.951	2.885	2.759	2.643	2.385	2.168	1.983	1.824	6
3.605	3.416	3.242	3.161	3.083	2.937	2.802	2.508	2.263	2.057	1.883	7
3.837	3.619	3.421	3.329	3.241	3.076	2.925	2.598	2.331	2.108	1.922	8
4.031	3.786	3.566	3.463	3.366	3.184	3.019	2.665	2.379	2.144	1.948	9
4.192	3.923	3.682	3.571	3.465	3.269	3.092	2.715	2.414	2.168	1.965	10
4.327	4.035	3.776	3.656	3.543	3.335	3.147	2.752	2.438	2.185	1.977	11
4.439	4.127	3.851	3.725	3.606	3.387	3.190	2.779	2.456	2.196	1.985	12
4.533	4.203	3.912	3.780	3.656	3.427	3.223	2.799	2.469	2.204	1.990	13
4.611	4.265	3.962	3.824	3.695	3.459	3.249	2.814	2.478	2.210	1.993	14
4.675	4.315	4.001	3.859	3.726	3.483	3.268	2.825	2.484	2.214	1.995	15
4.730	4.357	4.033	3.887	3.751	3.503	3.283	2.834	2.489	2.216	1.997	16
4.775	4.391	4.059	3.910	3.771	3.518	3.295	2.840	2.492	2.218	1.998	17
4.812	4.419	4.080	3.928	3.786	3.529	3.304	2.844	2.494	2.219	1.999	18
4.843	4.442	4.097	3.942	3.799	3.539	3.311	2.848	2.496	2.220	1.999	19
4.870	4.460	4.110	3.954	3.808	3.546	3.316	2.850	2.497	2.221	1.999	20
4.891	4.476	4.121	3.963	3.816	3.551	3.320	2.852	2.498	2.221	2.000	21
4.909	4.488	4.130	3.970	3.822	3.556	3.323	2.853	2.498	2.222	2.000	22
4.925	4.499	4.137	3.976	3.827	3.559	3.325	2.854	2.499	2.222	2.000	23
4.937	4.507	4.143	3.981	3.831	3.562	3.327	2.855	2.499	2.222	2.000	24
4.948	4.514	4.147	3.985	3.834	3.564	3.329	2.856	2.499	2.222	2.000	25
4.956	4.520	4.151	3.988	3.837	3.566	3.330	2.856	2.500	2.222	2.000	26
4.964	4.524	4.154	3.990	3.839	3.567	3.331	2.856	2.500	2.222	2.000	27
4.970	4.528	4.157	3.992	3.840	3.568	3.331	2.857	2.500	2.222	2.000	28
4.975	4.531	4.159	3.994	3.841	3.569	3.332	2.857	2.500	2.222	2.000	29
4.979	4.534	4.160	3.995	3.842	3.569	3.332	2.857	2.500	2.222	2.000	30
4.992	4.541	4.164	3.998	3.845	3.571	3.333	2.857	2.500	2.222	2.000	35
4.997	4.544	4.166	3.999	3.846	3.571	3.333	2.857	2.500	2.222	2.000	40
4.999	4.545	4.166	4.000	3.846	3.571	3.333	2.857	2.500	2.222	2.000	45
4.999	4.545	4.167	4.000	3.846	3.571	3.333	2.857	2.500	2.222	2.000	50

RATE
0.0%-0.9%

COMPOUNDING FACTOR FOR 1

Year	.0%	.1%	.2%	.3%	.4%
1	1.000 000	1.001 000	1.002 000	1.003 000	1.004 000
2	1.000 000	1.002 001	1.004 004	1.006 009	1.008 016
3	1.000 000	1.003 003	1.006 012	1.009 027	1.012 048
4	1.000 000	1.004 006	1.008 024	1.012 054	1.016 096
5	1.000 000	1.005 010	1.010 040	1.015 090	1.020 161
6	1.000 000	1.006 015	1.012 060	1.018 136	1.024 241
7	1.000 000	1.007 021	1.014 084	1.021 190	1.028 338
8	1.000 000	1.008 028	1.016 112	1.024 254	1.032 452
9	1.000 000	1.009 036	1.018 145	1.027 326	1.036 581
10	1.000 000	1.010 045	1.020 181	1.030 408	1.040 728
11	1.000 000	1.011 055	1.022 221	1.033 499	1.044 891
12	1.000 000	1.012 066	1.024 266	1.036 600	1.049 070
13	1.000 000	1.013 078	1.026 314	1.039 710	1.053 266
14	1.000 000	1.014 091	1.028 367	1.042 829	1.057 480
15	1.000 000	1.015 105	1.030 424	1.045 957	1.061 709
16	1.000 000	1.016 121	1.032 485	1.049 095	1.065 956
17	1.000 000	1.017 137	1.034 549	1.052 243	1.070 220
18	1.000 000	1.018 154	1.036 619	1.055 399	1.074 501
19	1.000 000	1.019 172	1.038 692	1.058 565	1.078 799
20	1.000 000	1.020 191	1.040 769	1.061 741	1.083 114
21	1.000 000	1.021 211	1.042 851	1.064 926	1.087 447
22	1.000 000	1.022 233	1.044 936	1.068 121	1.091 796
23	1.000 000	1.023 255	1.047 026	1.071 326	1.096 164
24	1.000 000	1.024 278	1.049 120	1.074 540	1.100 548
25	1.000 000	1.025 302	1.051 219	1.077 763	1.104 950
26	1.000 000	1.026 328	1.053 321	1.080 996	1.109 370
27	1.000 000	1.027 354	1.055 428	1.084 239	1.113 808
28	1.000 000	1.028 381	1.057 539	1.087 492	1.118 263
29	1.000 000	1.029 410	1.059 654	1.090 755	1.122 736
30	1.000 000	1.030 439	1.061 773	1.094 027	1.127 227
31	1.000 000	1.031 470	1.063 896	1.097 309	1.131 736
32	1.000 000	1.032 501	1.066 024	1.100 601	1.136 263
33	1.000 000	1.033 533	1.068 156	1.103 903	1.140 808
34	1.000 000	1.034 567	1.070 293	1.107 214	1.145 371
35	1.000 000	1.035 602	1.072 433	1.110 536	1.149 953
36	1.000 000	1.036 637	1.074 578	1.113 868	1.154 552
37	1.000 000	1.037 674	1.076 727	1.117 209	1.159 171
38	1.000 000	1.038 712	1.078 881	1.120 561	1.163 807
39	1.000 000	1.039 750	1.081 038	1.123 923	1.168 463
40	1.000 000	1.040 790	1.083 201	1.127 294	1.173 136
41	1.000 000	1.041 831	1.085 367	1.130 676	1.177 829
42	1.000 000	1.042 873	1.087 538	1.134 068	1.182 540
43	1.000 000	1.043 915	1.089 713	1.137 470	1.187 270
44	1.000 000	1.044 959	1.091 892	1.140 883	1.192 020
45	1.000 000	1.046 004	1.094 076	1.144 306	1.196 788
46	1.000 000	1.047 050	1.096 264	1.147 738	1.201 575
47	1.000 000	1.048 097	1.098 457	1.151 182	1.206 381
48	1.000 000	1.049 145	1.100 654	1.154 635	1.211 207
49	1.000 000	1.050 195	1.102 855	1.158 099	1.216 051
50	1.000 000	1.051 245	1.105 061	1.161 573	1.220 916

RATE
0.0%-0.9%

COMPOUNDING FACTOR FOR 1

.5%	.6%	.7%	.8%	.9%	Year
1.005 000	1.006 000	1.007 000	1.008 000	1.009 000	1
1.010 025	1.012 036	1.014 049	1.016 064	1.018 081	2
1.015 075	1.018 108	1.021 147	1.024 193	1.027 244	3
1.020 150	1.024 217	1.028 295	1.032 386	1.036 489	4
1.025 251	1.030 362	1.035 493	1.040 645	1.045 817	5
1.030 378	1.036 544	1.042 742	1.048 970	1.055 230	6
1.035 529	1.042 764	1.050 041	1.057 362	1.064 727	7
1.040 707	1.049 020	1.057 391	1.065 821	1.074 309	8
1.045 911	1.055 314	1.064 793	1.074 348	1.083 978	9
1.051 140	1.061 646	1.072 247	1.082 942	1.093 734	10
1.056 396	1.068 016	1.079 752	1.091 606	1.103 577	11
1.061 678	1.074 424	1.087 311	1.100 339	1.113 510	12
1.066 986	1.080 871	1.094 922	1.109 141	1.123 531	13
1.072 321	1.087 356	1.102 586	1.118 015	1.133 643	14
1.077 683	1.093 880	1.110 304	1.126 959	1.143 846	15
1.083 071	1.100 443	1.118 077	1.135 974	1.154 140	16
1.088 487	1.107 046	1.125 903	1.145 062	1.164 528	17
1.093 929	1.113 688	1.133 784	1.154 223	1.175 008	18
1.099 399	1.120 370	1.141 721	1.163 456	1.185 584	19
1.104 896	1.127 093	1.149 713	1.172 764	1.196 254	20
1.110 420	1.133 855	1.157 761	1.182 146	1.207 020	21
1.115 972	1.140 658	1.165 865	1.191 603	1.217 883	22
1.121 552	1.147 502	1.174 026	1.201 136	1.228 844	23
1.127 160	1.154 387	1.182 244	1.210 745	1.239 904	24
1.132 796	1.161 314	1.190 520	1.220 431	1.251 063	25
1.138 460	1.168 281	1.198 854	1.230 195	1.262 322	26
1.144 152	1.175 291	1.207 246	1.240 036	1.273 683	27
1.149 873	1.182 343	1.215 697	1.249 956	1.285 147	28
1.155 622	1.189 437	1.224 206	1.259 956	1.296 713	29
1.161 400	1.196 574	1.232 776	1.270 036	1.308 383	30
1.167 207	1.203 753	1.241 405	1.280 196	1.320 159	31
1.173 043	1.210 976	1.250 095	1.290 438	1.332 040	32
1.178 908	1.218 241	1.258 846	1.300 761	1.344 029	33
1.184 803	1.225 551	1.267 658	1.311 167	1.356 125	34
1.190 727	1.232 904	1.276 531	1.321 657	1.368 330	35
1.196 681	1.240 302	1.285 467	1.332 230	1.380 645	36
1.202 664	1.247 743	1.294 465	1.342 888	1.393 071	37
1.208 677	1.255 230	1.303 527	1.353 631	1.405 608	38
1.214 721	1.262 761	1.312 651	1.364 460	1.418 259	39
1.220 794	1.270 338	1.321 840	1.375 376	1.431 023	40
1.226 898	1.277 960	1.331 093	1.386 379	1.443 902	41
1.233 033	1.285 628	1.340 410	1.397 470	1.456 897	42
1.239 198	1.293 341	1.349 793	1.408 649	1.470 010	43
1.245 394	1.301 101	1.359 242	1.419 918	1.483 240	44
1.251 621	1.308 908	1.368 756	1.431 278	1.496 589	45
1.257 879	1.316 761	1.378 338	1.442 728	1.510 058	46
1.264 168	1.324 662	1.387 986	1.454 270	1.523 649	47
1.270 489	1.332 610	1.397 702	1.465 904	1.537 361	48
1.276 842	1.340 606	1.407 486	1.477 631	1.551 198	49
1.283 226	1.348 649	1.417 338	1.489 452	1.565 158	50

RATE
1.0%-1.9%

COMPOUNDING FACTOR FOR 1

Year	1.0%	1.1%	1.2%	1.3%	1.4%
1	1.010 000	1.011 000	1.012 000	1.013 000	1.014 000
2	1.020 100	1.022 121	1.024 144	1.026 169	1.028 196
3	1.030 301	1.033 364	1.036 434	1.039 509	1.042 591
4	1.040 604	1.044 731	1.048 871	1.053 023	1.057 187
5	1.051 010	1.056 223	1.061 457	1.066 712	1.071 988
6	1.061 520	1.067 842	1.074 195	1.080 579	1.086 995
7	1.072 135	1.079 588	1.087 085	1.094 627	1.102 213
8	1.082 857	1.091 464	1.100 130	1.108 857	1.117 644
9	1.093 685	1.103 470	1.113 332	1.123 272	1.133 291
10	1.104 622	1.115 608	1.126 692	1.137 875	1.149 157
11	1.115 668	1.127 880	1.140 212	1.152 667	1.165 246
12	1.126 825	1.140 286	1.153 895	1.167 652	1.181 559
13	1.138 093	1.152 829	1.167 741	1.182 831	1.198 101
14	1.149 474	1.165 510	1.181 754	1.198 208	1.214 874
15	1.160 969	1.178 331	1.195 935	1.213 785	1.231 883
16	1.172 579	1.191 293	1.210 287	1.229 564	1.249 129
17	1.184 304	1.204 397	1.224 810	1.245 548	1.266 617
18	1.196 147	1.217 645	1.239 508	1.261 740	1.284 349
19	1.208 109	1.231 039	1.254 382	1.278 143	1.302 330
20	1.220 190	1.244 581	1.269 434	1.294 759	1.320 563
21	1.232 392	1.258 271	1.284 668	1.311 591	1.339 051
22	1.244 716	1.272 112	1.300 084	1.328 641	1.357 798
23	1.257 163	1.286 105	1.315 685	1.345 914	1.376 807
24	1.269 735	1.300 253	1.331 473	1.363 411	1.396 082
25	1.282 432	1.314 555	1.347 450	1.381 135	1.415 627
26	1.295 256	1.329 015	1.363 620	1.399 090	1.435 446
27	1.308 209	1.343 635	1.379 983	1.417 278	1.455 542
28	1.321 291	1.358 415	1.396 543	1.435 703	1.475 920
29	1.334 504	1.373 357	1.413 302	1.454 367	1.496 583
30	1.347 849	1.388 464	1.430 261	1.473 273	1.517 535
31	1.361 327	1.403 737	1.447 424	1.492 426	1.538 780
32	1.374 941	1.419 178	1.464 793	1.511 828	1.560 323
33	1.388 690	1.434 789	1.482 371	1.531 481	1.582 168
34	1.402 577	1.450 572	1.500 159	1.551 391	1.604 318
35	1.416 603	1.466 528	1.518 161	1.571 559	1.626 779
36	1.430 769	1.482 660	1.536 379	1.591 989	1.649 553
37	1.445 076	1.498 969	1.554 816	1.612 685	1.672 647
38	1.459 527	1.515 458	1.573 474	1.633 650	1.696 064
39	1.474 123	1.532 128	1.592 355	1.654 887	1.719 809
40	1.488 864	1.548 981	1.611 464	1.676 401	1.743 886
41	1.503 752	1.566 020	1.630 801	1.698 194	1.768 301
42	1.518 790	1.583 246	1.650 371	1.720 270	1.793 057
43	1.533 978	1.600 662	1.670 175	1.742 634	1.818 160
44	1.549 318	1.618 269	1.690 217	1.765 288	1.843 614
45	1.564 811	1.636 070	1.710 500	1.788 237	1.869 425
46	1.580 459	1.654 067	1.731 026	1.811 484	1.895 597
47	1.596 263	1.672 262	1.751 798	1.835 033	1.922 135
48	1.612 226	1.690 657	1.772 820	1.858 889	1.949 045
49	1.628 348	1.709 254	1.794 094	1.883 054	1.976 332
50	1.644 632	1.728 056	1.815 623	1.907 534	2.004 000

COMPOUNDING FACTOR FOR 1

1.5%	1.6%	1.7%	1.8%	1.9%	Year
1.015 000	1.016 000	1.017 000	1.018 000	1.019 000	1
1.030 225	1.032 256	1.034 289	1.036 324	1.038 361	2
1.045 678	1.048 772	1.051 872	1.054 978	1.058 090	3
1.061 364	1.065 552	1.069 754	1.073 967	1.078 194	4
1.077 284	1.082 601	1.087 940	1.093 299	1.098 679	5
1.093 443	1.099 923	1.106 435	1.112 978	1.119 554	6
1.109 845	1.117 522	1.125 244	1.133 012	1.140 826	7
1.126 493	1.135 402	1.144 373	1.153 406	1.162 501	8
1.143 390	1.153 568	1.163 827	1.174 167	1.184 589	9
1.160 541	1.172 026	1.183 612	1.195 302	1.207 096	10
1.177 949	1.190 778	1.203 734	1.216 818	1.230 031	11
1.195 618	1.209 830	1.224 197	1.238 721	1.253 401	12
1.213 552	1.229 188	1.245 009	1.261 018	1.277 216	13
1.231 756	1.248 855	1.266 174	1.283 716	1.301 483	14
1.250 232	1.268 836	1.287 699	1.306 823	1.326 211	15
1.268 986	1.289 138	1.309 590	1.330 346	1.351 409	16
1.288 020	1.309 764	1.331 853	1.354 292	1.377 086	17
1.307 341	1.330 720	1.354 494	1.378 669	1.403 251	18
1.326 951	1.352 012	1.377 521	1.403 485	1.429 913	19
1.346 855	1.373 644	1.400 938	1.428 748	1.457 081	20
1.367 058	1.395 622	1.424 754	1.454 465	1.484 765	21
1.387 564	1.417 952	1.448 975	1.480 646	1.512 976	22
1.408 377	1.440 639	1.473 608	1.507 297	1.541 723	23
1.429 503	1.463 690	1.498 659	1.534 429	1.571 015	24
1.450 945	1.487 109	1.524 136	1.562 048	1.600 865	25
1.472 710	1.510 902	1.550 047	1.590 165	1.631 281	26
1.494 800	1.535 077	1.576 397	1.618 788	1.662 275	27
1.517 222	1.559 638	1.603 196	1.647 926	1.693 859	28
1.539 981	1.584 592	1.630 451	1.677 589	1.726 042	29
1.563 080	1.609 946	1.658 168	1.707 786	1.758 837	30
1.586 526	1.635 705	1.686 357	1.738 526	1.792 255	31
1.610 324	1.661 876	1.715 025	1.769 819	1.826 307	32
1.634 479	1.688 466	1.744 181	1.801 676	1.861 007	33
1.658 996	1.715 482	1.773 832	1.834 106	1.896 366	34
1.683 881	1.742 929	1.803 987	1.867 120	1.932 397	35
1.709 140	1.770 816	1.834 655	1.900 728	1.969 113	36
1.734 777	1.799 149	1.865 844	1.934 941	2.006 526	37
1.760 798	1.827 936	1.897 563	1.969 770	2.044 650	38
1.787 210	1.857 183	1.929 822	2.005 226	2.083 498	39
1.814 018	1.886 898	1.962 629	2.041 320	2.123 085	40
1.841 229	1.917 088	1.995 993	2.078 064	2.163 424	41
1.868 847	1.947 761	2.029 925	2.115 469	2.204 529	42
1.896 880	1.978 925	2.064 434	2.153 547	2.246 415	43
1.925 333	2.010 588	2.099 529	2.192 311	2.289 096	44
1.954 213	2.042 758	2.135 221	2.231 773	2.332 589	45
1.983 526	2.075 442	2.171 520	2.271 945	2.376 909	46
2.013 279	2.108 649	2.208 436	2.312 840	2.422 070	47
2.043 478	2.142 387	2.245 979	2.354 471	2.468 089	48
2.074 130	2.176 665	2.284 161	2.396 851	2.514 983	49
2.105 242	2.211 492	2.322 992	2.439 995	2.562 767	50

RATE
2.0%-2.9%

COMPOUNDING FACTOR FOR 1

Year	2.0%	2.1%	2.2%	2.3%	2.4%
1	1.020 000	1.021 000	1.022 000	1.023 000	1.024 000
2	1.040 400	1.042 441	1.044 484	1.046 529	1.048 576
3	1.061 208	1.064 332	1.067 463	1.070 599	1.073 742
4	1.082 432	1.086 683	1.090 947	1.095 223	1.099 512
5	1.104 081	1.109 504	1.114 948	1.120 413	1.125 900
6	1.126 162	1.132 803	1.139 477	1.146 183	1.152 922
7	1.148 686	1.156 592	1.164 545	1.172 545	1.180 592
8	1.171 659	1.180 880	1.190 165	1.199 513	1.208 926
9	1.195 093	1.205 679	1.216 349	1.227 102	1.237 940
10	1.218 994	1.230 998	1.243 108	1.255 325	1.267 651
11	1.243 374	1.256 849	1.270 457	1.284 198	1.298 074
12	1.268 242	1.283 243	1.298 407	1.313 734	1.329 228
13	1.293 607	1.310 191	1.326 972	1.343 950	1.361 129
14	1.319 479	1.337 705	1.356 165	1.374 861	1.393 797
15	1.345 868	1.365 797	1.386 001	1.406 483	1.427 248
16	1.372 786	1.394 479	1.416 493	1.438 832	1.461 502
17	1.400 241	1.423 763	1.447 656	1.471 925	1.496 578
18	1.428 246	1.453 662	1.479 504	1.505 780	1.532 496
19	1.456 811	1.484 189	1.512 053	1.540 413	1.569 275
20	1.485 947	1.515 357	1.545 318	1.575 842	1.606 938
21	1.515 666	1.547 179	1.579 315	1.612 086	1.645 505
22	1.545 980	1.579 670	1.614 060	1.649 164	1.684 997
23	1.576 899	1.612 843	1.649 569	1.687 095	1.725 437
24	1.608 437	1.646 713	1.685 860	1.725 898	1.766 847
25	1.640 606	1.681 294	1.722 949	1.765 594	1.809 251
26	1.673 418	1.716 601	1.760 854	1.806 203	1.852 673
27	1.706 886	1.752 649	1.799 593	1.847 745	1.897 138
28	1.741 024	1.789 455	1.839 184	1.890 243	1.942 669
29	1.775 845	1.827 034	1.879 646	1.933 719	1.989 293
30	1.811 362	1.865 401	1.920 998	1.978 195	2.037 036
31	1.847 589	1.904 575	1.963 260	2.023 693	2.085 925
32	1.884 541	1.944 571	2.006 451	2.070 238	2.135 987
33	1.922 231	1.985 407	2.050 593	2.117 853	2.187 251
34	1.960 676	2.027 100	2.095 706	2.166 564	2.239 745
35	1.999 890	2.069 669	2.141 812	2.216 395	2.293 499
36	2.039 887	2.113 132	2.188 932	2.267 372	2.348 543
37	2.080 685	2.157 508	2.237 088	2.319 522	2.404 908
38	2.122 299	2.202 816	2.286 304	2.372 871	2.462 625
39	2.164 745	2.249 075	2.336 603	2.427 447	2.521 728
40	2.208 040	2.296 306	2.388 008	2.483 278	2.582 250
41	2.252 200	2.344 528	2.440 544	2.540 393	2.644 224
42	2.297 244	2.393 763	2.494 236	2.598 822	2.707 685
43	2.343 189	2.444 032	2.549 110	2.658 595	2.772 670
44	2.390 053	2.495 357	2.605 190	2.719 743	2.839 214
45	2.437 854	2.547 759	2.662 504	2.782 297	2.907 355
46	2.486 611	2.601 262	2.721 079	2.846 290	2.977 131
47	2.536 344	2.655 889	2.780 943	2.911 755	3.048 583
48	2.587 070	2.711 662	2.842 124	2.978 725	3.121 749
49	2.638 812	2.768 607	2.904 651	3.047 236	3.196 671
50	2.691 588	2.826 748	2.968 553	3.117 322	3.273 391

COMPOUNDING FACTOR FOR 1

2.5%	2.6%	2.7%	2.8%	2.9%	Year
1.025 000	1.026 000	1.027 000	1.028 000	1.029 000	1
1.050 625	1.052 676	1.054 729	1.056 784	1.058 841	2
1.076 891	1.080 046	1.083 207	1.086 374	1.089 547	3
1.103 813	1.108 127	1.112 453	1.116 792	1.121 144	4
1.131 408	1.136 938	1.142 490	1.148 063	1.153 657	5
1.159 693	1.166 498	1.173 337	1.180 208	1.187 114	6
1.188 686	1.196 827	1.205 017	1.213 254	1.221 540	7
1.218 403	1.227 945	1.237 552	1.247 225	1.256 964	8
1.248 863	1.259 871	1.270 966	1.282 148	1.293 416	9
1.280 085	1.292 628	1.305 282	1.318 048	1.330 926	10
1.312 087	1.326 236	1.340 525	1.354 953	1.369 522	11
1.344 889	1.360 719	1.376 719	1.392 892	1.409 238	12
1.378 511	1.396 097	1.413 890	1.431 893	1.450 106	13
1.412 974	1.432 396	1.452 066	1.471 986	1.492 159	14
1.448 298	1.469 638	1.491 271	1.513 201	1.535 432	15
1.484 506	1.507 849	1.531 536	1.555 571	1.579 960	16
1.521 618	1.547 053	1.572 887	1.599 127	1.625 778	17
1.559 659	1.587 276	1.615 355	1.643 903	1.672 926	18
1.598 650	1.628 545	1.658 970	1.689 932	1.721 441	19
1.638 616	1.670 888	1.703 762	1.737 250	1.771 363	20
1.679 582	1.714 331	1.749 763	1.785 893	1.822 732	21
1.721 571	1.758 903	1.797 007	1.835 898	1.875 591	22
1.764 611	1.804 635	1.845 526	1.887 303	1.929 984	23
1.808 726	1.851 555	1.895 355	1.940 148	1.985 953	24
1.853 944	1.899 696	1.946 530	1.994 472	2.043 546	25
1.900 293	1.949 088	1.999 086	2.050 317	2.102 809	26
1.947 800	1.999 764	2.053 062	2.107 726	2.163 790	27
1.996 495	2.051 758	2.108 494	2.166 742	2.226 540	28
2.046 407	2.105 104	2.165 424	2.227 411	2.291 110	29
2.097 568	2.159 836	2.223 890	2.289 778	2.357 552	30
2.150 007	2.215 992	2.283 935	2.353 892	2.425 921	31
2.203 757	2.273 608	2.345 601	2.419 801	2.496 273	32
2.258 851	2.332 722	2.408 933	2.487 556	2.568 664	33
2.315 322	2.393 372	2.473 974	2.557 207	2.643 156	34
2.373 205	2.455 600	2.540 771	2.628 809	2.719 807	35
2.432 535	2.519 446	2.609 372	2.702 416	2.798 682	36
2.493 349	2.584 951	2.679 825	2.778 083	2.879 843	37
2.555 682	2.652 160	2.752 180	2.855 869	2.963 359	38
2.619 574	2.721 116	2.826 489	2.935 834	3.049 296	39
2.685 064	2.791 865	2.902 804	3.018 037	3.137 726	40
2.752 190	2.864 454	2.981 180	3.102 542	3.228 720	41
2.820 995	2.938 929	3.061 672	3.189 413	3.322 353	42
2.891 520	3.015 342	3.144 337	3.278 717	3.418 701	43
2.963 808	3.093 740	3.229 234	3.370 521	3.517 843	44
3.037 903	3.174 178	3.316 423	3.464 896	3.619 861	45
3.113 851	3.256 706	3.405 967	3.561 913	3.724 837	46
3.191 697	3.341 381	3.497 928	3.661 646	3.832 857	47
3.271 490	3.428 257	3.592 372	3.764 172	3.944 010	48
3.353 277	3.517 391	3.689 366	3.869 569	4.058 386	49
3.437 109	3.608 843	3.788 979	3.977 917	4.176 079	50

RATE
3.0%-3.9%

COMPOUNDING FACTOR FOR 1

Year	3.0%	3.1%	3.2%	3.3%	3.4%
1	1.030 000	1.031 000	1.032 000	1.033 000	1.034 000
2	1.060 900	1.062 961	1.065 024	1.067 089	1.069 156
3	1.092 727	1.095 913	1.099 105	1.102 303	1.105 507
4	1.125 509	1.129 886	1.134 276	1.138 679	1.143 095
5	1.159 274	1.164 913	1.170 573	1.176 255	1.181 960
6	1.194 052	1.201 025	1.208 031	1.215 072	1.222 146
7	1.229 874	1.238 257	1.246 688	1.255 169	1.263 699
8	1.266 770	1.276 643	1.286 582	1.296 590	1.306 665
9	1.304 773	1.316 218	1.327 753	1.339 377	1.351 092
10	1.343 916	1.357 021	1.370 241	1.383 577	1.397 029
11	1.384 234	1.399 089	1.414 089	1.429 235	1.444 528
12	1.425 761	1.442 461	1.459 340	1.476 399	1.493 642
13	1.468 534	1.487 177	1.506 038	1.525 121	1.544 426
14	1.512 590	1.533 279	1.554 232	1.575 450	1.596 936
15	1.557 967	1.580 811	1.603 967	1.627 439	1.651 232
16	1.604 706	1.629 816	1.655 294	1.681 145	1.707 374
17	1.652 848	1.680 341	1.708 263	1.736 623	1.765 425
18	1.702 433	1.732 431	1.762 928	1.793 931	1.825 449
19	1.753 506	1.786 136	1.819 342	1.853 131	1.887 514
20	1.806 111	1.841 507	1.877 561	1.914 284	1.951 690
21	1.860 295	1.898 593	1.937 642	1.977 456	2.018 047
22	1.916 103	1.957 450	1.999 647	2.042 712	2.086 661
23	1.973 587	2.018 131	2.063 636	2.110 121	2.157 607
24	2.032 794	2.080 693	2.129 672	2.179 755	2.230 966
25	2.093 778	2.145 194	2.197 822	2.251 687	2.306 819
26	2.156 591	2.211 695	2.268 152	2.325 993	2.385 251
27	2.221 289	2.280 258	2.340 733	2.402 751	2.466 349
28	2.287 928	2.350 946	2.415 636	2.482 041	2.550 205
29	2.356 566	2.423 825	2.492 937	2.563 949	2.636 912
30	2.427 262	2.498 964	2.572 710	2.648 559	2.726 567
31	2.500 080	2.576 432	2.655 037	2.735 961	2.819 270
32	2.575 083	2.656 301	2.739 998	2.826 248	2.915 125
33	2.652 335	2.738 646	2.827 678	2.919 514	3.014 240
34	2.731 905	2.823 544	2.918 164	3.015 858	3.116 724
35	2.813 862	2.911 074	3.011 545	3.115 382	3.222 692
36	2.898 278	3.001 318	3.107 915	3.218 189	3.332 264
37	2.985 227	3.094 358	3.207 368	3.324 389	3.445 561
38	3.074 783	3.190 284	3.310 004	3.434 094	3.562 710
39	3.167 027	3.289 182	3.415 924	3.547 419	3.683 842
40	3.262 038	3.391 147	3.525 234	3.664 484	3.809 093
41	3.359 899	3.496 273	3.638 041	3.785 412	3.938 602
42	3.460 696	3.604 657	3.754 458	3.910 331	4.072 514
43	3.564 517	3.716 401	3.874 601	4.039 372	4.210 980
44	3.671 452	3.831 610	3.998 588	4.172 671	4.354 153
45	3.781 596	3.950 390	4.126 543	4.310 369	4.502 194
46	3.895 044	4.072 852	4.258 592	4.452 611	4.655 269
47	4.011 895	4.199 110	4.394 867	4.599 548	4.813 548
48	4.132 252	4.329 283	4.535 503	4.751 333	4.977 209
49	4.256 219	4.463 490	4.680 639	4.908 127	5.146 434
50	4.383 906	4.601 859	4.830 420	5.070 095	5.321 413

RATE
3.0%-3.9%

COMPOUNDING FACTOR FOR 1

3.5%	3.6%	3.7%	3.8%	3.9%	Year
1.035 000	1.036 000	1.037 000	1.038 000	1.039 000	1
1.071 225	1.073 296	1.075 369	1.077 444	1.079 521	2
1.108 718	1.111 935	1.115 158	1.118 387	1.121 622	3
1.147 523	1.151 964	1.156 418	1.160 886	1.165 366	4
1.187 686	1.193 435	1.199 206	1.204 999	1.210 815	5
1.229 255	1.236 399	1.243 577	1.250 789	1.258 037	6
1.272 279	1.280 909	1.289 589	1.298 319	1.307 100	7
1.316 809	1.327 022	1.337 304	1.347 655	1.358 077	8
1.362 897	1.374 795	1.386 784	1.398 866	1.411 042	9
1.410 599	1.424 287	1.438 095	1.452 023	1.466 073	10
1.459 970	1.475 561	1.491 304	1.507 200	1.523 249	11
1.511 069	1.528 682	1.546 483	1.564 474	1.582 656	12
1.563 956	1.583 714	1.603 703	1.623 924	1.644 380	13
1.618 695	1.640 728	1.663 040	1.685 633	1.708 511	14
1.675 349	1.699 794	1.724 572	1.749 687	1.775 142	15
1.733 986	1.760 987	1.788 381	1.816 175	1.844 373	16
1.794 676	1.824 382	1.854 551	1.885 189	1.916 304	17
1.857 489	1.890 060	1.923 170	1.956 827	1.991 039	18
1.922 501	1.958 102	1.994 327	2.031 186	2.068 690	19
1.989 789	2.028 594	2.068 117	2.108 371	2.149 369	20
2.059 431	2.101 623	2.144 637	2.188 489	2.233 194	21
2.131 512	2.177 282	2.223 989	2.271 652	2.320 289	22
2.206 114	2.255 664	2.306 277	2.357 975	2.410 780	23
2.283 328	2.336 868	2.391 609	2.447 578	2.504 801	24
2.363 245	2.420 995	2.480 098	2.540 586	2.602 488	25
2.445 959	2.508 151	2.571 862	2.637 128	2.703 985	26
2.531 567	2.598 444	2.667 021	2.737 339	2.809 440	27
2.620 172	2.691 988	2.765 701	2.841 358	2.919 008	28
2.711 878	2.788 900	2.868 032	2.949 329	3.032 850	29
2.806 794	2.889 300	2.974 149	3.061 404	3.151 131	30
2.905 031	2.993 315	3.084 192	3.177 737	3.274 025	31
3.006 708	3.101 074	3.198 307	3.298 491	3.401 712	32
3.111 942	3.212 713	3.316 645	3.423 834	3.534 379	33
3.220 860	3.328 371	3.439 361	3.553 939	3.672 219	34
3.333 590	3.448 192	3.566 617	3.688 989	3.815 436	35
3.450 266	3.572 327	3.698 582	3.829 171	3.964 238	36
3.571 025	3.700 931	3.835 429	3.974 679	4.118 843	37
3.696 011	3.834 164	3.977 340	4.125 717	4.279 478	38
3.825 372	3.972 194	4.124 502	4.282 494	4.446 378	39
3.959 260	4.115 193	4.277 108	4.445 229	4.619 786	40
4.097 834	4.263 340	4.435 361	4.614 148	4.799 958	41
4.241 258	4.416 820	4.599 470	4.789 485	4.987 157	42
4.389 702	4.575 826	4.769 650	4.971 486	5.181 656	43
4.543 342	4.740 556	4.946 127	5.160 402	5.383 740	44
4.702 359	4.911 216	5.129 134	5.356 498	5.593 706	45
4.866 941	5.088 019	5.318 912	5.560 044	5.811 861	46
5.037 284	5.271 188	5.515 712	5.771 326	6.038 523	47
5.213 589	5.460 951	5.719 793	5.990 637	6.274 026	48
5.396 065	5.657 545	5.931 425	6.218 281	6.518 713	49
5.584 927	5.861 217	6.150 888	6.454 575	6.772 942	50

RATE
4.0%-4.9%

COMPOUNDING FACTOR FOR 1

Year	4.0%	4.1%	4.2%	4.3%	4.4%
1	1.040 000	1.041 000	1.042 000	1.043 000	1.044 000
2	1.081 600	1.083 681	1.085 764	1.087 849	1.089 936
3	1.124 864	1.128 112	1.131 366	1.134 627	1.137 893
4	1.169 859	1.174 365	1.178 883	1.183 415	1.187 960
5	1.216 653	1.222 513	1.228 397	1.234 302	1.240 231
6	1.265 319	1.272 637	1.279 989	1.287 377	1.294 801
7	1.315 932	1.324 815	1.333 749	1.342 735	1.351 772
8	1.368 569	1.379 132	1.389 766	1.400 472	1.411 250
9	1.423 312	1.435 676	1.448 136	1.460 692	1.473 345
10	1.480 244	1.494 539	1.508 958	1.523 502	1.538 172
11	1.539 454	1.555 815	1.572 334	1.589 013	1.605 852
12	1.601 032	1.619 604	1.638 372	1.657 340	1.676 509
13	1.665 074	1.686 007	1.707 184	1.728 606	1.750 276
14	1.731 676	1.755 134	1.778 886	1.802 936	1.827 288
15	1.800 944	1.827 094	1.853 599	1.880 462	1.907 689
16	1.872 981	1.902 005	1.931 450	1.961 322	1.991 627
17	1.947 900	1.979 987	2.012 571	2.045 659	2.079 258
18	2.025 817	2.061 167	2.097 099	2.133 622	2.170 746
19	2.106 849	2.145 675	2.185 177	2.225 368	2.266 259
20	2.191 123	2.233 647	2.276 955	2.321 059	2.365 974
21	2.278 768	2.325 227	2.372 587	2.420 864	2.470 077
22	2.369 919	2.420 561	2.472 235	2.524 962	2.578 760
23	2.464 716	2.519 804	2.576 069	2.633 535	2.692 226
24	2.563 304	2.623 116	2.684 264	2.746 777	2.810 684
25	2.665 836	2.730 664	2.797 003	2.864 888	2.934 354
26	2.772 470	2.842 621	2.914 477	2.988 079	3.063 465
27	2.883 369	2.959 169	3.036 885	3.116 566	3.198 258
28	2.998 703	3.080 494	3.164 435	3.250 578	3.338 981
29	3.118 651	3.206 795	3.297 341	3.390 353	3.485 896
30	3.243 398	3.338 273	3.435 829	3.536 138	3.639 276
31	3.373 133	3.475 142	3.580 134	3.688 192	3.799 404
32	3.508 059	3.617 623	3.730 500	3.846 785	3.966 578
33	3.648 381	3.765 946	3.887 181	4.012 196	4.141 107
34	3.794 316	3.920 350	4.050 442	4.184 721	4.323 316
35	3.946 089	4.081 084	4.220 561	4.364 664	4.513 542
36	4.103 933	4.248 408	4.397 824	4.552 344	4.712 137
37	4.268 090	4.422 593	4.582 533	4.748 095	4.919 472
38	4.438 813	4.603 920	4.774 999	4.952 263	5.135 928
39	4.616 366	4.792 680	4.975 549	5.165 211	5.361 909
40	4.801 021	4.989 180	5.184 522	5.387 315	5.597 833
41	4.993 061	5.193 736	5.402 272	5.618 969	5.844 138
42	5.192 784	5.406 680	5.629 168	5.860 585	6.101 280
43	5.400 495	5.628 354	5.865 593	6.112 590	6.369 736
44	5.616 515	5.859 116	6.111 948	6.375 431	6.650 005
45	5.841 176	6.099 340	6.368 650	6.649 575	6.942 605
46	6.074 823	6.349 413	6.636 133	6.935 507	7.248 079
47	6.317 816	6.609 739	6.914 850	7.233 733	7.566 995
48	6.570 528	6.880 738	7.205 274	7.544 784	7.899 943
49	6.833 349	7.162 848	7.507 896	7.869 210	8.247 540
50	7.106 683	7.456 525	7.823 227	8.207 586	8.610 432

RATE
4.0%-4.9%

COMPOUNDING FACTOR FOR 1

4.5%	4.6%	4.7%	4.8%	4.9%	Year
1.045 000	1.046 000	1.047 000	1.048 000	1.049 000	1
1.092 025	1.094 116	1.096 209	1.098 304	1.100 401	2
1.141 166	1.144 445	1.147 731	1.151 023	1.154 321	3
1.192 519	1.197 090	1.201 674	1.206 272	1.210 882	4
1.246 182	1.252 156	1.258 153	1.264 173	1.270 216	5
1.302 260	1.309 755	1.317 286	1.324 853	1.332 456	6
1.360 862	1.370 004	1.379 198	1.388 446	1.397 747	7
1.422 101	1.433 024	1.444 021	1.455 091	1.466 236	8
1.486 095	1.498 943	1.511 890	1.524 936	1.538 082	9
1.552 969	1.567 895	1.582 949	1.598 133	1.613 448	10
1.622 853	1.640 018	1.657 347	1.674 843	1.692 507	11
1.695 881	1.715 458	1.735 243	1.755 235	1.775 439	12
1.772 196	1.794 370	1.816 799	1.839 487	1.862 436	13
1.851 945	1.876 911	1.902 188	1.927 782	1.953 695	14
1.935 282	1.963 248	1.991 591	2.020 316	2.049 426	15
2.022 370	2.053 558	2.085 196	2.117 291	2.149 848	16
2.113 377	2.148 022	2.183 200	2.218 921	2.255 191	17
2.208 479	2.246 831	2.285 811	2.325 429	2.365 695	18
2.307 860	2.350 185	2.393 244	2.437 050	2.481 614	19
2.411 714	2.458 293	2.505 726	2.554 028	2.603 213	20
2.520 241	2.571 375	2.623 495	2.676 621	2.730 771	21
2.633 652	2.689 658	2.746 800	2.805 099	2.864 579	22
2.752 166	2.813 382	2.875 899	2.939 744	3.004 943	23
2.876 014	2.942 798	3.011 067	3.080 852	3.152 185	24
3.005 434	3.078 167	3.152 587	3.228 733	3.306 642	25
3.140 679	3.219 762	3.300 758	3.383 712	3.468 668	26
3.282 010	3.367 871	3.455 894	3.546 130	3.638 632	27
3.429 700	3.522 793	3.618 321	3.716 344	3.816 925	28
3.584 036	3.684 842	3.788 382	3.894 729	4.003 955	29
3.745 318	3.854 345	3.966 436	4.081 676	4.200 149	30
3.913 857	4.031 644	4.152 858	4.277 596	4.405 956	31
4.089 981	4.217 100	4.348 043	4.482 921	4.621 848	32
4.274 030	4.411 087	4.552 401	4.698 101	4.848 318	33
4.466 362	4.613 997	4.766 364	4.923 610	5.085 886	34
4.667 348	4.826 240	4.990 383	5.159 943	5.335 094	35
4.877 378	5.048 248	5.224 931	5.407 620	5.596 514	36
5.096 860	5.280 467	5.470 503	5.667 186	5.870 743	37
5.326 219	5.523 368	5.727 616	5.939 211	6.158 409	38
5.565 899	5.777 443	5.996 814	6.224 293	6.460 171	39
5.816 365	6.043 206	6.278 664	6.523 059	6.776 720	40
6.078 101	6.321 193	6.573 762	6.836 166	7.108 779	41
6.351 615	6.611 968	6.882 728	7.164 302	7.457 109	42
6.637 438	6.916 119	7.206 217	7.508 188	7.822 508	43
6.936 123	7.234 260	7.544 909	7.868 581	8.205 810	44
7.248 248	7.567 036	7.899 520	8.246 273	8.607 895	45
7.574 420	7.915 120	8.270 797	8.642 094	9.029 682	46
7.915 268	8.279 215	8.659 524	9.056 915	9.472 136	47
8.271 456	8.660 059	9.066 522	9.491 647	9.936 271	48
8.643 671	9.058 422	9.492 649	9.947 246	10.423 148	49
9.032 636	9.475 109	9.938 803	10.424 714	10.933 883	50

RATE
5.0%-5.9%

COMPOUNDING FACTOR FOR 1

Year	5.0%	5.1%	5.2%	5.3%	5.4%
1	1.050 000	1.051 000	1.052 000	1.053 000	1.054 000
2	1.102 500	1.104 601	1.106 704	1.108 809	1.110 916
3	1.157 625	1.160 936	1.164 253	1.167 576	1.170 905
4	1.215 506	1.220 143	1.224 794	1.229 457	1.234 134
5	1.276 282	1.282 371	1.288 483	1.294 619	1.300 778
6	1.340 096	1.347 772	1.355 484	1.363 233	1.371 020
7	1.407 100	1.416 508	1.425 969	1.435 485	1.445 055
8	1.477 455	1.488 750	1.500 120	1.511 565	1.523 088
9	1.551 328	1.564 676	1.578 126	1.591 678	1.605 334
10	1.628 895	1.644 475	1.660 188	1.676 037	1.692 022
11	1.710 339	1.728 343	1.746 518	1.764 867	1.783 392
12	1.795 856	1.816 488	1.837 337	1.858 405	1.879 695
13	1.885 649	1.909 129	1.932 879	1.956 901	1.981 198
14	1.979 932	2.006 495	2.033 388	2.060 617	2.088 183
15	2.078 928	2.108 826	2.139 125	2.169 829	2.200 945
16	2.182 875	2.216 376	2.250 359	2.284 830	2.319 796
17	2.292 018	2.329 411	2.367 378	2.405 926	2.445 065
18	2.406 619	2.448 211	2.490 481	2.533 440	2.577 098
19	2.526 950	2.573 070	2.619 987	2.667 713	2.716 262
20	2.653 298	2.704 297	2.756 226	2.809 101	2.862 940
21	2.785 963	2.842 216	2.899 550	2.957 984	3.017 539
22	2.925 261	2.987 169	3.050 326	3.114 757	3.180 486
23	3.071 524	3.139 514	3.208 943	3.279 839	3.352 232
24	3.225 100	3.299 630	3.375 808	3.453 671	3.533 252
25	3.386 355	3.467 911	3.551 350	3.636 715	3.724 048
26	3.555 673	3.644 774	3.736 020	3.829 461	3.925 147
27	3.733 456	3.830 658	3.930 293	4.032 422	4.137 105
28	3.920 129	4.026 021	4.134 669	4.246 141	4.360 508
29	4.116 136	4.231 348	4.349 671	4.471 186	4.595 976
30	4.321 942	4.447 147	4.575 854	4.708 159	4.844 158
31	4.538 039	4.673 951	4.813 799	4.957 692	5.105 743
32	4.764 941	4.912 323	5.064 116	5.220 449	5.381 453
33	5.003 189	5.162 851	5.327 450	5.497 133	5.672 051
34	5.253 348	5.426 157	5.604 478	5.788 481	5.978 342
35	5.516 015	5.702 891	5.895 911	6.095 271	6.301 173
36	5.791 816	5.993 738	6.202 498	6.418 320	6.641 436
37	6.081 407	6.299 419	6.525 028	6.758 491	7.000 074
38	6.385 477	6.620 689	6.864 329	7.116 691	7.378 078
39	6.704 751	6.958 344	7.221 274	7.493 876	7.776 494
40	7.039 989	7.313 220	7.596 781	7.891 051	8.196 424
41	7.391 988	7.686 194	7.991 813	8.309 277	8.639 031
42	7.761 588	8.078 190	8.407 388	8.749 668	9.105 539
43	8.149 667	8.490 178	8.844 572	9.213 401	9.597 238
44	8.557 150	8.923 177	9.304 490	9.701 711	10.115 489
45	8.985 008	9.378 259	9.788 323	10.215 902	10.661 725
46	9.434 258	9.856 550	10.297 316	10.757 344	11.237 458
47	9.905 971	10.359 234	10.832 776	11.327 484	11.844 281
48	10.401 270	10.887 555	11.396 081	11.927 840	12.483 872
49	10.921 333	11.442 821	11.988 677	12.560 016	13.158 002
50	11.467 400	12.026 404	12.612 088	13.225 697	13.868 534

RATE
5.0%-5.9%

COMPOUNDING FACTOR FOR 1

5.5%	5.6%	5.7%	5.8%	5.9%	Year
1.055 000	1.056 000	1.057 000	1.058 000	1.059 000	1
1.113 025	1.115 136	1.117 249	1.119 364	1.121 481	2
1.174 241	1.177 584	1.180 932	1.184 287	1.187 648	3
1.238 825	1.243 528	1.248 245	1.252 976	1.257 720	4
1.306 960	1.313 166	1.319 395	1.325 648	1.331 925	5
1.378 843	1.386 703	1.394 601	1.402 536	1.410 509	6
1.454 679	1.464 359	1.474 093	1.483 883	1.493 729	7
1.534 687	1.546 363	1.558 116	1.569 948	1.581 859	8
1.619 094	1.632 959	1.646 929	1.661 005	1.675 188	9
1.708 144	1.724 405	1.740 804	1.757 344	1.774 024	10
1.802 092	1.820 971	1.840 030	1.859 269	1.878 692	11
1.901 207	1.922 946	1.944 912	1.967 107	1.989 535	12
2.005 774	2.030 631	2.055 771	2.081 199	2.106 917	13
2.116 091	2.144 346	2.172 950	2.201 909	2.231 225	14
2.232 476	2.264 429	2.296 809	2.329 620	2.362 868	15
2.355 263	2.391 237	2.427 727	2.464 738	2.502 277	16
2.484 802	2.525 147	2.566 107	2.607 692	2.649 911	17
2.621 466	2.666 555	2.712 375	2.758 938	2.806 256	18
2.765 647	2.815 882	2.866 981	2.918 957	2.971 825	19
2.917 757	2.973 571	3.030 399	3.088 256	3.147 163	20
3.078 234	3.140 091	3.203 131	3.267 375	3.332 845	21
3.247 537	3.315 936	3.385 710	3.456 883	3.529 483	22
3.426 152	3.501 629	3.578 695	3.657 382	3.737 723	23
3.614 590	3.697 720	3.782 681	3.869 510	3.958 248	24
3.813 392	3.904 792	3.998 294	4.093 942	4.191 785	25
4.023 129	4.123 461	4.226 196	4.331 391	4.439 100	26
4.244 401	4.354 375	4.467 090	4.582 611	4.701 007	27
4.477 843	4.598 220	4.721 714	4.848 403	4.978 367	28
4.724 124	4.855 720	4.990 851	5.129 610	5.272 090	29
4.983 951	5.127 640	5.275 330	5.427 128	5.583 144	30
5.258 069	5.414 788	5.576 024	5.741 901	5.912 549	31
5.547 262	5.718 016	5.893 857	6.074 931	6.261 390	32
5.852 362	6.038 225	6.229 807	6.427 277	6.630 812	33
6.174 242	6.376 366	6.584 906	6.800 059	7.022 029	34
6.513 825	6.733 442	6.960 245	7.194 463	7.436 329	35
6.872 085	7.110 515	7.356 979	7.611 742	7.875 073	36
7.250 050	7.508 704	7.776 327	8.053 223	8.339 702	37
7.648 803	7.929 191	8.219 578	8.520 310	8.831 744	38
8.069 487	8.373 226	8.688 094	9.014 487	9.352 817	39
8.513 309	8.842 127	9.183 315	9.537 328	9.904 633	40
8.981 541	9.337 286	9.706 764	10.090 493	10.489 007	41
9.475 525	9.860 174	10.260 050	10.675 741	11.107 858	42
9.996 679	10.412 343	10.844 873	11.294 934	11.763 222	43
10.546 497	10.995 435	11.463 030	11.950 041	12.457 252	44
11.126 554	11.611 179	12.116 423	12.643 143	13.192 230	45
11.738 515	12.261 405	12.807 059	13.376 445	13.970 571	46
12.384 133	12.948 044	13.537 062	14.152 279	14.794 835	47
13.065 260	13.673 134	14.308 674	14.973 111	15.667 730	48
13.783 849	14.438 830	15.124 268	15.841 552	16.592 126	49
14.541 961	15.247 404	15.986 352	16.760 362	17.571 062	50

RATE
6.0%-6.9%

COMPOUNDING FACTOR FOR 1

Year	6.0%	6.1%	6.2%	6.3%	6.4%
1	1.060 000	1.061 000	1.062 000	1.063 000	1.064 000
2	1.123 600	1.125 721	1.127 844	1.129 969	1.132 096
3	1.191 016	1.194 390	1.197 770	1.201 157	1.204 550
4	1.262 477	1.267 248	1.272 032	1.276 830	1.281 641
5	1.338 226	1.344 550	1.350 898	1.357 270	1.363 666
6	1.418 519	1.426 567	1.434 654	1.442 778	1.450 941
7	1.503 630	1.513 588	1.523 602	1.533 673	1.543 801
8	1.593 848	1.605 917	1.618 066	1.630 295	1.642 605
9	1.689 479	1.703 878	1.718 386	1.733 003	1.747 731
10	1.790 848	1.807 814	1.824 926	1.842 182	1.859 586
11	1.898 299	1.918 091	1.938 071	1.958 240	1.978 600
12	2.012 196	2.035 095	2.058 231	2.081 609	2.105 230
13	2.132 928	2.159 235	2.185 842	2.212 750	2.239 965
14	2.260 904	2.290 949	2.321 364	2.352 154	2.383 322
15	2.396 558	2.430 697	2.465 289	2.500 339	2.535 855
16	2.540 352	2.578 969	2.618 136	2.657 861	2.698 150
17	2.692 773	2.736 286	2.780 461	2.825 306	2.870 831
18	2.854 339	2.903 200	2.952 849	3.003 300	3.054 565
19	3.025 600	3.080 295	3.135 926	3.192 508	3.250 057
20	3.207 135	3.268 193	3.330 354	3.393 636	3.458 060
21	3.399 564	3.467 553	3.536 835	3.607 435	3.679 376
22	3.603 537	3.679 073	3.756 119	3.834 704	3.914 856
23	3.819 750	3.903 497	3.988 999	4.076 290	4.165 407
24	4.048 935	4.141 610	4.236 317	4.333 096	4.431 993
25	4.291 871	4.394 248	4.498 968	4.606 081	4.715 641
26	4.549 383	4.662 297	4.777 904	4.896 265	5.017 442
27	4.822 346	4.946 698	5.074 134	5.204 729	5.338 558
28	5.111 687	5.248 446	5.388 731	5.532 627	5.680 226
29	5.418 388	5.568 601	5.722 832	5.881 183	6.043 760
30	5.743 491	5.908 286	6.077 647	6.251 697	6.430 561
31	6.088 101	6.268 692	6.454 462	6.645 554	6.842 117
32	6.453 387	6.651 082	6.854 638	7.064 224	7.280 012
33	6.840 590	7.056 798	7.279 626	7.509 270	7.745 933
34	7.251 025	7.487 262	7.730 963	7.982 354	8.241 672
35	7.686 087	7.943 985	8.210 282	8.485 242	8.769 139
36	8.147 252	8.428 568	8.719 320	9.019 813	9.330 364
37	8.636 087	8.942 711	9.259 918	9.588 061	9.927 508
38	9.154 252	9.488 217	9.834 032	10.192 109	10.562 868
39	9.703 507	10.066 998	10.443 742	10.834 212	11.238 892
40	10.285 718	10.681 085	11.091 254	11.516 767	11.958 181
41	10.902 861	11.332 631	11.778 912	12.242 323	12.723 504
42	11.557 033	12.023 921	12.509 205	13.013 590	13.537 809
43	12.250 455	12.757 380	13.284 776	13.833 446	14.404 229
44	12.985 482	13.535 581	14.108 432	14.704 953	15.326 099
45	13.764 611	14.361 251	14.983 154	15.631 365	16.306 969
46	14.590 487	15.237 287	15.912 110	16.616 141	17.350 616
47	15.465 917	16.166 762	16.898 661	17.662 958	18.461 055
48	16.393 872	17.152 934	17.946 378	18.775 724	19.642 562
49	17.377 504	18.199 263	19.059 053	19.958 595	20.899 686
50	18.420 154	19.309 418	20.240 714	21.215 000	22.237 266

RATE
6.0%-6.9%

COMPOUNDING FACTOR FOR 1

6.5%	6.6%	6.7%	6.8%	6.9%	Year
1.065 000	1.066 000	1.067 000	1.068 000	1.069 000	1
1.134 225	1.136 356	1.138 489	1.140 624	1.142 761	2
1.207 950	1.211 355	1.214 768	1.218 186	1.221 612	3
1.286 466	1.291 305	1.296 157	1.301 023	1.305 903	4
1.370 087	1.376 531	1.383 000	1.389 493	1.396 010	5
1.459 142	1.467 382	1.475 661	1.483 978	1.492 335	6
1.553 987	1.564 229	1.574 530	1.584 889	1.595 306	7
1.654 996	1.667 468	1.680 023	1.692 661	1.705 382	8
1.762 570	1.777 521	1.792 585	1.807 762	1.823 053	9
1.877 137	1.894 838	1.912 688	1.930 690	1.948 844	10
1.999 151	2.019 897	2.040 838	2.061 977	2.083 314	11
2.129 096	2.153 210	2.177 575	2.202 191	2.227 063	12
2.267 487	2.295 322	2.323 472	2.351 940	2.380 730	13
2.414 874	2.446 813	2.479 145	2.511 872	2.545 001	14
2.571 841	2.608 303	2.645 247	2.682 679	2.720 606	15
2.739 011	2.780 451	2.822 479	2.865 102	2.908 327	16
2.917 046	2.963 961	3.011 585	3.059 929	3.109 002	17
3.106 654	3.159 582	3.213 361	3.268 004	3.323 523	18
3.308 587	3.368 115	3.428 656	3.490 228	3.552 846	19
3.523 645	3.590 410	3.658 376	3.727 564	3.797 993	20
3.752 682	3.827 377	3.903 488	3.981 038	4.060 054	21
3.996 606	4.079 984	4.165 021	4.251 748	4.340 198	22
4.256 386	4.349 263	4.444 078	4.540 867	4.639 671	23
4.533 051	4.636 315	4.741 831	4.849 646	4.959 809	24
4.827 699	4.942 312	5.059 534	5.179 422	5.302 035	25
5.141 500	5.268 504	5.398 522	5.531 623	5.667 876	26
5.475 697	5.616 225	5.760 223	5.907 773	6.058 959	27
5.831 617	5.986 896	6.146 158	6.309 502	6.477 028	28
6.210 672	6.382 031	6.557 951	6.738 548	6.923 942	29
6.614 366	6.803 245	6.997 334	7.196 769	7.401 695	30
7.044 300	7.252 260	7.466 155	7.686 150	7.912 411	31
7.502 179	7.730 909	7.966 387	8.208 808	8.458 368	32
7.989 821	8.241 149	8.500 135	8.767 007	9.041 995	33
8.509 159	8.785 065	9.069 644	9.363 163	9.665 893	34
9.062 255	9.364 879	9.677 311	9.999 858	10.332 839	35
9.651 301	9.982 961	10.325 690	10.679 849	11.045 805	36
10.278 636	10.641 836	11.017 512	11.406 078	11.807 966	37
10.946 747	11.344 197	11.755 685	12.181 692	12.622 716	38
11.658 286	12.092 915	12.543 316	13.010 047	13.493 683	39
12.416 075	12.891 047	13.383 718	13.894 730	14.424 747	40
13.223 119	13.741 856	14.280 427	14.839 571	15.420 055	41
14.082 622	14.648 818	15.237 216	15.848 662	16.484 038	42
14.997 993	15.615 640	16.258 109	16.926 371	17.621 437	43
15.972 862	16.646 273	17.347 402	18.077 365	18.837 316	44
17.011 098	17.744 927	18.509 678	19.306 625	20.137 091	45
18.116 820	18.916 092	19.749 827	20.619 476	21.526 550	46
19.294 413	20.164 554	21.073 065	22.021 600	23.011 882	47
20.548 550	21.495 415	22.484 961	23.519 069	24.599 702	48
21.884 205	22.914 112	23.991 453	25.118 366	26.297 082	49
23.306 679	24.426 443	25.598 880	26.826 415	28.111 580	50

RATE
7.0%-7.9%

COMPOUNDING FACTOR FOR 1

Year	7.0%	7.1%	7.2%	7.3%	7.4%
1	1.070 000	1.071 000	1.072 000	1.073 000	1.074 000
2	1.144 900	1.147 041	1.149 184	1.151 329	1.153 476
3	1.225 043	1.228 481	1.231 925	1.235 376	1.238 833
4	1.310 796	1.315 703	1.320 624	1.325 558	1.330 507
5	1.402 552	1.409 118	1.415 709	1.422 324	1.428 964
6	1.500 730	1.509 165	1.517 640	1.526 154	1.534 708
7	1.605 781	1.616 316	1.626 910	1.637 563	1.648 276
8	1.718 186	1.731 075	1.744 047	1.757 105	1.770 249
9	1.838 459	1.853 981	1.869 619	1.885 374	1.901 247
10	1.967 151	1.985 613	2.004 231	2.023 006	2.041 939
11	2.104 852	2.126 592	2.148 536	2.170 686	2.193 043
12	2.252 192	2.277 580	2.303 231	2.329 146	2.355 328
13	2.409 845	2.439 288	2.469 063	2.499 173	2.529 622
14	2.578 534	2.612 478	2.646 836	2.681 613	2.716 814
15	2.759 032	2.797 964	2.837 408	2.877 371	2.917 858
16	2.952 164	2.996 619	3.041 701	3.087 419	3.133 780
17	3.158 815	3.209 379	3.260 704	3.312 800	3.365 680
18	3.379 932	3.437 245	3.495 474	3.554 635	3.614 740
19	3.616 528	3.681 289	3.747 149	3.814 123	3.882 231
20	3.869 684	3.942 661	4.016 943	4.092 554	4.169 516
21	4.140 562	4.222 590	4.306 163	4.391 311	4.478 060
22	4.430 402	4.522 394	4.616 207	4.711 876	4.809 436
23	4.740 530	4.843 484	4.948 574	5.055 843	5.165 335
24	5.072 367	5.187 371	5.304 871	5.424 920	5.547 570
25	5.427 433	5.555 674	5.686 822	5.820 939	5.958 090
26	5.807 353	5.950 127	6.096 273	6.245 868	6.398 988
27	6.213 868	6.372 586	6.535 205	6.701 816	6.872 513
28	6.648 838	6.825 040	7.005 740	7.191 048	7.381 079
29	7.114 257	7.309 618	7.510 153	7.715 995	7.927 279
30	7.612 255	7.828 600	8.050 884	8.279 263	8.513 898
31	8.145 113	8.384 431	8.630 547	8.883 649	9.143 926
32	8.715 271	8.979 726	9.251 947	9.532 155	9.820 577
33	9.325 340	9.617 286	9.918 087	10.228 002	10.547 300
34	9.978 114	10.300 113	10.632 189	10.974 647	11.327 800
35	10.676 581	11.031 422	11.397 707	11.775 796	12.166 057
36	11.423 942	11.814 652	12.218 342	12.635 429	13.066 345
37	12.223 618	12.653 493	13.098 062	13.557 815	14.033 255
38	13.079 271	13.551 891	14.041 123	14.547 536	15.071 716
39	13.994 820	14.514 075	15.052 084	15.609 506	16.187 023
40	14.974 458	15.544 574	16.135 834	16.749 000	17.384 862
41	16.022 670	16.648 239	17.297 614	17.971 677	18.671 342
42	17.144 257	17.830 264	18.543 042	19.283 609	20.053 021
43	18.344 355	19.096 213	19.878 141	20.691 313	21.536 945
44	19.628 460	20.452 044	21.309 367	22.201 779	23.130 679
45	21.002 452	21.904 139	22.843 642	23.822 508	24.842 349
46	22.472 623	23.459 333	24.488 384	25.561 551	26.680 683
47	24.045 707	25.124 946	26.251 548	27.427 545	28.655 054
48	25.728 907	26.908 817	28.141 659	29.429 756	30.775 527
49	27.529 930	28.819 343	30.167 859	31.670 120	33.052 917
50	29.457 025	30.865 516	32.339 944	33.883 331	35.498 832

RATE
7.0%-7.9%

COMPOUNDING FACTOR FOR 1

7.5%	7.6%	7.7%	7.8%	7.9%	Year
1.075 000	1.076 000	1.077 000	1.078 000	1.079 000	1
1.155 625	1.157 776	1.159 929	1.162 084	1.164 241	2
1.242 297	1.245 767	1.249 244	1.252 727	1.256 216	3
1.335 469	1.340 445	1.345 435	1.350 439	1.355 457	4
1.435 629	1.442 319	1.449 034	1.455 773	1.462 538	5
1.543 302	1.551 935	1.560 609	1.569 324	1.578 079	6
1.659 049	1.669 882	1.680 776	1.691 731	1.702 747	7
1.783 478	1.796 794	1.810 196	1.823 686	1.837 264	8
1.917 239	1.933 350	1.949 581	1.965 934	1.982 408	9
2.061 032	2.080 284	2.099 699	2.119 276	2.139 018	10
2.215 609	2.238 386	2.261 376	2.284 580	2.308 000	11
2.381 780	2.408 503	2.435 502	2.462 777	2.490 332	12
2.560 413	2.591 550	2.623 035	2.654 874	2.687 069	13
2.752 444	2.788 507	2.825 009	2.861 954	2.899 347	14
2.958 877	3.000 434	3.042 535	3.085 186	3.128 396	15
3.180 793	3.228 467	3.276 810	3.325 831	3.375 539	16
3.419 353	3.473 830	3.529 124	3.585 246	3.642 206	17
3.675 804	3.737 842	3.800 867	3.864 895	3.929 941	18
3.951 489	4.021 917	4.093 534	4.166 357	4.240 406	19
4.247 851	4.327 583	4.408 736	4.491 333	4.575 398	20
4.566 440	4.656 480	4.748 208	4.841 657	4.936 855	21
4.908 923	5.010 372	5.113 820	J.219 306	5.326 866	22
5.277 092	5.391 160	5.507 585	5.626 412	5.747 689	23
5.672 874	5.800 888	5.931 669	6.065 272	6.201 756	24
6.098 340	6.241 756	6.388 407	6.538 363	6.691 695	25
6.555 715	6.716 129	6.880 314	7.048 355	7.220 339	26
7.047 394	7.226 555	7.410 099	7.598 127	7.790 745	27
7.575 948	7.775 773	7.980 676	8.190 781	8.406 214	28
8.144 144	8.366 732	8.595 188	8.829 662	9.070 305	29
8.754 955	9.002 604	9.257 018	9.518 375	9.786 859	30
9.411 577	9.686 802	9.969 808	10.260 809	10.560 021	31
10.117 445	10.422 999	10.737 483	11.061 152	11.394 263	32
10.876 253	11.215 147	11.564 270	11.923 921	12.294 410	33
11.691 972	12.067 498	12.454 718	12.853 987	13.265 668	34
12.568 870	12.984 628	13.413 732	13.856 598	14.313 656	35
13.511 536	13.971 459	14.446 589	14.937 413	15.444 434	36
14.524 901	15.033 290	15.558 976	16.102 531	16.664 545	37
15.614 268	16.175 820	16.757 018	17.358 529	17.981 044	38
16.785 339	17.405 183	18.047 308	18.712 494	19.401 546	39
18.044 239	18.727 976	19.436 951	20.172 068	20.934 268	40
19.397 557	20.151 303	20.933 596	21.745 490	22.588 076	41
20.852 374	21.682 802	22.545 483	23.441 638	24.372 534	42
22.416 302	23.330 695	24.281 485	25.270 086	26.297 964	43
24.097 524	25.103 827	26.151 159	27.241 152	28.375 503	44
25.904 839	27.011 718	28.164 798	29.365 962	30.617 168	45
27.847 702	29.064 609	30.333 488	31.656 507	33.035 924	46
29.936 279	31.273 519	32.669 167	34.125 715	35.645 762	47
32.181 500	33.650 306	35.184 692	36.787 521	38.461 777	48
34.595 113	36.207 730	37.893 914	39.656 947	41.500 257	49
37.189 746	38.959 517	40.811 745	42.750 189	44 778 778	50

RATE
8.0%-8.9%

COMPOUNDING FACTOR FOR 1

Year	8.0%	8.1%	8.2%	8.3%	8.4%
1	1.080 000	1.081 000	1.082 000	1.083 000	1.084 000
2	1.166 400	1.168 561	1.170 724	1.172 889	1.175 056
3	1.259 712	1.263 214	1.266 723	1.270 239	1.273 761
4	1.360 489	1.365 535	1.370 595	1.375 669	1.380 757
5	1.469 328	1.476 143	1.482 983	1.489 849	1.496 740
6	1.586 874	1.595 711	1.604 588	1.613 507	1.622 466
7	1.713 824	1.724 963	1.736 164	1.747 428	1.758 754
8	1.850 930	1.864 685	1.878 530	1.892 464	1.906 489
9	1.999 005	2.015 725	2.032 569	2.049 539	2.066 634
10	2.158 925	2.178 999	2.199 240	2.219 650	2.240 231
11	2.331 639	2.355 497	2.379 578	2.403 881	2.428 411
12	2.518 170	2.546 293	2.574 703	2.603 403	2.632 397
13	2.719 624	2.752 542	2.785 829	2.819 486	2.853 518
14	2.937 194	2.975 498	3.014 267	3.053 503	3.093 214
15	3.172 169	3.216 514	3.261 436	3.306 944	3.353 044
16	3.425 943	3.477 051	3.528 874	3.581 420	3.634 700
17	3.700 018	3.758 692	3.818 242	3.878 678	3.940 014
18	3.996 019	4.063 147	4.131 338	4.200 609	4.270 975
19	4.315 701	4.392 261	4.470 107	4.549 259	4.629 737
20	4.660 957	4.748 035	4.836 656	4.926 848	5.018 635
21	5.033 834	5.132 625	5.233 262	5.335 776	5.440 201
22	5.436 540	5.548 368	5.662 389	5.778 645	5.897 178
23	5.871 464	5.997 786	6.126 705	6.258 273	6.392 541
24	6.341 181	6.483 607	6.629 095	6.777 710	6.929 514
25	6.848 475	7.008 779	7.172 681	7.340 260	7.511 593
26	7.396 353	7.576 490	7.760 841	7.949 501	8.142 567
27	7.988 061	8.190 185	8.397 230	8.609 310	8.826 543
28	8.627 106	8.853 590	9.085 803	9.323 882	9.567 972
29	9.317 275	9.570 731	9.830 839	10.097 765	10.371 682
30	10.062 657	10.345 961	10.636 967	10.935 879	11.242 903
31	10.867 669	11.183 983	11.509 199	11.843 557	12.187 307
32	11.737 083	12.089 886	12.452 953	12.826 572	13.211 041
33	12.676 050	13.069 167	13.474 095	13.891 178	14.320 768
34	13.690 134	14.127 769	14.578 971	15.044 146	15.523713
35	14.785 344	15.272 119	15.774 446	16.292 810	16.827 705
36	15.968 172	16.509 160	17.067 951	17.645 113	18.241 232
37	17.245 626	17.846 402	18.467 523	19.109 657	19.773 495
38	18.625 276	19.291 961	19.981 860	20.695 759	21.434 469
39	20.115 298	20.854 610	21.620 372	22.413 507	23.234 964
40	21.724 521	22.543 833	23.393 243	24.273 828	25.186 701
41	23.462 483	24.369 883	25.311 489	26.288 555	27.302 384
42	25.339 482	26.343 844	27.387 031	28.470 506	29.595 784
43	27.366 640	28.477 695	29.632 767	30.833 557	32.081 830
44	29.555 972	30.784 389	32.062 654	33.392 743	34.776 704
45	31.920 449	33.277 924	34.691 792	36.164 340	37.697 947
46	34.474 085	35.973 436	37.536 519	39.165 981	40.864 575
47	37.232 012	38.887 284	40.614 514	42.416 757	44.297 199
48	40.210 573	42.037 154	43.944 904	45.937 348	48.018 163
49	43.427 419	45.442 164	47.548 386	49.750 148	52.051 689
50	46.901 610	49.122 979	51.447 353	53.879 410	56.424 031

RATE
8.0%-8.9%

COMPOUNDING FACTOR FOR 1

8.5%	8.6%	8.7%	8.8%	8.9%	Year
1.085 000	1.086 000	1.087 000	1.088 000	1.089 000	1
1.177 225	1.179 396	1.181 569	1.183 744	1.185 921	2
1.277 289	1.280 824	1.284 366	1.287 913	1.291 468	3
1.385 859	1.390 975	1.396 105	1.401 250	1.406 409	4
1.503 657	1.510 599	1.517 566	1.524 560	1.531 579	5
1.631 468	1.640 510	1.649 595	1.658 721	1.667 890	6
1.770 142	1.781 594	1.793 109	1.804 689	1.816 332	7
1.920 604	1.934 811	1.949 110	1.963 501	1.977 985	8
2.083 856	2.101 205	2.118 683	2.136 289	2.154 026	9
2.260 983	2.281 909	2.303 008	2.324 283	2.345 734	10
2.453 167	2.478 153	2.503 370	2.528 820	2.554 505	11
2.661 686	2.691 274	2.721 163	2.751 356	2.781 855	12
2.887 930	2.922 723	2.957 904	2.993 475	3.029 441	13
3.133 404	3.174 078	3.215 242	3.256 901	3.299 061	14
3.399 743	3.447 048	3.494 968	3.543 508	3.592 677	15
3.688 721	3.743 495	3.799 030	3.855 337	3.912 425	16
4.002 262	4.065 435	4.129 545	4.194 606	4.260 631	17
4.342 455	4.415 062	4.488 816	4.563 732	4.639 828	18
4.711 563	4.794 758	4.879 343	4.965 340	5.052 772	19
5.112 046	5.207 107	5.303 846	5.402 290	5.502 469	20
5.546 570	5.654 918	5.765 280	5.877 692	5.992 189	21
6.018 028	6.141 241	6.266 860	6.394 929	6.525 493	22
6.529 561	6.669 388	6.812 076	6.957 682	7.106 262	23
7.084 574	7.242 955	7.404 727	7.569 958	7.738 720	24
7.686 762	7.865 849	8.048 938	8.236 115	8.427 466	25
8.340 137	8.542 313	8.749 196	8.960 893	9.177 510	26
9.049 049	9.276 951	9.510 376	9.749 451	9.994 309	27
9.818 218	10.074 769	10.337 779	10.607 403	10.883 802	28
10.652 766	10.941 199	11.237 166	11.540 854	11.852 460	29
11.558 252	11.882 143	12.214 799	12.556 450	12.907 329	30
12.540 703	12.904 007	13.277 486	13.661 417	14.056 082	31
13.606 663	14.013 751	14.432 628	14.863 622	15.307 073	32
14.763 229	15.218 934	15.688 266	16.171 621	16.669 402	33
16.018 104	16.527 762	17.053 146	17.594 723	18.152 979	34
17.379 642	17.949 150	18.536 769	19.143 059	19.768 594	35
18.856 912	19.492 777	20.149 468	20.827 648	21.527 999	36
20.459 750	21.169 156	21.902 472	22.660 481	23.443 991	37
22.198 828	22.989 703	23.807 987	24.654 604	25.530 506	38
24.085 729	24.966 817	25.879 282	26.824 209	27.802 722	39
26.133 016	27.113 964	28.130 779	29.184 739	30.277 164	40
28.354 322	29.445 765	30.578 157	31.752 996	32.971 831	41
30.764 439	31.978 100	33.238 457	34.547 260	35.906 324	42
33.379 417	34.728 217	36.130 203	37.587 419	39.101 987	43
36.216 667	37.714 844	39.273 530	40.895 111	42.582 064	44
39.295 084	40.958 320	42.690 327	44.493 881	46.371 868	45
42.635 166	44.480 736	46.404 386	48.409 343	50.498 964	46
46.259 155	48.306 079	50.441 567	52.669 365	54.993 372	47
50.191 183	52.460 402	54.829 984	57.304 269	59.887 782	48
54.457 434	56.971 996	59.600 192	62.347 045	65.217 795	49
59.086 316	61.871 588	64.785 409	67.833 585	71.022 178	50

RATE
9.0%-9.9%

COMPOUNDING FACTOR FOR 1

Year	9.0%	9.1%	9.2%	9.3%	9.4%
1	1.090 000	1.091 000	1.092 000	1.093 000	1.094 000
2	1.188 100	1.190 281	1.192 464	1.194 649	1.196 836
3	1.295 029	1.298 597	1.302 171	1.305 751	1.309 339
4	1.411 582	1.416 769	1.421 970	1.427 186	1.432 416
5	1.538 624	1.545 695	1.552 792	1.559 915	1.567 064
6	1.677 100	1.686 353	1.695 649	1.704 987	1.714 368
7	1.828 039	1.839 811	1.851 648	1.863 550	1.875 518
8	1.992 563	2.007 234	2.022 000	2.036 861	2.051 817
9	2.171 893	2.189 892	2.208 024	2.226 289	2.244 688
10	2.367 364	2.389 172	2.411 162	2.433 333	2.455 688
11	2.580 426	2.606 587	2.632 989	2.659 633	2.686 523
12	2.812 665	2.843 787	2.875 224	2.906 979	2.939 056
13	3.065 805	3.102 571	3.139 744	3.177 328	3.215 327
14	3.341 727	3.384 905	3.428 601	3.472 820	3.517 568
15	3.642 482	3.692 932	3.744 032	3.795 792	3.848 219
16	3.970 306	4.028 988	4.088 483	4.148 801	4.209 952
17	4.327 633	4.395 626	4.464 624	4.534 639	4.605 688
18	4.717 120	4.795 628	4.875 369	4.956 361	5.038 622
19	5.141 661	5.232 030	5.323 903	5.417 302	5.512 253
20	5.604 411	5.708 145	5.813 702	5.921 111	6.030 404
21	6.108 808	6.227 586	6.348 563	6.471 775	6.597 262
22	6.658 600	6.794 297	6.932 630	7.073 650	7.217 405
23	7.257 874	7.412 578	7.570 432	7.731 499	7.895 841
24	7.911 083	8.087 122	8.266 912	8.450 529	8.638 050
25	8.623 081	8.823 050	9.027 468	9.236 428	9.450 027
26	9.399 158	9.625 948	9.857 995	10.095 416	10.338 330
27	10.245 082	10.501 909	10.764 931	11.034 289	11.310 133
28	11.167 140	11.457 583	11.755 304	12.060 478	12.373 285
29	12.172 182	12.500 223	12.836 792	13.182 103	13.536 374
30	13.267 678	13.637 743	14.017 777	14.408 038	14.808 793
31	14.461 770	14.878 778	15.307 413	15.747 986	16.200 819
32	15.763 329	16.232 747	16.715 695	17.212 549	17.723 696
33	17.182 028	17.709 927	18.253 539	18.813 316	19.389 724
34	18.728 411	19.321 530	19.932 864	20.562 954	21.212 358
35	20.413 968	21.079 790	21.766 688	22.475 309	23.206 320
36	22.251 225	22.998 050	23.769 223	24.565 513	25.387 714
37	24.253 835	25.090 873	25.955 991	26.850 105	27.774 159
38	26.436 680	27.374 142	28.343 942	29.347 165	30.384 930
39	28.815 982	29.865 189	30.951 585	32.076 451	33.241 113
40	31.409 420	32.582 922	33.799 131	35.059 561	36.365 778
41	34.236 268	35.547 967	36.908 651	38.320 101	39.784 161
42	37.317 532	38.782 833	40.304 247	41.883 870	43.523 872
43	40.676 110	42.312 070	44.012 238	45.779 070	47.615 116
44	44.336 960	46.162 469	48.061 364	50.036 523	52.090 937
45	48.327 286	50.363 253	52.483 009	54.689 920	56.987 485
46	52.676 742	54.946 309	57.311 446	59.776 083	62.344 308
47	57.417 649	59.946 424	62.584 099	65.335 258	68.204 673
48	62.585 237	65.401 548	68.341 836	71.411 437	74.615 913
49	68.217 908	71.353 089	74.629 285	78.052 701	81.629 809
50	74.357 520	77.846 220	81.495 179	85.311 602	89.303 011

RATE
9.0%-9.9%

COMPOUNDING FACTOR FOR 1

9.5%	9.6%	9.7%	9.8%	9.9%	Year
1.095 000	1.096 000	1.097 000	1.098 000	1.099 000	1
1.199 025	1.201 216	1.203 409	1.205 604	1.207 801	2
1.312 932	1.316 533	1.320 140	1.323 753	1.327 373	3
1.437 661	1.442 920	1.448 193	1.453 481	1.458 783	4
1.574 239	1.581 440	1.588 668	1.595 922	1.603 203	5
1.723 791	1.733 258	1.742 769	1.752 323	1.761 920	6
1.887 552	1.899 651	1.911 817	1.924 050	1.936 350	7
2.066 869	2.082 018	2.097 264	2.112 607	2.128 049	8
2.263 222	2.281 891	2.300 698	2.319 643	2.338 725	9
2.478 228	2.500 953	2.523 866	2.546 967	2.570 259	10
2.713 659	2.741 045	2.768 681	2.796 570	2.824 715	11
2.971 457	3.004 185	3.037 243	3.070 634	3.104 362	12
3.253 745	3.292 587	3.331 856	3.371 556	3.411 693	13
3.562 851	3.608 675	3.655 045	3.701 969	3.749 451	14
3.901 322	3.955 108	4.009 585	4.064 762	4.120 647	15
4.271 948	4.334 798	4.398 515	4.463 108	4.528 591	16
4.677 783	4.750 939	4.825 171	4.900 493	4.976 921	17
5.122 172	5.207 029	5.293 212	5.380 741	5.469 636	18
5.608 778	5.706 903	5.806 654	5.908 054	6.011 130	19
6.141 612	6.254 766	6.369 899	6.487 043	6.606 232	20
6.725 065	6.855 224	6.987 779	7.122 774	7.260 249	21
7.363 946	7.513 325	7.665 594	7.820 805	7.979 014	22
8.063 521	8.234 605	8.409 156	8.587 244	8.768 937	23
8.829 556	9.025 127	9.224 845	9.428 794	9.637 061	24
9.668 364	9.891 539	10.119 655	10.352 816	10.591 130	25
10.586 858	10.841 126	11.101 261	11.367 392	11.639 652	26
11.592 610	11.881 875	12.178 083	12.481 397	12.791 978	27
12.693 908	13.022 534	13.359 358	13.704 573	14.058 384	28
13.899 829	14.272 698	14.655 215	15.047 622	15.450 164	29
15.220 313	15.642 877	16.076 771	16.522 289	16.979 730	30
16.666 242	17.144 593	17.636 218	18.141 473	18.660 723	31
18.249 535	18.790 474	19.346 931	19.919 337	20.508 135	32
19.983 241	20.594 359	21.223 583	21.871 432	22.538 440	33
21.881 649	22.571 418	23.282 271	24.014 833	24.769 745	34
23.960 406	24.738 274	25.540 651	26.368 286	27.221 950	35
26.236 644	27.113 148	28.018 094	28.952 378	29.916 923	36
28.729 126	29.716 011	30.735 849	31.789 711	32.878 699	37
31.458 393	32.568 748	33.717 227	34.905 103	36.133 690	38
34.446 940	35.695 347	36.987 798	38.325 803	39.710 925	39
37.719 399	39.122 101	40.575 614	42.081 732	43.642 307	40
41.302 742	42.877 822	44.511 449	46.205 742	47.962 895	41
45.226 503	46.994 093	48.829 059	50.733 904	52.711 222	42
49.523 020	51.505 526	53.565 478	55.705 827	57.929 633	43
54.227 707	56.450 057	58.761 329	61.164 998	63.664 666	44
59.379 340	61.869 262	64.461 178	67.159 168	69.967 468	45
65.020 377	67.808 711	70.713 913	73.740 766	76.894 248	46
71.197 313	74.318 348	77.573 162	80.967 361	84.506 778	47
77.961 057	81.452 909	85.097 759	88.902 163	92.872 949	48
85.367 358	89.272 388	93.352 242	97.614 575	102.067 371	49
93.477 257	97.842 538	102.407 409	107.180 803	112.172 041	50

RATE
10.0%-10.9%

COMPOUNDING FACTOR FOR 1

Year	10.0%	10.1%	10.2%	10.3%	10.4%
1	1.100 000	1.101 000	1.102 000	1.103 000	1.104 000
2	1.210 000	1.212 201	1.214 404	1.216 609	1.218 816
3	1.331 000	1.334 633	1.338 273	1.341 920	1.345 573
4	1.464 100	1.469 431	1.474 777	1.480 137	1.485 512
5	1.610 510	1.617 844	1.625 204	1.632 592	1.640 006
6	1.771 561	1.781 246	1.790 975	1.800 749	1.810 566
7	1.948 717	1.961 152	1.973 655	1.986 226	1.998 865
8	2.143 589	2.159 228	2.174 967	2.190 807	2.206 747
9	2.357 948	2.377 310	2.396 814	2.416 460	2.436 249
10	2.593 742	2.617 419	2.641 289	2.665 355	2.689 619
11	2.853 117	2.881 778	2.910 701	2.939 887	2.969 339
12	3.138 428	3.172 837	3.207 592	3.242 695	3.278 150
13	3.452 271	3.493 294	3.534 766	3.576 693	3.619 078
14	3.797 498	3.846 117	3.895 313	3.945 092	3.995 462
15	4.177 248	4.234 575	4.292 635	4.351 437	4.410 990
16	4.594 973	4.662 267	4.730 483	4.799 635	4.869 733
17	5.054 470	5.133 156	5.212 993	5.293 997	5.376 186
18	5.559 917	5.651 604	5.744 718	5.839 279	5.935 309
19	6.115 909	6.222 416	6.330 679	6.440 725	6.552 581
20	6.727 500	6.850 880	6.976 408	7.104 119	7.234 049
21	7.400 250	7.542 819	7.688 002	7.835 844	7.986 390
22	8.140 275	8.304 644	8.472 178	8.642 936	8.816 975
23	8.954 302	9.143 413	9.336 340	9.533 158	9.733 941
24	9.849 733	10.066 898	10.288 647	10.515 073	10.746 270
25	10.834 706	11.083 654	11.338 089	11.598 126	11.863 882
26	11.918 177	12.203 103	12.494 574	12.792 733	13.097 726
27	13.109 994	13.435 617	13.769 021	14.110 384	14.459 890
28	14.420 994	14.792 614	15.173 461	15.563 754	15.963 718
29	15.863 093	16.286 668	16.721 154	17.166 820	17.623 945
30	17.449 402	17.931 622	18.426 711	18.935 003	19.456 835
31	19.194 342	19.742 716	20.306 236	20.885 308	21.480 346
32	21.113 777	21.736 730	22.377 472	23.036 495	23.714 302
33	23.225 154	23.932 140	24.659 974	25.409 254	26.180 590
34	25.547 670	26.349 286	27.175 292	28.026 407	28.903 371
35	28.102 437	29.010 563	29.947 171	30.913 127	31.909 321
36	30.912 681	31.940 630	33.001 783	34.097 179	35.227 891
37	34.003 949	35.166 634	36.367 965	37.609 188	38.891 592
38	37.404 343	38.718 464	40.077 497	41.482 935	42.936 317
39	41.144 778	42.629 029	44.165 402	45.755 677	47.401 694
40	45.259 256	46.934 561	48.670 273	50.468 512	52.331 470
41	49.785 181	51.674 952	53.634 641	55.666 768	57.773 943
42	54.763 699	56.894 122	59.105 374	61.400 446	63.782 433
43	60.240 069	62.640 428	65.134 122	67.724 691	70.415 806
44	66.264 076	68.967 111	71.777 803	74.700 335	77.739 050
45	72.890 484	75.932 789	79.099 138	82.394 469	85.823 911
46	80.179 532	83.602 001	87.167 251	90.881 099	94.749 598
47	88.197 485	92.045 803	96.058 310	100.241 853	104.603 556
48	97.017 234	101.342 429	105.856 258	110.566 703	115.482 326
49	106.718 957	111.578 015	116.653 596	121.955 140	127.492 488
50	117.390 853	122.847 394	128.552 263	134.516 520	140.751 707

RATE
10.0%-10.9%

COMPOUNDING FACTOR FOR 1

10.5%	10.6%	10.7%	10.8%	10.9%	Year
1.105 000	1.106 000	1.107 000	1.108 000	1.109 000	**1**
1.221 025	1.223 236	1.225 449	1.227 664	1.229 881	**2**
1.349 233	1.352 899	1.356 572	1.360 252	1.363 938	**3**
1.490 902	1.496 306	1.501 725	1.507 159	1.512 607	**4**
1.647 447	1.654 915	1.662 410	1.669 932	1.677 481	**5**
1.820 429	1.830 336	1.840 288	1.850 285	1.860 327	**6**
2.011 574	2.024 351	2.037 198	2.050 115	2.063 103	**7**
2.222 789	2.238 933	2.255 179	2.271 528	2.287 981	**8**
2.456 182	2.476 259	2.496 483	2.516 853	2.537 371	**9**
2.714 081	2.738 743	2.763 607	2.788 673	2.813 944	**10**
2.999 059	3.029 050	3.059 312	3.089 850	3.120 664	**11**
3.313 961	3.350 129	3.386 659	3.423 554	3.460 816	**12**
3.661 926	3.705 243	3.749 031	3.793 297	3.838 045	**13**
4.046 429	4.097 998	4.150 178	4.202 973	4.256 392	**14**
4.471 304	4.532 386	4.594 247	4.656 895	4.720 339	**15**
4.940 791	5.012 819	5.085 831	5.159 839	5.234 856	**16**
5.459 574	5.544 178	5.630 015	5.717 102	5.805 455	**17**
6.032 829	6.131 861	6.232 427	6.334 549	6.438 250	**18**
6.666 276	6.781 838	6.899 296	7.018 680	7.140 019	**19**
7.366 235	7.500 713	7.637 521	7.776 698	7.918 281	**20**
8.139 690	8.295 788	8.454 736	8.616 581	8.781 374	**21**
8.994 357	9.175 142	9.359 392	9.547 172	9.738 544	**22**
9.938 764	10.147 707	10.360 847	10.578 266	10.800 045	**23**
10.982 335	11.223 364	11.469 458	11.720 719	11.977 250	**24**
12.135 480	12.413 041	12.696 690	12.986 557	13.282 770	**25**
13.409 705	13.728 823	14.055 236	14.389 105	14.730 592	**26**
14.817 724	15.184 078	15.559 146	15.943 128	16.336 226	**27**
16.373 585	16.793 590	17.223 975	17.664 986	18.116 875	**28**
18.092 812	18.573 711	19.066 940	19.572 804	20.091 615	**29**
19.992 557	20.542 524	21.107 103	21.686 667	22.281 601	**30**
22.091 775	22.720 032	23.365 563	24.028 827	24.710 295	**31**
24.411 412	25.128 355	25.865 678	26.623 940	27.403 717	**32**
26.974 610	27.791 961	28.633 306	29.499 326	30.390 722	**33**
29.806 944	30.737 909	31.697 069	32.685 253	33.703 311	**34**
32.936 673	33.996 127	35.088 656	36.215 261	37.376 972	**35**
36.395 024	37.599 717	38.843 142	40.126 509	41.451 062	**36**
40.216 501	41.585 286	42.999 358	44.460 172	45.969 228	**37**
44.439 234	45.993 327	47.600 289	49.261 870	50.979 874	**38**
49.105 354	50.868 620	52.693 520	54.582 152	56.536 680	**39**
54.261 416	56.260 693	58.331 727	60.477 025	62.699 178	**40**
59.958 864	62.224 327	64.573 222	67.008 543	69.533 388	**41**
66.254 545	68.820 105	71.482 557	74.245 466	77.112 528	**42**
73.211 272	76.115 036	79.131 190	82.263 976	85.517 793	**43**
80.898 456	84.183 230	87.598 228	91.148 486	94.839 232	**44**
89.392 794	93.106 653	96.971 238	100.992 522	105.176 709	**45**
98.779 037	102.975 958	107.347 160	111.899 714	116.640 970	**46**
109.150 836	113.891 409	118.833 306	123.984 884	129.354 836	**47**
120.611 674	125.963 899	131.548 470	137.375 251	143.454 513	**48**
133.275 900	139.318 072	145.624 157	152.211 778	159.091 055	**49**
147.269 869	154.083 576	161.205 941	168.050 650	176.431 980	**50**

USING THESE TABLES

The tables in this book can be used for most project preparation purposes. Illustrations of common applications for the factors in the tables are given below. They are followed by examples of their use in computing discounted measures of project worth.

The tables in this book and illustrations of their uses

Compounding and discounting tables. The basic tables are the compounding and discounting tables, pages 2-101. Most factors in these tables are computed to 6 decimal places, but where the factor is 10,000 or more it is given to 10 significant places and the decimal point is "floated"—that is, placed in its proper position in the 10 digit sequence. These tables give the compounding factor for 1, the compounding factor for 1 per annum, the sinking fund factor, the discount factor, the present worth of an annuity factor, and the capital recovery factor for each whole percentage point from 1% through 50% for 50 years.

Summary present worth tables. For most project purposes only the discount factor and the present worth of an annuity factor are needed and 3 decimal places are sufficient. Hence, for convenience, summary 3 decimal tables with just these two factors have been included, pages 102-105. The intervals have been selected to include the most common discount rates for benefit-cost ratio and net present worth calculations and to provide convenient intervals from which to interpolate when the internal rate of return technique is used to estimate the internal economic return or the internal financial return. Three decimal present worth calculations will permit estimating the benefit-cost ratio to the nearest tenth of a unit ratio value and permit estimating the internal economic or financial return using the internal rate of return technique to the nearest whole percentage point—as precise an estimate as is justified in a development project.

Narrow interval compounding tables. When evaluating projects there is sometimes need to project growth rates using smaller percentage intervals than the whole percentage points included in the first two tables. To meet this need, narrow interval compounding tables have been included on pages 106-127 which give the compounding factor for 1 for each tenth of a percentage point from 0.0% through 10.9%.

Fractional interest rates and more detailed tables. For some project purposes there may arise a need for factors for fractional interest rates or for periods longer than 50 years. For commercial and legal purposes more than 6 decimal places may be needed. A convenient set of 10 decimal tables which includes many fractional interest rates and very long periods may be found in Charles H. Gushee, *ed. Financial Compound Interest and Annuity Tables.* 3rd. ed. (Boston: Financial Publishing Company, 1961). A number of other sources are also available.

Time notation. The factors in these tables have been computed assuming they fall on the last day of the year for which they are stated.

In project preparation, it is often convenient to think in terms of project years rather than calendar years. The point in time at which all values are to be equated through the compounding and discounting process may then be termed t_0. Often t_0 is established as being the present, but it should be clear t_0 can be any point in time and may be chosen simply on the basis of convenience. Those values which arise *before* t_0 are increased to their equivalent value at t_0 through compounding by the appropriate interest rate; those values which arise *after* t_0 are brought back to their equivalent value at t_0 (often termed the present worth) through discounting by the appropriate interest rate. Commonly in project evaluation all values are brought back by discounting to t_0 which is established as being just before the beginning of a project (and which may be thought of as the 0th year). The first project year is then termed t_1, the second t_2, and so forth. The examples of compounding and discounting in this section make this assumption.

In most project evaluation, it is sufficiently accurate and quite convenient to assume all values fall at the *end* of the project year in which they occur. Thus, in these examples, both costs and returns are assumed to fall at the end of the project year, including those incurred in the first project year (t_1) and all costs and all returns, including those arising in the first year, are discounted to the beginning of the project (t_0).

Since these tables are intended primarily for project evaluation, for convenience the intervals are referred to as years. The tables can, of course, be used for intervals other than years by simply considering the "year" column as a "period" column.

1. COMPOUNDING FACTOR FOR 1—*What an initial amount becomes when growing at compound interest.* (Compound interest factor; amount of 1.)

A road has 353 vehicles passing over it on the average each day in 1971 (t_0). The transport economists forecast traffic growth at 9% a year for 10 years. What will be the average number of vehicles passing over the road in 1981 (t_{10})?

353	×	2.367	=	836
Number of vehicles a day in 1971 (t_0)		9% compounding factor for 1 for 10 years (column 1, page 18)		Average number of vehicles a day in 1981 (t_{10})

Rs. 2,045 is deposited at 7% compound interest and left for 8 years. How much will be the balance at the end of the 8th year?

Rs. 2,045	×	1.718	=	Rs. 3,513
Original amount deposited (at t_0)		7% compounding factor for 1 for 8 years		Balance at the end of the 8th year (t_8)

The rice production target for the 5 year plan is to increase output by 3.5% a year. If the 1972 production is 2.63 million tons, what is the target production for 1977?

For this, the narrow interval compounding factor for 1 table may be consulted.

2.63 million tons	×	1.188	=	3.12 million tons
1972 production (t_0)		3.5% compounding factor for 1 for 5 years (column 1, page 113)		1977 target production (t_5)

In Brazil, FAO reports cattle numbers rose from 58.4 million as an average from 1951/52-1955/56 to 89.9 million in 1967/68. Taking the average number of animals as being representative of the number of cattle in the midpoint year of 1953/54, what is the average annual rate of growth in cattle numbers in the 14 years between 1953/54 and 1967/68?

To determine this, an approximation from the narrow interval compounding tables may be used. The total increase from 1953/54 to 1967/68 expressed in percentage terms is:

89.9 million	÷	58.4 million	=	1.539	=	54%
Number of cattle in 1967/68 (t_{14})		Number of cattle in 1953/54 (t_0)		Proportionate increase in cattle in 14 years (t_0-t_{14})		Total percentage increase in cattle numbers

Not allowing for the influence of compounding, the average rate of growth may be estimated as somewhere in the vicinity of 3.9% a year (54% ÷ 14 = 3.9%). This, of course, overestimates the true compound rate. To find a more accurate estimate which allows for compounding, the narrow interval compounding tables may be consulted for the factor opposite 14 years which is closest to 1.539. The hunt may conveniently begin at the factor for 3.9% for 14 years = 1.708 511 (column 5, page 113). As expected, this is greater than 1.539. Proceeding leftward along the line, the figure 1.533 279 is reached which is the factor for 3.1% (column 2, page 112). This is closer to 1.539 than either the factor for 3.0% (which is 1.512 590) or the factor for 3.2% (which is 1.554 232). Hence, the average annual growth in cattle numbers between 1953/54 and 1967/68 may be reported as 3.1% to the nearest tenth of a percentage point.

2. COMPOUNDING FACTOR FOR 1 PER ANNUM—*Growth of equal year-end deposits all growing at compound interest.* (Compound interest factor for 1 per annum; amount of 1 per annum.)

This factor permits calculating the value to which a constant amount deposited at the *end* of *each* year will grow by the end of a stated year at a stated interest rate.

On December 31 of each year for 9 years the amount of M$782 is deposited into an account that earns 6% interest. What will be the balance at the end of the 9th year?

M$782	×	11.491	=	M$8,986
Amount deposited at end of each year from 1st to 9th year (t_1-t_9)		6% compounding factor for 1 per annum for 9 years (column 2, page 12)		Amount on deposit at end of 9th year (t_9) (including 9th year deposit)

3. SINKING FUND FACTOR—*Level deposit required each year to reach 1 by a given year.*

This factor permits calculating the level annual payment that must be set aside each year, to be invested at compound interest, in order to have a predetermined sum at a given time. It is used primarily to determine how much must be put into a fund in order to have recovered the amount of an investment at the end of its useful life. (Note, however, that this is a very mechanistic depreciation rule and may not be good management practice in many circumstances.)

When a new irrigation scheme was installed, it was decided farmers should be charged an amount sufficient to replace the pumps when they wear out—that is, *farmers will pay a replacement charge. It is decided that the money collected from the farmers should be invested in government bonds bearing 11% interest. To replace the pumps in 15 years will cost US$875,000. How much should be the annual collection from the farmers?*

US$875,000	×	.029 065	=	US$25,432
Replacement cost in 15 years (t_{15})		11% sinking fund factor for 15 years (column 3, page 22)		Annual amount to be collected from farmers (and to be invested in government bonds at 11%)

A bus company buys 10 new buses for a total of Rs. 33,250,000. The buses last on the average 7 years and can be sold at a salvage value of 20% of their original purchase price. What is an appropriate sinking fund provision, assuming the money set aside can be invested at 10%?

First, the total depreciation must be determined.

Original purchase price	Rs. 33,250,000
LESS salvage value of 20% of the purchase price	– 6,650,000
Total depreciation	Rs. 26,600,000

Rs. 26,600,000	×	.105 405	=	Rs. 2,803,773
Amount that will be needed in the sinking fund account in 7 years (t_7)		10% sinking fund factor for 7 years		Amount to be allocated to the sinking fund account every year (and invested at 10%)

Note that the sinking fund factor is just the opposite of the compounding factor for 1 per annum (that is, it is the reciprocal). This relationship may be used to check the sinking fund calculation. The amount to be deposited annually at 10%, Rs. 2,803,773, may be multiplied by the 10% compounding factor for 1 per annum factor for 7 years to determine if the result equals the amount that will be needed in the sinking fund account in 7 years.

Rs. 2,803,773	×	9.487 171	=	Rs. 26,599,874
Amount to be allocated to the sinking fund account every year (and invested at 10%)		10% compounding factor for 1 per annum for 7 years		Amount that will be needed in the sinking fund account in 7 years (t_7)

4. DISCOUNT FACTOR—*How much 1 at a future date is worth today.* (Present worth of 1.)

This factor permits determining the value today of an amount received or paid out in the future. The process of finding the present worth in project preparation is generally referred to as discounting. Note that the discount factor is the reciprocal of the compounding factor for 1. Hence, it is common to hear expressions such as, "discounted at an interest rate of 14%."

The most common use of discounting in project evaluation is to find the present worth of future costs or future benefits (see pages 135-138).

The net benefit of the Hounslow Irrigation Scheme in Jamaica in the 14th year of the project was estimated to be J\$173,831. Discounted at an interest rate of 21%, what is the present worth at the beginning of the project (t_0)?

J\$173,831	×	.069	=	J\$11,994
Actual value at the future time (t_{14})		21% discount factor for 14th year (column 1, page 43)		Present worth at beginning of the project (t_0)

A cement plant will produce Tcs. 1,180,000 worth of cement in its first full year of operation in 1975, the 4th year of the project (t_4). Discounted at 12%, what is the present worth of that output on December 31, 1971 (t_0)?

Tcs. 1,180,000	×	.636	=	Tcs. 750,480
Value of output in 1975 (t_4)		12% discount factor for 4th year		Present worth at the end of 1971 (t_0) of the 1975 output

A dam will still be in place 50 years in the future. If the value of that dam at that time is considered to be its replacement cost and this will amount to US\$1,200,000–and still using the convention of only 3 decimals in the discounting process–what is the present worth of the dam discounted at 17%?

US\$1,200,000	×	.000	=	US\$0
Value 50 years in the future (t_{50})		17% discount factor for 50th year to 3rd decimal		Present worth at t_0

5. PRESENT WORTH OF AN ANNUITY FACTOR–*How much 1 received or paid annually is worth today.* (Present worth of 1 per annum; discount factor for a stream of income.)

This factor enables determination of the present worth of a constant amount received each year for some length of time in the future. It is a great time saver in the computations necessary for project evaluation. Its use is direct and simple if it is used for a constant stream of money which begins in the first year and lasts to some future year, say the 11th year of the project (from t_1 to t_{11}). But it may also be used to determine the present worth today (t_0) of a constant stream of money which begins some time other than the first year of the project–say which begins in the 7th year and continues through the 15th year (from t_7 to t_{15}), although this takes some additional manipulation.

Note that the present worth of an annuity factor for any given number of years is the total of the discount factors for all years through the last–that is, in the compounding and discounting tables, column 2 on every right hand page is the running subtotal of column 1.

In Pakistan a farmer with 15 acres who invests in a tubewell is estimated, on the average, to earn an incremental net income of Rs. 4,415 each year over the 15 year life of the well. Discounted at 18%, what is the present worth of this stream of income to the farmer at the time of his investment (t_0)?

Rs. 4,415	×	5.092	=	Rs. 22,481
Annual amount received each year from 1st through the 15th year (t_1-t_{15})		18% present worth of an annuity factor for 15 years (column 2, page 37)		Present worth of the stream of income at t_0

Returning to the example of the cement plant in section 4, it may be noted how the factor for the present worth of an annuity can be used when the stream of future values begins at some time other than the first year.

Once a cement factory is in full production in 1977, the 6th year of the project (t_6), it will produce cement valued at Tcs. 1,475,000 annually over the economic life of the plant, taken to be 15 years. What is the present worth of the cement production from 1977 through 1986 (t_6-t_{15}) discounted at 12%?

In order to proceed, the factor by which to multiply the annual value of cement production must first be calculated. This involves finding that part of the factor for computing the present worth of an annuity which arises from the 6th through the 15th years. The procedure is to subtract the value of the factor for 5 years (note that it is *not* the factor for 6 years) from the value of the factor for 15 years.

12% present worth of an annuity factor for 15 years (t_{15})	6.811
LESS 12% present worth of an annuity factor for 5 years (t_5)	–3.605
12% present worth of an annuity factor for the 6th through the 15th years (t_6-t_{15}) (= sum of the discount factors for these 10 years)	3.206

Note that the value of 3.206 computed for the 10 years from the 6th through the 15th (t_6-t_{15}) is *not* the same as the value of the factor for the first 10 years (t_1-t_{10}) which is 5.650. The reason is that the 10 years from the 6th through the 15th years (t_6-t_{15}) lie further off in the future than the first 10 years (t_1-t_{10}).

The computation of the factor can be checked (allowing for rounding errors) by taking advantage of the fact that the present worth of an annuity factor is simply the running subtotal of the discount factors, as noted above.

Year	Discount factor 12%	Year	Discount factor 12%
6	.507	11	.287
7	.452	12	.257
8	.404	13	.229
9	.361	14	.205
10	.322	15	.183
		Total	3.207

The factor determined by computation can then be applied to determine the present worth of the stream of future income.

Tcs. 1,475,000	×	3.206	=	Tcs. 4,728,850
Annual output from 6th through 15th years (t_6-t_{15})		12% present worth of an annuity factor from the 6th through the 15th years which we have computed		Present worth of the future stream of income at t_0

6. CAPITAL RECOVERY FACTOR—*Annual payment that will repay a $1 loan in X years with compound interest on the unpaid balance.* (Partial payment factor.)

This factor permits calculating what constant annual payments would be necessary to repay a loan over a given period of time at a stated interest rate. The total payment is a varying combination of both interest and repayment of principal.

Note this factor is the reciprocal of the present worth of an annuity factor.

The Agricultural Development Bank of Pakistan lends to farmers at 8% interest to finance tubewells. If a farmer borrows Rs. 8,790 for a tubewell to be repaid in 10 years, what is the amount of his combined interest and principal payment?

Rs. 8,790	×	0.149 029	=	Rs. 1,310
Amount initially borrowed at the beginning of the first year (t_0)		8% capital recovery factor for a 10 year period (t_{10}) (column 3, page 17)		Amount of annual payment from end of first year through end of 10th year (t_1-t_{10})

The government has agreed to make a 20 year loan of US$500,000 at 12% interest to a toll road authority. It will take the first 3 years of the loan period to build the road, and the government has agreed to "capitalize" the interest until the road is completed and toll collection has begun in the 4th year. The amount to be spent on construction in the first year (t_1) is to be US$100,000. In both the 2nd and 3rd years (t_2 and t_3) construction expenditures are to be US$200,000. What is the annual amount the toll road authority must pay the government in a combined interest and principal payment if it repays the loan in the remaining 17 years of the loan period from the 4th through the 20th years (t_4-t_{20})?

By agreeing to "capitalize" the interest during the first 3 years of the loan, the government has, in effect, agreed not to collect the interest which would otherwise be due but rather to add the interest due to the principal of the loan (hence the term "to capitalize") and to charge 12% interest on the new total.

Considering the drawdown for the first year (t_1) as an example, it may be seen that the government will permit the toll road authority to continue to add the interest due to the original capital drawdown for 3 years through the end of the 3rd year (t_3). Thus, the amount due at the end of the 3rd year (t_3) will be the original principal with interest compounded for 3 years. The compounding factor for 1 is used to determine that the amount due for the drawdown of US$100,000 during the first year (t_1) by the end of the 3rd year (t_3) is US$100,000 x 1.404 928 = US$140,493. For the drawdown of the 2nd year (t_2), the capitalization process only applies to the 2nd and 3rd years (t_2 and t_3), so the compounding factor for 1 for 2 years is used. Thus, the amount due for the drawdown of US$200,000 during the 2nd year (t_2) is US$200,000 x 1.254 400 = US$250,880. A similar process is followed for the 3rd year. These amounts are then totalled to show the amount of principal and capitalized interest due at the end of the 3rd year (t_3) as shown below.

Project Year	Amount of loan drawdown (US$)	Compound interest factor to end of 3rd year (12%)	Due at end of 3rd year (US$)
t_1	100,000	1.404 928	140,493
t_2	200,000	1.254 400	250,880
t_3	200,000	1.120 000	224,000
	Total principal and interest due at end of 3rd year		615,373

The 12% capital recovery factor may now be applied to the amount owed at the beginning of the 4th year (= end of t_3) to determine the level payment of principal and interest necessary for the toll road authority to be able to repay the government.

US$615,373	×	.140 457	=	US$86,433
Total amount including principal and capitalized interest owed at end of 3rd year (t_3) [= beginning of 4th year (t_4)]		12% capital recovery factor for 17 years		Amount of repayment each year from 4th through 20th years (t_4-t_{20})

Discounted measures of project worth

In project preparation, the discount factor and the present worth of an annuity factor are commonly used to permit comparing the wealth generating potential of one project with that of alternative projects.

Benefit-cost comparisons. Three discounted measures of project worth are commonly used which are comparisons of benefits in relation to costs:

$$\text{Benefit-cost ratio} = \frac{\text{Present worth of benefits}}{\text{Present worth of costs}}$$

$$\text{Net present worth} = \begin{bmatrix}\text{Present worth}\\ \text{of benefits}\end{bmatrix} - \begin{bmatrix}\text{Present worth}\\ \text{of costs}\end{bmatrix}$$

$$\text{Internal rate of return} = \text{That discount rate such that} \begin{bmatrix}\text{Present worth}\\ \text{of benefits}\end{bmatrix} = \begin{bmatrix}\text{Present worth}\\ \text{of costs}\end{bmatrix}$$

These three measures are essentially the same. For any investment-type project, there exists an interest rate which is the internal rate of return and at which the benefit-cost ratio equals 1 and the net present worth is zero.

The benefit-cost ratio is commonly employed as a tool to help evaluate public sector projects, most often those of a water resource nature. Only rarely is it used for private sector projects or for such public sector investments as those contemplated by government corporations. The internal rate of return is commonly used to help evaluate both public and private investment projects. Its use is especially prevalent in larger corporations and among international lending agencies. The net present worth measure is used primarily to evaluate public sector investments and for determining the least cost combination in project optimization.

In the World Bank, the internal rate of return is the most frequently employed measure, although both the benefit-cost ratio and the net present worth are occasionally employed.

Opportunity cost of capital. All three discounted measures of project worth must be related to the opportunity cost of capital. For private enterprise the opportunity cost of capital will be a weighted average of the borrowing rate for funds and an acceptable price-earnings ratio for equity shares.

For the society as a whole, the opportunity cost of capital is the return on the last (that is, marginal) investment which could be made were all the available capital fully invested in the most remunerative alternative manner. Determining the opportunity cost of capital for a society is difficult, but economists generally consider it to lie between 8% and 15% in most developing countries.

Benefit-cost ratio. In economic discussions, "cost-benefit ratio" and "benefit-cost ratio" are used interchangeably. In all instances, however, the computation referred to is the same. Both the benefit stream and the cost stream are discounted by an interest rate considered to be close to the opportunity cost of capital and the ratio between the present worth of the benefits divided by the present worth of the costs is determined.

Table 1 illustrates computation of a benefit-cost ratio for a population project in Trinidad and Tobago financed in part by a World Bank loan.

Net present worth. Net present worth (often referred to as net present value) is simply the present worth of the net benefits of a project discounted at the opportunity cost of capital. In table 1, it can be seen that the net present worth is the present worth of the benefits less the present worth of the costs, TT$90,462,000 − TT$26,004,000 = TT$64,458,000. Often it is computationally simpler to determine the incremental net benefit stream (generally referred to as the "cash flow" in project evaluation) and to discount that stream. This is illustrated in columns (7), (8), and (9) of table 2 where the incremental net benefit stream or cash flow is discounted assuming an opportunity cost of capital of 12% to find a net present worth of Ur$2,462,000,000.

Internal rate of return. The internal rate of return must be determined by trial and error. The measure represents the return over the life of the project to the resources engaged in the project. (Contrary to what is often stated, no reinvestment assumption need be made.) The cash flow is discounted to determine its present worth. By trial and error one discount rate is found which is too low and which leaves a positive present worth and another discount rate is found which is too high and which leaves a negative present worth of the cash flow stream. This brackets the true internal rate of return which may then be estimated by interpolation. The interpolation rule is:

$$\text{Internal rate of return} = \text{Lower discount rate} + \text{Difference between the two discount rates}\left[\frac{\text{Present worth of the cash flow at the lower discount rate}}{\text{Absolute difference between the present worths of the cash flow streams at the two discount rates}}\right]$$

This procedure is followed at the bottom of table 2. The interpolation gives an internal rate of return of 21% (which in this case is the internal economic return because of the way the values in the table have been chosen). If it were exactly 21%,

Table 1. TRINIDAD AND TOBAGO: Population Project Illustrating Computation of Benefit-Cost Ratio (Thousand Trinidad and Tobago Dollars)

(1) Year	(2) Costs[a]	(3) D.F. 10%	(4) P.W. 10%	(5) Benefits[b]	(6) D.F. 10%	(7) P.W. 10%
1974	3,206	.909	2,914	—	.909	—
1975	5,228	.826	4,318	179	.826	148
1976	4,048	.751	3,040	534	.751	401
1977	3,630	.683	2,479	1,042	.683	712
1978	2,328	.621	1,446	1,729	.621	1,074
1979	2,168			2,486	.564	1,402
1980	2,168			3,729	.513	1,913
1981	2,168			5,428	.467	2,535
1982	2,168			7,525	.424	3,191
1983	2,168			10,093	.386	3,896
1984	2,168			12,857	.350	4,500
1985	2,168			15,727	.319	5,017
1986	2,168			17,912	.290	5,194
1987	2,168			20,618	.263	5,423
1988	2,168			22,692	.239	5,423
1989	2,168	5.446*	11,807	24,465	.218	5,333
1990	2,168			26,145	.198	5,177
1991	2,168			27,817	.180	5,007
1992	2,168			29,456	.164	4,831
1993	2,168			31,044	.149	4,626
1994	2,168			32,585	.135	4,399
1995	2,168			34,066	.123	4,190
1996	2,168			35,472	.112	3,973
1997	2,168			33,426	.102	3,409
1998	2,168			34,156	.092	3,142
1999	2,168			34,603	.084	2,907
2000	2,168			34,724	.076	2,639
Total	66,136	9.236	26,004	500,510	9.238	90,462

Source: Analysis prepared by Miss I. Z. Husain, Population Projects Department, IBRD.

*The present worth of an annuity factor for the 6th through 27th years was calculated following the procedure explained on page 133. The present worth of the constant stream of costs from 1979 through 2000 as given in column 2 is obtained by multiplying the costs for one year by the present worth of an annuity factor as computed (TT$2,168 thousand x 5.446 = TT$11,807 thousand).

a. Costs include capital and recurring costs for operating the project.

b. Benefits are savings arising from births averted and include costs of food and clothing saved, education costs saved, and health costs saved.

$$\text{Benefit-cost Ratio} = \frac{90,462}{26,004} = 3.5$$

then the present worth of the cash flow at the 21% discount rate would be 0. If it is somewhat above or below 21%, the present worth will be closer to 0 at the 21% rate than it is at either 20% or 22%. Thus the interpolation may be checked by discounting at the internal rate of return estimated through interpolation.

A present worth of an annuity factor was computed for the 6th through the 11th years to save computation. The factor in column (10), for example, was derived as follows:

20% present worth of an annuity factor for 11 years	4.327
LESS 20% present worth of an annuity factor for 5 years	−2.991
20% present worth of an annuity factor from the 6th through the 11th years	1.336

(It may be noted that the sum of the discount factors for all 12 years is the same as the present worth of an annuity factor for 12 years allowing for rounding errors. This provides a quick internal check.)

Depreciation allowances. In the above examples of discounted measures of project worth depreciation is *not* deducted as a cost. Discounted measures of project worth automatically take care of depreciation. If the undiscounted benefit-cost ratio is at least 1, if the undiscounted net present worth is at least 0, or if the undiscounted internal rate of return is at least 0, then the resources invested have been recovered. If the benefit-cost ratio at some positive discount rate is at least equal to 1, the net present worth at some positive discount rate is 0, or the internal rate of return is positive, then in addition to the return *of* capital there is also a return *to* capital.

Minimum-cost test and cross-over discount rate. The use of a minimum-cost test is frequent in economic appraisals. It is used (a) for many projects whose benefits cannot be quantified and (b) to make certain that a project's technology, design standards, and construction phasing have been correctly chosen. Minimum-cost tests are found most frequently in the public utilities and transportation sectors. The test consists of calculating the present worth of the cost streams associated with alternative project technologies, design standards, or phasing for a range of discount rates. Some examples are comparisons between hydro and thermal cost streams to carry out a power program; a comparison of different water resources, pipe sizes, pumping arrangements, and expansion phasing in water systems; or alternative road design standards, maintenance costs, and future up-grading work to satisfy an expected pattern of growth. Project economic analysis frequently consists of an examination of the alternatives that have been compared in the feasibility and design studies and of the methods and assumptions used in making the comparisons.

The preference ranking of the alternatives (indicated by the cost stream with the lowest present worth) may change between lower and higher discount rates. The discount rate at which the preference changes is known as the cross-over discount rate. The cross-over discount rate itself has limited significance; the more significant point is determined by the discount rate representing the opportunity cost of capital which allows one to identify the least-cost alternative according to the economic cost of capital in the country concerned.

Table 2. URUGUAY: Third Livestock Development Project
Net Present Worth at 12% and Internal Economic Return
(Million Uruguayan Pesos)

(1) Year	(2) Aggregate of ranchers incremental net cash balances	(3) Taxes[a]	(4) Subsidies[b]	(5) Technical services	(6) On-ranch invest-ment	(7) Incremental benefits (=cash flow)	(8) D.F. 12%	(9) Present worth 12%	(10) D.F. 20%	(11) Present worth 20%	(12) D.F. 25%	(13) Present worth 25%
1	− 438	− 120	−299	−315	−2,271	− 3,443	.893	−3,075	.833	−2,868	.800	−2,754
2	− 1,269	+ 55	− 80	− 40	—	− 1,334	.797	−1,063	.694	− 926	.640	− 854
3	+ 710	+ 114	− 80	− 40	—	+ 704	.712	+ 501	.579	+ 408	.512	+ 360
4	+ 1,133	+ 214	− 80	− 40	—	+ 1,227	.636	+ 780	.482	+ 591	.410	+ 503
5	+ 1,270	+ 286	− 80	− 40	—	+ 1,436	.567	+ 814	.402	+ 577	.328	+ 471
6-11	+ 1,230	+ 286	—	− 40	—	+ 1,476	2.333*	+3,444	1.336*	+1,972	.967*	+1,427
12	+ 3,884[c]	+ 286	—	− 40	—	+ 4,130	.257	+1,061	.112	+ 463	.069	+ 285
Total	+12,670	+2,551	−619	−755	−2,271	+11,576	6.195	+2,462	4.438	+ 217	3.726	− 562

Source: IBRD. Third Livestock Development Project—Uruguay. Report No. PA-38a. Washington: IBRD, 1970. Annex 9, p. 1.

*The present worth of an annuity factor for the 6th through the 11th years was calculated following the procedure explained on pages 133 and 138. The present worth of the constant stream of the cash flow from years 6 through 11 as given in column 9, for example, is obtained by multiplying the cash flow for one year by the present worth of an annuity factor as computed (Ur$1,476 million x 2.333 = Ur$3,444 million).

a. See text of original report for details of export and other taxes. The negative tax entry in year 1 is the amount of tax revenue foregone as a result of the investment program.

b. Fertilizer subsidy estimated at 33% of total cost in project year 1, 10% of total cost in project years 2 through 5, and 0 thereafter.

c. Includes $2,654 million for incremental herd value at the end of the project (= salvage value or net residual assets).

Net Present Worth at 12% Opportunity Cost of Capital = Ur$2,462 million

$$\text{Internal Economic Return} = 20 + 5\left(\frac{217}{779}\right) = 21\%$$

In El Salvador two alternatives existed for expanding the capacity of a transmission line. One alternative, which postponed the heavy investment as long as possible, was to convert an existing 69 kV line to 115 kV in years 1 and 2 and to add a parallel 115 kV line in years 6 and 7. Its total undiscounted cost is larger. The other alternative, involving the greater immediate expenditure but the smaller total undiscounted cost, was to construct a parallel line in years 1 and 2 and to convert the 69 kV line to 115 kV in years 6 and 7. If the opportunity cost of capital in El Salvador is taken to be 10%, which alternative is preferable? What is the cross-over discount rate?

The computations are laid out in table 3. If the opportunity cost of capital is taken to be 10%, the early investment alternative has the lower present worth and is preferable. (But note that if the opportunity cost of capital were 15%, the postponed investment alternative would have the lower present worth and would be preferred.)

The cross-over discount rate may be found either graphically or by computation. The graphic method is illustrated in Figure 1. The present worths of the postponed investment are plotted at 10% and at 15% and the two points joined by a straight line. Similarly, the present worths of the early investment alternative at 10% and 15% are plotted and the points joined by a line. Where the two lines cross is the cross-over discount rate (which in this case may be read from the graph to be 11.6%).

The cross-over discount rate may be computed by finding that discount rate which equalizes the present worths of the cost streams of the two alternative technologies. In practice, this is found by subtracting the undiscounted cost stream year by year of the cheaper alternative from that of the more expensive alternative and

Figure 1. EL SALVADOR: Choice between Power Line Alternatives Illustrating Cross-over Discount Rate

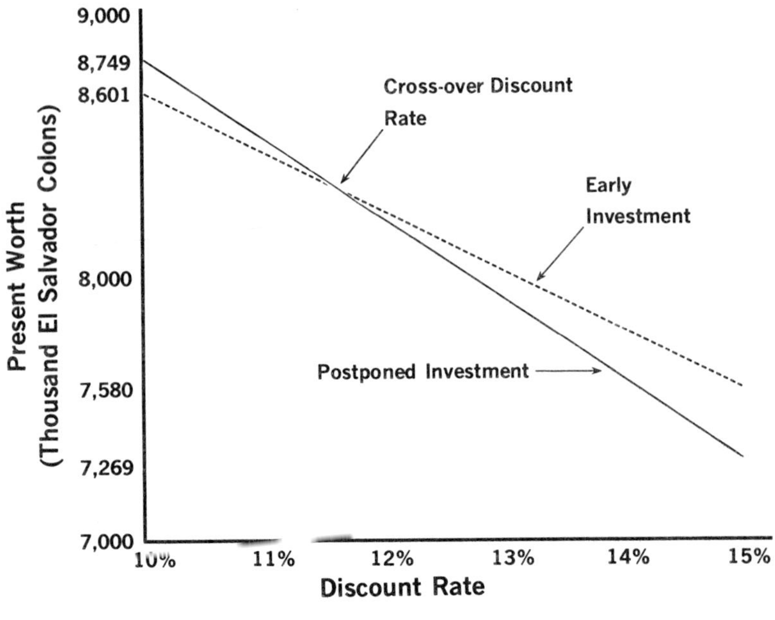

Table 3. EL SALVADOR: Choice between Power Line Alternatives Illustrating Cross-over Discount Rate (Thousand El Salvador Colons)

Year	Postponed Investment			Early Investment			Cross-over Discount Rate		
	Cost Stream[a]	Present Worth 10%	Present Worth 15%	Cost Stream[a]	Present Worth 10%	Present Worth 15%	Differences between Cost Streams	Present Worth 10%	Present Worth 15%
1	¢ 770	¢ 700	¢ 670	¢ 2,100	¢1,909	¢1,827	¢–1,330	¢–1,209	¢–1,157
2	4,075	3,366	3,081	5,000	4,130	3,780	– 925	– 764	– 699
3	206	155	136	360	270	237	– 154	– 116	– 101
4	210	143	120	360	246	206	– 150	– 102	– 86
5	216	134	107	360	224	179	– 144	– 89	– 72
6	2,390	1,348	1,032	1,105	623	477	+1,285	+ 725	+ 555
7	5,332	2,735	2,005	2,010	1,031	756	+3,322	+1,704	+1,249
8	360	168	118	360	168	118	0	0	0
Total	¢13,559	¢8,749	¢7,269	¢11,655	¢8,601	¢7,580	¢+1,904	¢+ 149	¢– 311

Source: IBRD. Appraisal of the Soyapango Gas Turbine Project (Fifth Power Project). Washington: IBRD, December 1970. Annex 11, pp. 5-6. [Report No. PU-55a]

a. Capital plus operating and maintenance costs.

Cross-over discount rate $= 10 + 5\left(\frac{149}{460}\right) = 11.6\%$

then finding through trial and error the discount rate which will exactly make the present worth of the stream of differences equal zero. This is illustrated in table 3. The first step is to find the present worth of the stream of differences at 10% (chosen to be low enough to give a *positive* present worth) and at 15% (chosen to be high enough to give a *negative* present worth). The cross-over discount rate is found by linear interpolation between the positive and the negative values to determine the rate which makes the present worth of the differences between the costs equal zero. (Interpolation is discussed in more detail in connection with discounted measures of project worth, page 136. The error introduced by using linear interpolation is not significant in most cases and may be ignored.) At a discount rate below 11.6% the early investment alternative is preferred; at a discount rate above 11.6%, the postponed investment is preferred. At 11.6% the decision maker is indifferent between alternative technologies.

Since the data from which cross-over discount rates are computed are at best approximations, it is probably better to state the cross-over discount rate in some form such as "at discount rates of 11% or below the early investment alternative is preferred; at discount rates of 12% or above the postponed investment alternative is preferred."

MATHEMATICAL APPENDIX

The tables in this book were computed under the direction of the World Bank Computing Activities Department using the standard formulas below.

1. Compounding factor for 1

$$s = (1 + i)^n$$

where

s = sum at end of period
i = interest rate
n = number of periods

2. Compounding factor for 1 per annum

$$s_{\overline{n}|} = \frac{(1 + i)^n - 1}{i}$$

3. Sinking fund factor

$$\frac{1}{s_{\overline{n}|}} = \frac{i}{(1 + i)^n - 1}$$

4. Discount factor

$$v^n = \frac{1}{(1 + i)^n}$$

where

v^n = present worth of 1 at the end of period n with an interest rate of i per period

5. Present worth of an annuity factor

$$a_{\overline{n}|} = \frac{1 - \dfrac{1}{(1 + i)^n}}{i}$$

where

$a_{\overline{n}|}$ = present worth of an annuity of 1 per period for n periods with an interest rate of i per period

6. Capital recovery factor

$$\frac{1}{a_{\overline{n}|}} = \frac{i}{1 - \dfrac{1}{(1 + i)^n}}$$

The following rounding convention has been used in this book. When a value of less than 5 is to be dropped, the digit to the left remains unchanged. When a value of more than 5 is to be dropped, the digit to the left is increased by 1. When a value of exactly 5 is to be dropped, the digit to the left if *even* is left unchanged. If *odd*, it is raised by 1. The effect of this rule is that all numbers which have been rounded by dropping an exact 5 will be reported as even numbers.